STORIES

OF

WORLD WAR II

Smoky Valley Writers
from
McPherson County, Kansas
2011

Ann Parr, Editor

Stories of World War II

Copyright © 2011 by Smoky Valley Writers

No part of this book may be reproduced or transmitted in any form or by any means electronic or mechanical, including photocopying or by any information storage without permission in writing from the copyright owner.

Cover design by Liz Knaus

Text design and layout by Jim L. Friesen

Library of Congress Control Number: 2011940180

International Standard Book Number: 978-0-984001-81-1

Printed in the United States of America by Mennonite Press, Inc., Newton, KS, www.mennonitepress.com

CONTENTS

History and Dedication

How we did the project:

Smoky Valley Writers was formed to collect World War II stories from twenty Lindsborg, McPherson, Smolan, Inman, and Marquette, Kansas, area residents who served on the warfront or supported warfront efforts on the homefront. They partnered with sixth graders who entered the stories on computers and prepared pictures for twenty individual books. High school and college students supported technology efforts along the way. The age gap had less and less significance as each group gained respect for each other's experiences. They learned more about each other and more about America's history. It was truly an intergenerational effort of grace.

Smoky Valley Writers met weekly from January 11 through April 13, 2011, when final pages of their books went to the publisher. The stories replaced yellowed newspaper articles in dresser drawers, crinkled photographs stuffed in attics, and events talked about on porch swings at family reunions. They came out of hiding and were tucked into hardbound books for safe keeping. To further ensure their legacy, this book, *Smoky Valley Writers Volume 1,* places all twenty stories in one place.

An intergenerational project with our middle school partners:

Sixth graders from Smoky Valley Middle School joined with writers to provide technical support. The intergenerational partnerships turned out to be one of the brightest spots of the project. In their own words, sixth graders say:

> "When I found out I was chosen for the project, I knew I had to do a good job. It was a privilege and I wanted to do my best. A neat thing about working with my partner was knowing that he had learned Morse Code many years ago, and he could still remember how to do it. About older people? I'd tell my friends to listen to them. They have cool stories to tell." —Yohannes Apel

> "My partner wrote blueprints for airplanes. That's awesome. I also found out how much families worried about their loved ones who were in the service. Sometimes they didn't know where they were or what they were doing, or most of all, if they would come back. It must have been awful." —Lindsey Johnson

> "I learned about how different the weapons were from what we know about now, and how dangerous it was to be in the war. I have so much respect for what the soldiers did for us during World War II." —Alyssa Patrick

"I was really surprised to be chosen. At first I was not sure what we would be doing, but after we got into it, it was really fun. I learned so much about the war in the Pacific. We had studied about the war in Europe, but now I know that was only a part of it. Most of all, I learned how wise older people are. They have more respect for everything, including us students, and they value life because they have seen so much. It was exciting to have my classmates ask where we were and what we were doing, and then be able to tell them about the project." —Maxwell Howe

"My family comes from Germany, and now I know more about what tough times they had. There were so many small wars before all the countries got involved. It must have been an awful time. I had fun, and at first, I thought older people were not much fun, but I changed my mind. I liked helping them with their books." —Jacob Bryan

"I expected a slow process, since we would be working with older people, and that we'd have to remind them of what was next. No way. It went very fast. It was easy to work with them. I loved looking at all their pictures, knowing that they meant so many memories for them—both hard times and good times. It was an honor to be asked." —Abby Rishel

"I expected it to be like a school assignment, not something where I'd get close to my partner, but I did. I've adopted my partner as a new grandmother for me. We talk all the time, and she's going to my first volleyball game this week. I didn't know how hard the women worked during the war and how everyone was involved. It was awesome to get to know these people. They're so nice, and they make me happy." —Rilee Carson

"I was surprised to know that my partner's brother was missing in action for a very long time and how much pain that made for the family. Actually, I was surprised to learn about so many different stories about the war from the writers. I loved how they took all the time we needed to understand their stories. They wanted to make us happy because we were helping them." —Halle McClure

"I expected to learn more about World War II, and I did. It became real to me, brought it to life instead of just reading or hearing about it. I found out older people appreciate things more than we do. They went through more and worked hard. I loved the chance to connect with people I wouldn't have otherwise." —Delaney Johnson

"I expected it to be hard and didn't think it would be much fun. I was wrong. It was lots of fun. I thought it was really cool to learn about my partner's work with the USO and learn about the other older people's stories. They have many stories, but don't tell us unless we ask, like this project did. I liked talking to my partner about World War II, but about other things too. She was lots of fun." —Katie Patterson

"I was excited to be chosen. It was really cool to be with people who had been in World War II. I couldn't get over how many of my partner's family members had been in the military—all the wars since her husband was in World War II. I had heard about Pearl

Harbor, but had no idea what a big "shocker" it was to our country. I found out these older people had been through a lot and were happy to share their stories with us kids. It was fun being with them, traveling to other places to make presentations and hear more about their experiences." —Meredith Galloway

Honor and gratitude:

We honor the *Smoky Valley Writers* for this book and for the price this 1940s adult generation paid to insure our country's commitment to democracy. We give them our highest regard and our biggest thank you, and we dedicate this project to all who have told their stories and to all who did not have a chance to leave a personal legacy such as this.

As one of our college writers states in her book about Glenferd Funk: "History isn't made up of distant, abstract figures and events that are locked up in dusty books and atlases. History is sitting right next to you in church, your next-door neighbor, or even that crotchety man ahead of you in the checkout line. History has gnarled hands and peppermints in its pockets, and occasionally, blue hair. By grasping those hands, one can discover that history isn't solely made up of radical figures. It is made up of everyone. Every individual has a part to play. And while we are looking for the next Napoleon, Washington, or Churchill, we may overlook the ordinary men and women who cheered or jeered them into existence. And they are slipping away from us faster than we can learn to appreciate them."

Dawn to Sunrise:
A Father and Daughter Remember Pearl Harbor

by Jeanne Ahlers

THIS BOOK IS DEDICATED TO:

STEPHEN A. KALLIS, JR.

Stephen
Major, 64th CA (AA)

August 7, 1942

*Stephen A.
Kallis*

It is now exactly eight months since the slant eyes caught us with our pants at half mast, and for my own sake and that of the officers who didn't have that exciting experience, I'll try to amplify the simple entries that appeared on the station and record of events section of B-41's morning reports of the first few days of the war.

Strictly speaking the Alert of November 27th was not a war move but that Alert helped direct our actions of the first hectic hours so it must be included. At about 5:00 p.m. (as it was still known) November 27, the alert siren at Fort Kamehameha blew. The men boiled out of the barracks, while I went directly to Fort Headquarters, slinging on my field belt and gas mask as I went. Reporting to Major Venn, CO of the 41st, I was informed that it was an anti-sabotage alert and that I was to take my anti-sabotage position, protecting the Pearl Harbor Groupment Headquarters and telephone exchange at Battery Hasbrouck, setting up our two .50 cal. M1 machine guns on the parapet and our two .30 cal. machine guns to cover the ground approaches. Strong patrols covered the adjoining lumber yard, while a guard of six posts was organized and the war reserve of small arms ammunition was drawn and placed in one of the magazines at Hasbrouck.

In the next week, the alert was relaxed to the point of reducing the guard to six men and returning the machine guns to their normal storage place, about a mile away from Hasbrouck. We were about to do some .50 cal. balloon firing so 1800 rounds of belted ammunition was drawn from Ordnance and stored with the guns. The remainder of the battery and both officers went on dust control project

December 1st, so the ammunition was not fired and was immediately available on the seventh.

Jeanne's family.

Jeanne
Age 6 at the time

Because my birthday was in November, I had not been admitted to first grade until after Thanksgiving. I found school wonderful – I had not been to kindergarten, so this was my first school experience – and my life had been rather solitary before we came to Hawaii. For the first time I had the experience of being part of a group. I remember we must have already been preparing for Christmas, because we made lanterns out of construction paper: black frames, orange interior, yellow flame. Salt was sprinkled onto paste to give the effect of snow on the lanterns.

I also had my first crush on a boy. His name was Henry. I came home Friday, December 5, quite heartbroken because Henry and his family were going to move to Hickam Field, the Air Corps base, away from Fort Kamehameha, where we lived. He would be leaving our school!

It was my first experience of something that would trouble me all the time I was growing up: the nomadic quality of military life. Friendships made, only to be broken by a set of "orders."

On that Friday, our teacher had arranged for us to have what she called an "assembly." It involved our sitting in a circle of chairs pulled out from the desks, while she probably read us a story. The recess bell rang, and the teacher asked Henry and me to stay behind and put back the chairs. I saw a Heaven-sent opportunity. There we were, he and I and a number of chairs. So I said, "Henry … kiss me!" He hit me over the head with a chair.

Ah, the trials of young love!

Stephen

December 7th dawned, the usual clear beautiful day. Lieutenant Macauley and I had been to a dinner dance at the Pearl Harbor Navy Club on Saturday night, and with one thing and another, had retired late. The usual percentage of enlisted men was on overnight pass, and since there was no Sunday reveille, the majority of the remainder slept late.

I was awakened by a crash at about 0755. Several more explosions sounded and I tried to figure out why anyone should be firing on a Sunday. Suddenly I heard machine gun fire interposed with the crashes, and noticed that the house was shaking terribly with each explosion. I slid hastily into my uniform, and stepped to the lanai. As I stepped out the door, I saw a plane, silver and blue, passing along parallel to Officers' Row at about 500 feet altitude. The plane had wheel pants and I could see the red ball on the fuselage, just behind the cockpit. I looked out to sea and saw what seemed to be dozens more planes coming in at extremely low altitudes. Another series of explosions sounded from the direction of Hickam Field.

I started immediately for the barracks on foot. The whole effect was nightmarish. The very houses and trees of the Post, long familiar to me, seemed strange. The atmosphere was like that which preceded a thunder storm on the mainland, each feature of the view standing out with an almost menacing clarity. The same dreamlike effect was apparent in my progress. My feet fairly flew but I felt as if I was traveling at a snail's pace. As I ran down the street, I noticed sparks bouncing from the pavement near my feet. I glanced back over my shoulder and saw a plane on me. I jumped out of the road and travelled the next hundred yards among the hibiscus hedges and coconut trees. A car driven by Lieutenant Pomeroy came along, and he slowed down to pick me up. He was Ordnance Officer, so we exchanged a dozen words about supplies before he dropped me at the office.

Jeanne

I thought I heard thunder, and I was terrified of thunder; always had been, as far back as I could remember. When we were going to move to Hawaii, my parents tried to reassure me that the move would be good, because, for one thing, it never thundered in Hawaii. But … I heard what I heard!

So I went into my parents' room. Shaking them frantically, I said, "You said it never thunders in Hawaii. But it's thundering!"

My father sat up in bed. "Ethel," he said to my mother, "I think it's the Japs."

Grabbing his bathrobe, he ran outside and came back looking grim.

"Get dressed," he told my mother. "Get the children dressed, and stay by the phone until I tell you what to do."

My mother patted my head. "There, there, dear," she said to me. "Go get dressed. It isn't thunder. It's only bombs."

Reassured, I trotted off to my room to get dressed.

Meanwhile, she went with my father to the front door to see him off. As he started down the street, a Japanese plane approached, flying so low that she could see the gunner's gold tooth glinting in the sun. He shot one bullet at her, then took off after my father. The bullet hit the sidewalk, digging a dent about four inches long in the cement, and slithered up to her feet, the armor belt peeled back. She picked it up and took it into the house with her. She would keep it as a symbol of all the things that could happen, but didn't.

Stephen

It couldn't have been much after 0805 when I got to the office. The First Sergeant was there, and he and I went to the supply room. Sergeant Duzyk was already issuing out ammunition to the long line of half-dressed men. I decided to move the battery to Hasbrouck, since my greatest fear was that the Japanese would combine their bombing assault with the dropping of parachute troops. Hasbrouck was the closest position to Hickam Field, a key point of the Harbor Defenses of Pearl Harbor and, incidentally, where the remainder of my small arms ammunition was stored. A 2½ ton truck reported in and I detailed Sgt. Cowd and a couple of men to go down and

The bullet intended for Jeanne's mother.

secure the machine guns. Lieutenant Macauley, who had been caught by the blitz just outside Hickam Gate, appeared at this time and I directed him to take the battery up to Hasbrouck, the First Sergeant and I remaining behind until the last man had cleared. The battery moved out in extended order and I was gratified to observe that there was bunching up as they proceeded up the street, even though the strafing was continuous. The barracks had also been strafed while the ammunition was being issued and the men formed up for the move, but owing to the broad veranda, there was no direct vision from the air and nearly all of the bullets struck in the squad rooms, which were already deserted.

The First Sergeant and I waited for the men to leave and then started up the street. We got a lift from Lieutenant Harnett and arrived just after the first of the battery. There was a bunch of civilian workers, mostly Orientals, under the trees and Lieutenant Macauley had sent a couple of men to watch them for fear of attempts at sabotage. We arrived just in time to see our men moving towards the workers with fixed bayonets. The workers started to move off and one of the men said, in the coldest voice I had ever heard, "Don't run. You're not going anywhere!"

The engineer in charge of them took over and volunteered their services wherever they could be used. He was told to stand by in case of fires.

As soon as I arrived at Hasbrouck, I climbed to the old B.C. station on top of the emplacement and looked over Hickam Field and the Navy Yard. It looked like any of the war movies that we always thought were pure Hollywood. The background was an immense pall of smoke from Pearl Harbor. It seemed to come from the oil tanks, but was actually the explosion and burning of the *Arizona*.

Hickam Barracks was also burning and there were five or six planes along the Warm Up Apron that were blazing fiercely, sending up huge clouds of pitch black smoke. A large hangar bellied up, and seemed to explode as I looked. The whole sky was dotted with black smoke puffs from the antiaircraft with an occasional yellow-gray burst among them. Everywhere Jap planes dived and zoomed, for all the world like gnats over a trout stream, sliding down to just above the barrage to release their bombs, then diving through or circling out over the sea to come in low for ground strafing. A B-17E came in to land, then reared up like a horse and tore away, with two Japs after it but unable to catch it. The din was unimaginable. With tracers whipping past me in my exposed position, I stayed only long enough to see that there were no parachutists in sight, then slid down and reported to Col. Rhein that all was clear. He had a teletype in his hand. He instructed me to take all the battery down to the gun position, leaving only 20 men as a security guard, since the teletype reported Jap transports only 20 miles off Barber's Point.

We started the men back down the road, picking up the .50s which had just arrived, but leaving the .30s for the guard. The First Sergeant and both of the officers rode down in the recon, a silly way of putting all the eggs in one basket, but, although fired on, we were not hit. We broke some regulations about speed, however. We arrived at the guns long before the first of the men got down and took cover in an old sand bag emplacement, left from the September maneuvers. The lack of buildings between us and Hickam Field gave up a clear view of the damage being done, while the beach in front of our position was the turning point of the ground strafers, many of whom favored us with a burst as they came over us. We had time to observe the sight that gave us the biggest kick of the day, the destroyers leaving Pearl Harbor. It was heartening to see them roar out the channel heading for what might well have been, from our inaccurate reports, certain death at the hands of a large Japanese fleet. The Japanese planes could see the channel very clearly from the air, and they concentrated their bombs at the channel mouth. Destroyer after destroyer sped out of the harbor, all guns blazing away, and disappeared into the waterspouts, lost to view as they made their turn in the midst of the bombs, and streaked back into sight, apparently unscathed, heading for the horizon and the enemy fleet

Jeanne

My brother and I got dressed, and our mother gave us breakfast. Although it was a bright sunny morning, the window shades were all the way down. My brother stood facing the window, and noticed a beam of sunlight coming through a space at the side of the shade. It was filled with dancing dust motes. This would be one of his most enduring memories of that day.

At some point the phone rang, and our mother told us to come with her. We went out the door and up the street.

It was a strange sight. Small black and white clouds dotted the sky, reminding me of the stuffed toy dog I had lost a day or two earlier, and I stared fascinated at them as we walked. A bus came along and slowed down for us. Our mother more or less pushed us into the bus, boarded it herself, and we headed for an abandoned mortar station. It was an odd sort of bus with wicker seats, which were not very comfortable. But it wasn't a very long ride, after all.

We arrived at a flat-facaded building that

Pearl Harbor, December 7, 1941.

seemed to be made of cement, and went inside. Many other people were there, including a woman who had brought oranges with her and she distributed orange segments to all of the children. Another woman had brought waffles, and gave pieces to the children. There was no butter or syrup, and the waffles were cold, but we ate them happily enough.

We would have to stay there for the time being, we were told. The conditions were very crowded, and the floor was full of cockroaches. My mother, a former schoolteacher, taught me to count to 100 by stepping on dirty cockroaches, one after another. It didn't make an appreciable difference.

Boys are always boys, and they discovered an old mortar launcher, which would turn around if cranked by hand. My brother joined them, and they had fun taking turns standing on it, until a soldier noticed them and chased them off the turntable.

Sleeping arrangements were simple, to say the least: more or less curling up wherever one happened to be. And sanitation was a slit trench at the side of the building.

Stephen

As the first of our men appeared, we put them into trucks and sent them to the magazines to draw shells and powder. We spotted a small dump near each gun and manned the plotting car and the two guns we had personnel for. A detachment of C-41 made this possible. The .50s were set up in the duckweed and could fire on a series of enemy planes, two of which they damaged badly. A fifty pound bomb landed between the guns but luckily did not explode. Our machine guns chattered away, and many of the men cut loose with Springfields, probably doing little or no damage, but giving vent to the anger that was our prime emotion.

As I try to recapture our mood during the attack, what stood out at all times was anger. Nearly everyone was scared, all were filled with self disgust at the way we were caught napping, but sheer rage was the dominant response. Men rejoined after a wild ride from the city and an even wilder ride through Hickam Field, and each had picked up stories, mainly false, about events downtown and about casualties and damage to Military and Naval installations. Each succeeding tale made us madder. The water was reported as poisoned by higher authority, and although there was a hydrant nearby, we could not drink from it. Being under fire makes a man extremely thirsty. I sent a truck up to the mess hall to get the milk out of the ice box, and when they arrived the kitchen blew up in their faces. No food, no drink, and a lot of Battery Fund property smashed to fragments. All of this fanned the flame.

I had been concerned, before the blitz, as to how we would act under fire. None of us, with the exception of the First Sergeant, had been under fire and I had wondered how the men would react, especially in a situation where it was not a question of fighting but largely a matter of taking a pasting without being able to fight back. An officer has to watch over his men, and the responsibility helps steady his nerves. This is also true of the noncoms, especially the sergeants, but the privates had to make do by taking cover in a place where there was no cover. I circulated around among the men to calm them, if necessary, but it wasn't needed. Many had the same lump in their stomachs as I had in mine, a very unpleasant feeling that someone is tying knots in your intestines. Some were pale, as I imagine I was, but all were functioning at top speed.

Our reinforcements were taken away, and a detachment of our own men with them. Those of us that remained took cover and watched the bombing. We had a grandstand seat from where we were. Two flights of level bombers came in at about 15,000 feet and we could see them open their bomb bays and lay their eggs. The sunlight glinted on the bombs as they fell, and they were visible all the way down. A series of explosions merging one into another marked their arrival on the hangar line. The effect was theatrical in the extreme, flash after flash, growing into a billow of dirty brown smoke, with girders and huge slabs of roofing spinning through the air. It looked as if there would be nothing left of Hickam Field, but when I saw the damage on

December 8, I noticed most of the string had fallen neatly in a road and much of the damage could be repaired with a bulldozer. Many other seemingly incredible escapes occurred. One of the men approaching the gun park stopped for a moment to speak to another and a 20mm shot struck the pavement close enough to tear his shoe. Two girls from the post exchange, passing through Hickam, were put under a truck until a lull came. Bullets sprayed around the truck, not hitting it. When they got out from under they discovered they had been under a filled gasoline truck.

The raid quieted down in the afternoon and we were able to get a little food but no water. After dark, I took over the group from Major Venn, who went to Honolulu to arrange for moving the two batteries to field positions. He returned about 9:00 p.m. The creepiest experience I had that whole day was walking about a mile in the pitch black night through invisible troops with very itchy trigger fingers. The entire night was full of shooting, as a gunner would test his gun by firing a burst in the air, and every gun within earshot would do the same. The sight was awe inspiring, tracer seems to float slowly up and the field and fort seemed to be full of Roman candles. This was especially noticeable during the last short raid at about 10:30 when considerable lead went flying skyward. The sight was so beautiful that I stood out on the open watching the fireworks display until two tracer bullets went between my feet, reminding me that the display was lethal as well as beautiful.

Jeanne

Life under crowded conditions at the old mortar battery was anything but comfortable, but as small children we were not particularly aware of specific discomforts. Being herded together into one building was in some ways merely an interesting experience. I have no distinct recollection of how we passed the three days, but I am sure the adults found some ways of channeling our natural energies.

The attack, of course, had taken place on a Sunday, so all the refrigerators contained the Sunday roasts.

On Monday, some soldiers went through all the quarters and took the roasts and cooked them up into a kind of stew. The rumor went that one of the officers had been hunting and had brought down a mountain goat that also went into the pot.

I don't believe anyone really complained about the food. Under the circumstances just having something to eat was comforting.

Stephen

With morning came more rumors, all as cheering and as false as the discouraging ones of the day before. We got orders to move to our field position but had to wait for another battery to move first, so were not able to do more than make up the train on the 8th. The night of the 8th, my second sleepless one, was marked by some imaginary gliders that were being tracked faithfully for an hour or two. These proved to be as false as the stories of parachute troops on the North Shore and the transports off Harbor's Point had been on Sunday.

We moved out Tuesday morning, in two trains. Troops, equipment and armament in one train, ammunition, with six BAR armed guards in the other. The little matter of some 46 bridges and culverts to cross combined with authentic reports of sniping, made me issue orders to shoot to kill anyone observed tampering with bridges, switches or the like. We cleaned out the barracks of everything that we could use in the field and took off. Our communications and observing sections had been transported the day before so that we could be ready to fire as soon as we got into position. It is hard to recall now, but at that time we expected the Japs back any day, before we could draw on the Mainland for reinforcements. As a result we worked under terrific pressure and a fairly high nervous tension, trying to be ready for "Nichi Nichi" when he came back.

I reported to Col. Anderson, a Field Artilleryman who commanded a composite Groupment with Coast Artillery batteries from two regiments and three Field Artillery batteries. To make it more

complicated, he had three Naval officers from damaged ships attached for duty. I got a cordial reception and was offered the use of fifty civilian laborers to help construct my position. I jumped at the chance and we used them for the next two weeks.

Back to the battery at dusk, and I saw the emplacing of the two guns we could man was progressing. Lieutenant Macauley and I oriented the guns with a compass and flashlight. That sounds simple, but a railroad gun is quite a mass of metal and it also rides on steel rails, both conditions which have strong influence on a compass needle. Well, we did it, posted our crews, set out our guards and then went to a tent that had been pitched for our first sleep of the war.

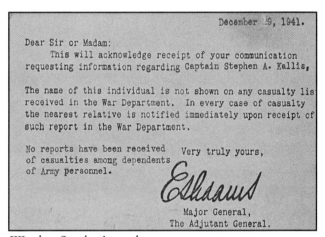

Word to Stephen's mother.

Jeanne

Christmas proverbially comes once a year, including 1941, and including Pearl Harbor. December 7 had been named as the day by which all mail going to the mainland had to be sent, so in some ways Christmas 1941 was fairly well on its way by the day of the attack.

Life, of course, for the time being, had to go on. My brother remembers that flashlights had to be covered with blue cellophane, about three layers of it, so the light could not be seen from the air; the spot of light was to be directed toward the sidewalk. He remembers the flashlight patterns vividly to this day. "It was an article of faith," he adds, "that the glow of cigarettes could be seen from the air, for that matter, so anyone smoking had to do so in a way that would block the cigarette tip glow from shining upwards."

The holiday generally was subdued. The commanding officers of the various companies did the best they could to promote a holiday feeling. Christmas dinners were served to the troops, and, except for critical positions, the men were given free time over the holidays.

My mother told me, "We personally had a little tree on a table, and had our own quiet celebration on Christmas Day. It wasn't a pleasant holiday." I have no clear recollection of it.

Still, some holiday spirit was there. For one thing, we were still alive! In the final analysis, that was a gift not to be ignored.

During the days immediately following the attack, my mother wrote to her mother from the bomb shelter, telling her that we were all "safe and splendid." That letter certainly made my grandmother's Christmas better.

The school had taken a direct hit, so we had no more school in Hawaii.

Evacuation of dependents began the last of January and first of February. We were among the last families to leave, boarding the ship on May 4, 1942. We were not allowed to follow the usual ritual of leaving Hawaii – tossing our leis overboard – for fear that the Japanese submarines would spot them and sink us.

It was very different from our voyage to Hawaii. We had to wear life preservers around our waists at all times, even when sleeping. That was uncomfortable, to say the least.

Our trip home was quite circuitous, as we had to avoid Japanese submarines that were between Hawaii and the mainland. We went as far north as the Arctic Circle before finally landing in San Francisco. At the time we children, at least, never knew the reason why the trip was so long…and so cold!

My father, of course, remained behind. He returned to the mainland and had a few months in Georgia before being sent to Europe. His return was just in time for Christmas 1942. Except for a ten-week course at Fort Leavenworth, he did not return to the United States until late 1945.

Jeanne and her brother with gas masks.

Epilogue

Jeanne

My father, as a career Army officer, also took part in the Korean War. After a year in Korea, he was posted to Sendai, Japan, where we joined him in March of 1952. I was a junior in high school at that time.

Cherry blossoms were in snowy evidence, spring in its first flush, brilliant sunshine on April 28 of that year, a date I will never forget.

The peace treaty between Japan and the United States had been drawn up and approved by the U.N. It was to be signed in Tokyo and in Washington, D.C., and at the same time in Sendai, before the eyes of the whole post, an impressive ceremony was to take place.

Two flagpoles stood in front of XVI Corps Headquarters. One had flown the American flag and on the other the flag of the United Nations, its white emblem

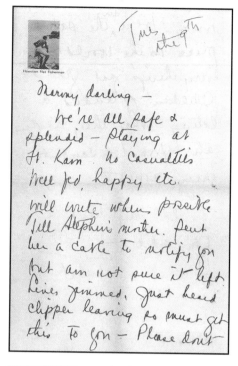

would become an independent, sovereign nation again, and for once the Japanese people would be allowed, almost unchecked, to come onto the American post. All the town, prefecture, and district officials were given reserved seats on the Headquarters lawn, and there were to be speeches by both Japanese and Americans.

The flag-raising took place at eleven that morning, and the Japanese staff helpers at the school were let off at that time. The school was dismissed at ten minutes to eleven, and we students walked over to Headquarters two by two.

A crowd had already gathered in front of XVI Corps Headquarters, where the American flag was flying alone against an intensely blue sky. The pole that normally held the U.N. flag stood in stark relief, the focus of everyone's eyes. We students stood across the street from Headquarters, where many chairs for the Japanese dignitaries had been placed. This was to our left as we faced it. To the right stood a column of soldiers, probably all of XVI Corps; the Signal Corps battalion stood on the students' side of the street, facing the scene. Another organization was to the students' left; American and Japanese civilians, including the students, in the center of the street. Two bands, the American and the Japanese, were on the scene, also to the left.

When the American band played "The Star Spangled Banner," everyone stood at attention, and I thought it had never sounded more thrilling, the flag never more beautiful, fluttering high and gracious against the shiny blue of the sky.

After a speech in English and one in Japanese, the Japanese flag slowly went up, and the Japanese band played their national anthem, the "Kiminaya." Embodied in the slow, deliberate melody was all the sorrow of the ages, the defeat they had suffered, the half-sad, solemn gladness they must have been feeling that day. It moved me, even though I knew it was the regulation, to see the Americans, even the third-graders from school, standing as much at attention for the Japanese anthem as for their own. Some of the grade school boys were solemnly giving their Boy Scout salutes.

My classmate Liz said, in a low voice, "My mother wonders if, now that they're free, they'll revolt against our being here."

on a blue background symbolizing the hope of world peace even in a country only a couple of hundred miles from an active war.

On April 28, 1952, however, this changed, at least for the day. The U.N. flag would not be raised that morning; instead, for the first time in nearly seven years, the Japanese flag would fly. On that day, Japan

I wished she hadn't spoken. I said, "I think it will depend on what we do." I didn't really want to talk at all. It was no moment for superficial chatter, I thought.

Looking at the Japanese women in their traditional kimonos, lining the street up past the athletic fields, their babies on their backs in obis, the old men who had seen so much of Japan as it had once been, as it had later become, the old women in black, our color of mourning, theirs for rejoicing … I wondered what they were feeling. Was a deep, overwhelming gladness rising within them? Surely they must be moved beyond words to see their flag flying free against the sky. Years of training in being impassive in public, hiding their emotions, fled. Some openly wept, unashamed of their tears, which glistened in the brilliant sun.

Their sun had risen again in the Land of the Rising Sun.

I looked at the flags flying side by side, and in that moment I hoped, indeed prayed, that those two flags might always remain on the same side, always allies, always friends.

The course of two nations was changed. The groundwork had been laid and now it would be up to the Americans to see that the newly formed friendship endured. On each of our shoulders would be the responsibility of helping it hold.

I remember Sendai as it was in 1953, with the hope—and belief—that it will fully recover from the earthquake and tsunami of March 2011. The Japanese have a saying, "Bend with the wind.

Jeanne graduating from high school, Sendai, Japan.

Jeanne now

Japanese and American flags, rising side by side.

AUTHOR PAGE

Jeanne was five years old when her father, an ROTC graduate of Columbia University in New York, moved the family to Hawaii where he would be stationed as an Army Reservist in World War II. He gave thirty-three years to an Army career, going active after his service during World War II. The family moved continually, ending with Jeanne's last year of high school in Sendai, Japan.

After moving from place to place and attending thirteen schools before she graduated from high

Stephen A. Kallis

school, Jeanne Ahlers claims Boston as her hometown. When she arrived there following high school graduation, she attended Tufts University for four years, and was not willing to budge from a place she could call home, even though Dad had been assigned to France at that time. She did relinquish and travel to Europe once to study in Germany. In Boston, she also met her future husband, Peter, through their affiliation with a Lutheran church choir. A native of Germany, he was a student at the Harvard Divinity

School, soon to change his focus to the study of the German language, which he taught at Beloit College in Beloit, Wisconsin, before coming to Bethany College in Lindsborg in 1972.

While in Lindsborg, Jeanne worked at the Lindsborg News Record and the Lindsborg Community Library and the United Methodist Church. Her life changed drastically January 24, 1975, when she and the family were involved in a tragic car accident. Six weeks prior, she and Peter had adopted a three and one-half year old Korean boy, whom they named Michael. Jeanne and Michael escaped serious injury, but Peter became permanently disabled after months of rehabilitation at Craig Hospital in Denver. He was able to teach two more years at Bethany before the German major was discontinued.

The family traveled to Germany in 2006 where Peter could renew family acquaintances and Michael could meet his new relatives. Jeanne continued to work at the newspaper and the library following Peter's death February 15, 2007.

Jeanne is a veteran writer. Her Pearl Harbor story has shown up as a college paper, a feature in the Lindsborg News Record, and now as a published book. She began a novel—*You've Made Your Bed*—as a college senior, put it away for several years, and revisited the manuscript while she was in Wisconsin with Peter. She finished it, published it, and enjoys knowing that copies reside in several Lindsborg homes as well as the public library and is available for purchase through national distribution sites.

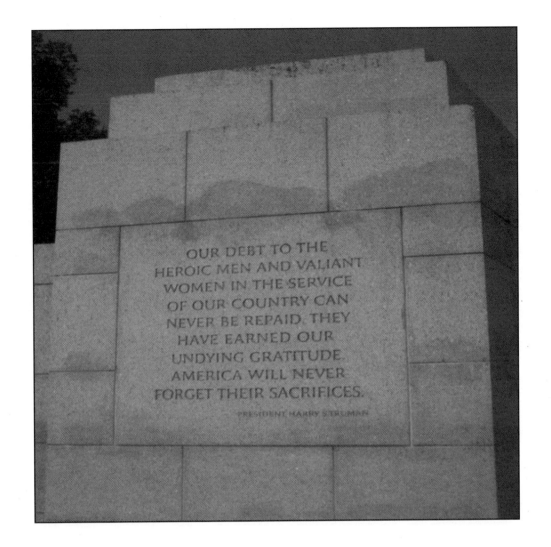

OUR DEBT TO THE
HEROIC MEN AND VALIANT
WOMEN IN THE SERVICE
OF OUR COUNTRY CAN
NEVER BE REPAID. THEY
HAVE EARNED OUR
UNDYING GRATITUDE.
AMERICA WILL NEVER
FORGET THEIR SACRIFICES.
PRESIDENT HARRY STRUMAN

JUST DOING OUR JOB

by Angel Andrewson

THIS BOOK IS DEDICATED TO:

The men and women who gave everything to the common good during WW II.

"Over There"

The following pages are stories from men and women who were 'over there,' in the midst of the war being fought on land, or sea or air. These are the heroes who shaped our country and gave their all for those left at home and for generations to come. Each story is titled by the name of the individual whose story you are reading; they are from different branches of the service and had completely different jobs or assignments, all of whom are heroes in my mind. These are their stories, and I am proud to be the one to pass them on and preserve them for future generations.

Ellery Wayne Einfeldt

There are events in our lives which forever

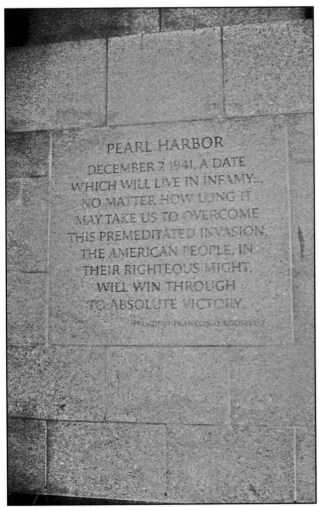

WW II Memorial, Washington, D.C.

remain etched in our minds; we recall exactly where we were when they occurred; what song was playing, which TV show we were watching, even the scents that were in the air around us when a major event took place. Sometimes these songs, scents, and shows can take us back to that moment in time, and in our memory, we can recall the specific details about that day.

The attack on Pearl Harbor is such an event. Anyone who was alive at the time of this terrible attack on our country can tell you what they were doing, where they were, the emotions they felt, and what they did in the moments and days following.

This was an event which the world remembers and which forever shaped the lives of people around the world, but especially Americans. The unsuspected bombing of our ships in the harbor was the beginning of a terrible war which killed hundreds of thousands of men and women around the world and left a wave of mass destruction when all was said and done.

Ellery Wayne Einfeldt, my dad's older brother, was in the United States Navy, stationed at Pearl Harbor on December 7, 1941. His ship assignment was the California, but he was on the Arizona at the time of the attack by the Japanese at 8:00 am that fateful day. When the ship went down, it was, indeed, hell on and below deck of that ship as it burst into flames. The fire burned black and heated the steel hull of the ship as well as the water surrounding it and others in the harbor that day. Men panicked below deck and locked themselves in rooms where they thought they would be safe from the fiery hell above them. Ellery knew that to do so would mean sure death for these men, and he physically carried and otherwise led these young men above deck through burning flames, blinding smoke, and unbearable heat to the safety of lifeboats and/or the water where they could swim to a safe place away from the burning hull of the massive ship. Ellery was a quiet, unassuming man and took no credit for what he did to save these young men. He, like so many other men of his time, 'was only doing his job,' keeping his men and his brother sailors safe, as they would have done for him.

The humility of these many men is incredible, and you can hear story after similar story of this type of bravery from these unsung heroes. These are the men who made our country safe and built the foundation to keep it the greatest country in the world.

WW II Memorial, Washington, D.C.

Lowell Miller

The terrifying wail of air raid sirens struck fear in the young corpsman; his feet seemed weighted in concrete as he ran for shelter. The horrible explosions of bombs outside had him believing that this was the end, as a nun in the shelter hurriedly and repeatedly recited the Hail Mary amidst the panic. When suddenly all was quiet, the young soldier was still very much alive, and often has wondered since, if it was indeed the prayers of the nun that saved them.

Bombings weren't new; he had seen and felt their destruction as they fell all around in the European theater where he was stationed. Once he watched in horror as a cemetery was bombed and coffins shot up from the war-torn earth, as if mocking the oft-used epitaph 'Rest In Peace.' Lowell recounts, "I could lie and say I was brave and courageous, but I was scared to death."

Lowell Miller, now a Lindsborg, Kansas, resident, spent his military time as a corpsman in England and in North Africa. As if worrying about bombs weren't enough, there were many inherent

dangers just being in the country of Africa. One night, Lowell was sent to deliver malaria swabs to a lab, and when he arrived, there were two lions by the door. Eerily, in the background, he heard a young girl singing "Santa Lucia," a stark contrast to the predators staring at him. He waited, very still, and the lions eventually left their post, and Lowell was able to deliver his package and return to his base safely.

As if bombs weren't enough!

Thank you, Lowell, for your courageous service!

Ruth (Rush) Johnson

Amidst the turmoil and destruction during times of war, there were also times, events, and places that provided soldiers a chance to relax, recreate, and enjoy some semblance of normality. It was with enlisted military personnel like Corporal Ruth (Rush) Johnson, that these opportunities were put in place. Ruth was a member of the Air Transport Command branch of the US Army, and played trumpet in the band.

Ruth Johnson's Honorable Discharge.

Unable to attend college due to financial constraints, Ruth made the decision to join the service, as all of her friends had left to college or military already. So, from Jamestown, Kansas, Ruth signed up to serve her country. Ruth didn't choose her branch of the military; she was assigned to the Army and left for Ft. Des Moines, Iowa, for training. She was very homesick the first night, even though she was in a barracks with 49 other young women. However, the homesickness was short lived as they began their training the next day and there was no time for anything but Army life. She was so tired at the end of the day that she fell into bed and slept.

Because she played trumpet, Ruth also doubled as the company bugler. After seven months of training and band practice, Ruth, as part of the WAC Band, traveled to Wales, Germany and France, to provide entertainment for the troops around the world.

The band provided concerts and dances, but that was not the only entertainment that these band personnel provided as they traveled from country to country, base to base. They also helped set up libraries and recreation at the bases they visited, (basketball teams for the men, and softball for the women) as well as publishing a newsletter on the bases. Ruth reports that it was "a plum job, really" and that she enjoyed her time traveling around the world.

Travel from base to base was by train, and Ruth got used to thinking of the train as home and she did get tired of riding them. She never tired of meeting the people and enjoying the cultures wherever she went. One thing she could have done without was Brussels sprouts, and it seemed that everyone served them, no matter where she was! Another thing Ruth enjoyed about her time in the military was the friends she made, both in the military and in the countries where she traveled. She kept in touch with many of them until they died. Ruth especially liked the Welsh, they were beautiful people, and enjoyed the food they prepared. She said the best cooks were the Germans. The food reminded her of home cooked meals, as it was more meat and potatoes than what they served elsewhere.

There was no leave overseas, so Ruth never got to go home till the war was over, but she did get to see her brother while in Wales, as he got a two-day pass and came to see her. She kept in contact with her family back home with letters, which were sent free to all military personnel-no postage was required.

When it was announced that the war was over, there began the celebrating-dancing and yelling and singing and, of course, drinking, in the streets, the pubs (where, on V-E and V-Day, drinks were free), and the homes. Then, the work began to close up bases. This meant destroying everything they had built, all that they had done to provide for the soldiers, now was to be destroyed. For Ruth, this was

the hardest part of her job, which until then had been enjoyable most of the time. The part that really got to her was when they destroyed the libraries; buildings, furniture, and the books.

"The books, that hurt" said Ruth. She loved books and reading, and the library was a favorite place for her. But, it was her job, and she did as she was told, but she didn't like it.

Ruth went to Chicago, and was discharged there and went home to Kansas. She was ready to begin the rest of her life, which included going to college on the G.I. Bill to get her teaching degree. Ruth taught in a one-room schoolhouse for five years, then got married to Vivian Johnson and raised a family. From time to time when her children were young and misbehaving, Ruth would get out her Good Conduct Medal to show to them it was even important to the Army to be on your best behavior! Adorning Ruth's uniform were also the Victory Medal, European African Middle Eastern Theater Ribbon, and two overseas Service Bars. When Ruth thinks about her service, she says "I was proud to be in the military, proud to wear the uniform"

Who wouldn't be? Thank you, Ruth!

Pip Nelson

Life in the Army during WWII was seen as "just doin' our job," as Phillip 'Pip' Nelson related. It is his words that became the title and premise of this book, and a recurring theme you will see reading the stories.

Pip was raised in Smolan, Kansas, and was drafted in July of 1941 at the age of 24 and completed boot camp in Texas near Galveston. "It was the longest trip I'd ever taken so far," says Pip. From there, Pip began a much longer trip when he boarded a ship and ended up in Germany. From there he was sent to Czechoslovakia, where he spent most of the next four and a half years as a gunner on a 155mm cannon.

Pip says it seemed like forever instead of just four years. During his service, Pip recalls that he really never felt afraid or scared. He just did what he was told and that kept him safe. He says that they

Pip Nelson

told him to aim over there and he did, and that "I never did see anything I was shooting at" because of the range of the cannon. He did see the destruction of the bombings that had taken place before he and his company arrived, and he said it was massive, and his overall view of being 'over there' was, "it was loud and it wasn't very pleasant."

Pip was a Corporal with the 805th field artillery and was finally able to get home in January of 1946, returning to Smolan and eventually marrying.

He and his wife ended up building their own home and Pip opened a service station in the town, which he ran until he retired, and he lived in Smolan until 2008 when he moved to Bethany Home in Lindsborg. Pip is one of those men who still is laid back and humble about his service, as so many of these veterans are. They all seem to sing the same refrain, "We were just doing our job."

I for one am so glad they did!

Royer Barclay

Royer Barclay of Lindsborg, spent his time during WWII in the Navy, assigned first to a radar technology lab in Patuxent, Maryland. He then

spent 30 days on a boat between there and Trinidad. The over-the-sea ride was the toughest part of his assignments. There were sixty-three sailors on the 'banana boat.' He was in charge of them, most of them much younger than Royer's 31 years. He had told them when the boat began to pitch in the rough waters to get up on deck if they were going to be seasick, but, alas, most of them didn't make it that far!

Royer spent a good portion of this trip on deck holding on for dear life as the waves crashed over him and he, too, gave in to seasickness. He remembers telling the boys to hang on and help one another, but as they all became ill, it was every man for himself and some of them didn't seem to care if they went overboard or not.

Royer recalls that it was immensely important for him to get back home intact, as he had a wife and baby boy waiting for him. The boat continued to pitch with the stormy sea seemingly in cahoots with the enemy, attempting to sink them, but they made it to their destination. A little worse for wear, but at least alive!

According to Royer, the time on Trinidad was not noteworthy as the Germans had surrendered by the time they got there, but this humble sailor would never take credit for any accolades. As far as he was concerned, he was just a man doing his duty to insure the freedom of the country in which his young son would live and grow.

Wally Drevitts - In His Own Words

The company formed up in Richmond, Virginia, and most of the boys came from the east, the smart ones that is. (laughs) I came from Kansas, the Smolan area. My wife Esther and I lived there after we were married. After our unit was formed up and we went through basic, she joined me and we got an apartment. I was part of the 864th Army unit attached to the US Air Force. We were to build up supplies, build roads, airports and the like.

I shipped to New York and trained. Then, the Queen Mary waited for us — 16,000 troops on that ship! We were just a small part of that group. Now, the Queen Mary didn't run in convoy, she was too fast a ship. So we were on our own out there, watching for German subs, which were all over the seas. The subs sunk a lot of ships, but we never had a lot of trouble. We put up in Scotland, in the Perth of Clyde. Then they put us on trains and we shipped to England, where we dug in with a base that was already started.

We had rock crushers, scrapers, trucks, and I was in charge of keeping them running. Hardly any of us had any experience with the Letourneau scrapers, so when we went to get them, no one knew how to drive them. They were steered with steering clutches, no front wheels, and some of the guys had trouble with that. It was a scraper mounted on the back of a tractor with drive wheels, and there were wheels on the scraper. There were no front wheels or steering wheels. If you were going downhill and the load was pushing you, well, then you had to cross clutch. If you wanted to go right, you pulled the other way, and a few of the boys had trouble with that and went off the road a few times! A few men had some experience with them, but it was my job to keep them all going. They were my responsibility and I took it seriously.

We landed on Normandy, after dozers and others had been in and begun building up the front. We laid back 30 miles and dug-in in a man's apple orchard, in two-man foxholes. We actually slept pretty good! We never got bombed or strafed, not that we couldn't have, we just happened to be lucky,

Letourneau scraper.

I guess. The only thing is that one night there was a false gas attack, and we had to lay there with our gas masks on. I guess it was just a test, and they wanted to be sure we were ready for anything. We never had any bombings or anything the whole time I was in. The early landing, of course, lost a lot of men. It was bombed and finally taken.

Before we went in, they had been in and begun to clear roadways and runways and were beginning to get things built up. Our company went in and continued to build the roads and runways, following the front. Never saw much fire, but when we first got in I found some German gun placements that hadn't been touched. It was where there was a machine gun and a pile of ammunition.

We built runways, the surveyors laid out strips for evacuation and supplies drops, we put down the dirt work, and put in pierced plank runways. These were steel with holes in 'em and they locked together; they were for single or double engine planes, not real big. I got to land on one after the war in Germany on leave to Paris, dropped off a friend of mine on one of the runways they had built. I was in the nose cone on this plane, and when we landed on that pierce plank runway, and they put on the brakes, that runway just rolled up like a wave. I think they put me in the nose just so they could scare me. It worked!

Well, when the war ended, I was one of the early ones who got to go home. I went home in one piece. I was one of the lucky ones. I've thought about that, that my mother's prayers have followed me most of my life. I didn't enlist, you know. I had been married about a year, I guess. Worked there in Smolan for a local International dealer. We lived in my mother's house. When we shipped out to New York, Esther was pregnant. When I came home, I had a 16-month old little girl to get acquainted with. When I came home, that little girl looked at me, like, who are you? But they had shown her pictures of me, and it didn't take long for her and me to get to know each other.

Now, there was no job left for me in Smolan. The International dealer had sold out, and I had a wife and a little girl to take care of. I had decided to take a vacation before going back to work, but I quickly got bored with that. We bought a home in Smolan, and I went to Salina and went to one place, and the guy I was supposed to see wasn't there, so I went to another place, and they hired me. I worked there 34 years, repairing big equipment, and we had a little boy, David, and we lived there and raised those two kids in Smolan.

On the Home Front

WWII was won not only by men and women in the military, by any means. If not for the support back home in the good ol' USA, we may not have come away with victory. Those left at home to "keep the home fires burning" also built the planes, battleships, and tanks that carried our military over land, air and sea. Also, as the saying goes, "an army crawls on it belly." Those tireless folks who grew the food for our army were every bit an integral part of the war effort.

Earl Swenson

One of these young farmers who served our country on the home front was Earl Swenson, of Lindsborg, Kansas. Earl was just old enough to enlist when the news of Pearl Harbor rocked the country, and the world. Young men showed up in droves to sign up to serve and protect our country, and Earl was no exception. Problem was, they were not so eager to take Earl at the recruiting station. Earl was one of those in McPherson County who had a deferment because he was a farmer. Had he lived in Saline County, he could have enlisted and been on his way to fighting in the trenches with his peers. Living in McPherson County, however, kept him at home on the farm, as there weren't nearly as many in that county to stay and raise the much needed food to continue to fuel our country and our military's nutritional needs. So, much to his chagrin, Earl remained at home and continued working on the farm to do his part in the war effort.

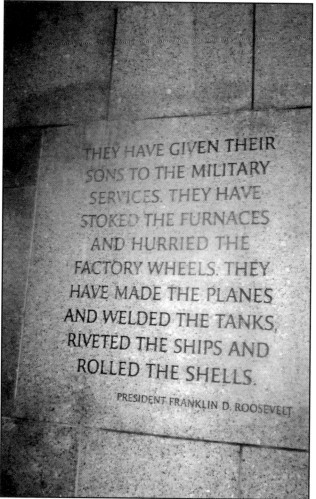

WW II Memorial, Washington, D.C.

Earl recounts that they raised corn, and he shucked that corn by hand, going row by row with his trusty team of horses (one black nag and one white one) pulling a buckboard wagon. Earl would shuck the corn of each cob and toss the cob in the wagon in one seemingly fluid motion, and then the next and the next and so on until the wagon was full. Earl became the fastest corn shucker ever to be seen in the area-he could shuck 106 bushels in one day!

Earl loved hard work and though he felt bad about not being able to serve in the military, he knew his job at home was just as important. There were, however, those who begged to differ and would look down on Earl and other young men who were at home 'safe and sound' while their sons were 'over there' fighting for our country and our freedoms.

More than once did Earl overhear conversations in grocery stores, community gatherings or on the street, regarding him and how he just stayed where he was safe and didn't have to put his life on the line like their young men did. How unfair it was that Earl was able to stay home with his family and their sons were over there dying. Earl felt bad about that, but it was not his choice to stay home.

And so it was…many young men stayed home, seeing to crops and livestock to keep the economy going and a nation fed at a time when food would be rationed and purse strings and belts tightened more than they had ever known before.

To all those who stayed behind to keep the country running, "I salute You !"

Russel James (Jim) Thomas
(Courtesy Don C. Thomas)

Jim Thomas was another of those men who didn't fight the war overseas or in the military, but he fought tooth and nail every day on the home front to survive and see that his family and the neighbors were taken care of during the hard years of WWII. His son, Don Thomas, now of Lindsborg, relates the story of his hero, his dad.

Accompanying his dad to the Poheta Cemetery south of Solomon, Kansas, one day, Don Thomas watched as his dad cleared weeds around a gravestone, taking care to clean it up and make it look respectable. Don asked him if they were good friends. His dad replied, "Yes, they saved my life."

Don inquired further and Jim related the story of Mr. and Mrs. Reese of Solomon. This couple served as the Selective Service officers for the township in which the Thomas family lived south of Solomon. When the war started and the call went out for men to sign up to serve in the military, Jim went to their house to do just that. They told him that it wasn't possible, that they couldn't let him sign up.

Jim replied, "No, it's my duty," to which they replied, "You can't go."

When he asked why, they said, "Well, for one, you have a wife and six children at home. Who's going to take care of them? And who's going to grease the windmills, and plaster the cisterns, and take care of all the things you do for everyone around here? We can't keep things going if you aren't here!"

So, Jim, a brick mason, plasterer, painter, and basically a jack of all trades in the community, continued to do just that, taking care of things big and small in the community.

The Thomas family, as most families in the area, farmed for a living, so Jim was kept busy with his own farm and home and family, but also took time to take care of the needs of his neighbors. He would check their cisterns and repair them, he would make 'baskets' out of chicken wire and fill them with charcoal, then hang them under the gutters so the rainwater would pass through the charcoal before going to the cistern to help filter the drinking water.

Windmill such as Jim Thomas worked on.

He climbed the windmills (up until he was 75!) "He loved to climb, loved high places" and greased and repaired them to insure water pumped to the tanks. He also painted, wallpapered, repaired, and fixed things in and around the community until he died in 1994 at age 89.

So, yes, Jim was grateful that the couple wouldn't let him join the military (because of course, there's a good chance he may not have come back), and so were the neighbors in and around Solomon, Kansas, for they wouldn't have had his expertise to keep their farms and households running while the war was being fought.

The Thomas family increased by two more before the war was won, the last one being Don C. Thomas, who passed this story of his dad on to me. Don, too, is glad Jim didn't join the military, or he may very well not have been born!

To Russel 'Jim' Thomas: may the memories and the lessons from your life of selflessness and neighboring never be forgotten!

War is indeed hell, as General MacArthur not so poetically stated. And not just for those on the battlefield, of which he was speaking. No, being on the home front brought its own sense of hell to those surviving the war without their loved ones, without benefit of internet or Skype to keep in contact with them, or overnight mail or phone calls to assure families of their whereabouts and that they were even alive. It also was a hard time for those left to man the factories and the farms, the grocery stores, the feed mills, you name it. The country had to keep going, despite the fact that 16.1 million men and women had answered the call to serve in the military.

Because so many of our men were gone, women stepped up and began entering the work force; an entirely new generation of women was born of this war. Women found an independence they had never known before, and many remained employed after the war was over, starting a trend that continues today. Women no longer were relegated to being only homemakers and mothers. They could also work the factories, the mills, basically whatever was needed to keep our country on its feet.

Marty Tubbs

One of these women was Martha Tubbs, (deceased) of Lindsborg, a young farm girl who heard the call for help during WWII and, along with her two sisters, answered it, joining many other young women in Oregon, building, of all things, battleships! What a far cry from working on the family farm, milking cows, plowing fields, cutting wheat, baking bread, sewing and mending, and other domestic duties.

Martha and her young sisters had been taught another very worthwhile task while growing up on the farm: they all knew how to weld. Their father had taught them so they could help repair farm equipment when needed, and so they took that knowledge to Portland, Oregon, and built battleships till the end of the war.

All was not fun and games, though. Working in factories was not easy work, most of them were hot, stifling buildings and the work was tedious and much of it was overhead. At the end of the day, they often felt as though *they* had been through battle. Martha and her sisters were used to hard work on the farm, but working a factory found them experiencing a new kind of fatigue and new aches and pains in muscles they didn't know they had. But they were doing it to keep the wheels of our country's military rolling, enduring conditions reminiscent of war.

Yes, war is hell on the home front too.

Marie Nelson

Soldiers in WWII were not all overseas, and not all were in the midst of battle, but they all enjoyed the entertainment and distraction from the war which often times came to them courtesy of the USO. The USO (United Service Organization) was organized in April of 1941 to serve the religious, spiritual and educational needs of the men and women in the armed forces. The USO clubs were financed largely through public donations. The USO also provided entertainment options for service personnel including dances, sporting events, and dinners at the homes of families where they were stationed.

Because there were so many agencies seeking funds during the war, the government created the National War Fund. It was based on the idea of a Community Chest — consolidating many causes in one large fund drive. The flag of the National War Fund often hung in USO clubs. To receive funds an agency had to be approved as being essential to the war effort by the president's War Relief Control Board. The USO received nearly half of the money collected by the National War Fund in 1944.

These clubs were set up where there were military bases, and Salina, Kansas, was one such city, with Schilling Air Force Base on the west edge of town, and Camp Phillips just down the road. Marie Nelson, now of Lindsborg, Kansas, was just 17 and a college freshman attending Kansas Wesleyan University when the war broke out. The girls in her sorority were all going to join the USO, so Marie went also, but they said at 17, she was too young. The others all actively spoke in her favor and, because she was a college freshman, they finally allowed her to join. Thus began a very enjoyable and memorable chapter in Marie's life.

On Friday nights, a bus would come and pick up the girls and they would go to the dance at the Schilling Air Force Base in Salina. On Saturday nights, they went to the Masonic Temple. The dances provided live bands and on several occasions they were treated to the Glenn Miller Orchestra, Sammy Kaye and other big name bands of the times. One weekend, the 4th Division came to the dance, and they were all young college boys, about 300 of them. There had been a chickenpox outbreak in Salina, and only 14 of the girls were able to come to the dance. "Fourteen girls to 300 men, boy, that was fun!" Marie says.

One evening, there was a 'strapping boy from the South' who 'had red hair, just like mine,' and they danced and visited throughout the night. When the dance was over, he asked if he could carry her home. Marie said, "No, I can walk, thanks, but you could walk me home," and so he did.

There were other aspects to the USO besides providing dances on the weekends, and the Presbyte-

rian Church was the site of a 'soldier center,' a place where the soldiers could come and play cards (old maid, fish, Chinese checkers, etc. NO pinochle or bridge allowed!), badminton or volleyball with the members of the USO. Marie enjoyed this aspect also, and it gave her a chance to visit with the soldiers, a bit of normalcy to the military life they were living.

Visiting one evening with friends at the soldiers' center, Marie overheard a soldier who walked by say, "Boy, her seams are crooked." "Oh, look at hers-they're perfect. Oh, look at hers…" You see, at this time the hose women wore had seams up the backs, and it was very difficult to get and keep those seams straight up the backs of the leg. Marie and her friends all looked at each other and together ran to the bathroom to inspect seams and make sure theirs were all straight!

All the dances and friends and fun times often made it hard to believe that there was a war. Marie said she feels a little ashamed that we had fun, but we did, but, that's what the soldiers needed, a distraction from the war they were fighting.

There was one thing that brought the war to the forefront in Marie's life on a weekly basis, and that was the air raid drills. Marie's father was the neighborhood air raid warden, and once a week, a drill was conducted and he would go from house to house to be sure no light could be seen in any houses, and that everyone was indoors.

Marie's home had a center room with only one window, so during the drills, they shut out all the lights and went into that room with a small gas lantern and covered the window with black curtains. It was an eerie feeling to see all the houses completely dark, but that was necessary in case we were being bombed, they couldn't see where the population centers were if it was pitch black everywhere. Thankfully these were only drills and they never had an actual air raid.

Eventually, the war was over, and Marie recalls that on V-E day, there was dancing in the streets, and everyone was yelling and screaming and, "I'd never been kissed by so many men as I was that day." It was a day of rejoicing and happiness after a devastating war around the world. At this point, Marie was graduating college with a degree in business administration with a major in history and a minor in Spanish. She went to work for Grace E. Stewart, a local school, and then married in 1952. "Many of the girls found their husbands through the USO, but I wasn't one of them. I found mine after college and I had a job."

Well, maybe Marie didn't find her husband in the USO, but she and the other members helped a lot of young soldiers cope with military life through their time in the USO, providing entertainment venues for them and spending time visiting and getting to know them. I'm sure the soldiers appreciated the opportunity to step away from the military for a little while each week, courtesy of the USO.

Thanks, ladies, for your part in maintaining the morale of our troops!

Chester Peterson, Jr.
In His Own Words

February 1942 is remembered as the time the U.S Army virtually confiscated farmland to make Camp Phillips to train the 94th Infantry Division, the Smoky Hill Air Corps Base—now Schilling airport—for B-17s and later the B29s, and the German POW camp.

My father had worked so hard during the Depression (keep in mind, it really was World War II that took the county out of the Depression) that by 1942 he and Grandma Alphild had 880 acres. The government took 800 acres from the family, leaving just the homeplace of 80 acres! Grandma and my father were able to buy an adjoining 80 acres, and that was it, until the late 1940s. Years later they eventually got the closest 160 acres bought back. All the rest is still in the Smoky Hill Bombing Range.

One of these repurchased 80s owned by Grandma Alphild was the basis of my 4-H Club land project and resulted in state championships in Soil Conservation and Grasses and Legumes.

Although Uncle Sam paid the lowest rate possible for the land to the farmers who were displaced

and/or had farmland for Camp Phillips, the farmers had to invest the money within a year or pay capital gains taxes. My father wanted grassland, and first investigated the famous Flint Hills. However, I remember him saying several times that he didn't think the grass and water there were worth the prices being asked. He checked out a ranch in extreme northeast Ellsworth County and liked what he saw: Several good springs, the potential for some new ponds, good grass, and reasonable fences. He and Grandma Alphild immediately bought the "Ranch."

The first thing they did was have the Soil Conservation Service (now Natural Resources Conservation Services) produce a complete conservation plan. Waterways were constructed on the cropland, followed by the building of terraces when the grass in the waterways was established. Five ponds were built, for a total of six, which allowed more uniform and efficient cattle grazing. Later, my mother approved cross-fencing which allowed even more efficiency via rotation grazing.

My job on this Ellsworth ranch was seemingly never ending: Digging postholes so the fences could be improved. I think on average there was maybe four inches of soil and then small shards of limestone all the way down to bedrock. Toward the close of a long day on the way back home my father would pull the pickup into the filling station Highway 40 at Carneiro. He'd buy me a bottle of pop—only a nickel—and leave another penny for a deposit on the bottle.

Camp Phillips began west right across the road and railroad track in front of the farmstead. The Army shot 105mm and 155mm cannons from there to the western boundary--which, even though their vibrations loosened plaster in our house, we greatly preferred they shoot from east to west!

City boy soldiers would abandon their foxholes when the creek began overflowing after heavy rains. My father always let them stay in the bunkhouse until they could return across the road.

Farmers could hire German POWs to work by the day then. We often had a pair, Tony and Matteus, that were like family. They'd been captured as teenagers while serving in Rommel's Afrika Korps. Civilians couldn't buy oranges or Hershey bars, so they'd buy them at their PX and bring them to us.

After WWII was over, the government rented out all the land to big operators who no doubt paid some graft money. They burned and disked the ground up and down the hills, raping and pillaging the soil for three years. Then the original owners had the option of buying back some of the land. Unfortunately, 640 acres, a full section of our family's land, is still owned by the government and is part of the Smoky Hill bombing range.

As for unexploded bombs and shells, that was one advantage of having someone else farm the ground at first. Because every so often, we'd hear about an employee having the front of this tractor blown off by an abandoned live bomb.

I never hit a bomb. However, once I straightened out an outside duckfoot blade shank that was 1x1½ inches of steel by inadvertently running it into an unseen foxhole dug by some soldier. A year or two after the war some friends and I, while out exploring, found a bomb under the big bridge that adjoined some of our land. I still wonder if it's being trundled down the Smoky Hill-Kaw-Missouri-Mississippi Rivers with every flood. Look out, New Orleans!

One day in what must have been in either late 1941 or early 1942, Grandma Alphild was outside and yelled, "Come out, come out and see this!!" And 'this', was a biplane flying overhead, the first airplane I'd ever seen. It was no doubt scouting out the government's later mandatory land purchase.

Oh, my, but did we see a lot of them later on. All right, it's a slight, but only slight exaggeration to say the sky was dark with B-17 bombers flying from the Smoky Hill Army Air Base southwest of Salina. Later in WWII, B-29s replaced them practicing formation flying. These fighters would stretch from horizon to horizon, like an aluminum cloud.

Newcomers often are puzzled why the road from the Saline County line north of Lindsborg to Smolan is called the Burma Road. During WWII it was a sand country road over which infantry recruits were marched mile after mile after mile.

B-17 (The Mighty Fortress) at Salina, KS airport 2011.

Because central Kansas can get slightly warm and humid in mid-summer—actually 'slightly' should be amended to 'grossly'—the soldiers likened their forced marching the road over which the cruel Japanese forced POWs to prison camp in steamy Burma.

Just before Christmas 1943 we four, Chester Sr., Erma, Grandma Alphild, who lived with us, and I, drove to Morro Bay, California. We spent Christmas with the Tonsings where Uncle Ernest was an Army officer and chaplain. We took the southern route, and so on the way we went into Old Mexico at Ciudad Juarez across from El Paso, Texas.

Gas rationing was in effect, although my father had all the gas windshield stickers 'A','B', and 'C', which helped. Rubber tires were also rationed, and just about impossible for civilians to buy. Tires certainly didn't last as long as they do now either. Farmers, however, could purchase four-wheel trailers with new rubber tires. By an amazing coincidence with our desire to travel to the West Coast, my father just happened to buy a trailer that used the same size tires as the family Pontiac. Just lucky, I guess.

During the war years we also rounded up all the scrap metal we could find and donated it to the war effort. War bonds could be purchased for $18.75 for a $25 bond payable in ten years on up. Or, you could buy war bond stamps and paste them into a booklet, then turn it in when it was full for a bond.

My father bought the first war bond sold in Saline County. I still have the first war bond I was able to buy via stamps. I probably should have cashed it in years ago, but it looks good on my office wall.

WWII also was the precursor that meant not only would I never be an accomplished speller, but even being adequate was a real stretch. Back in those days there were six or eight families on each telephone 'party line' operated by Ed and Goldy at Salemsburg. When there was a community emergency, Goldy, the usual switchboard operator, would plug in all the lines at once and give one l-o-n-g ring.

Keep in mind that I always brought home a lot of books to read. I kept track and read exactly 100 during the eight months of my fifth grade year. I brought home my first 'study' book, my spelling textbook, when I was in the second grade. I was on the word 'squirrel' when the line call came: a B29 bomber had crashed just off the Falun-Assaria road just two miles from home. Unfortunately, only one airman managed to bail out, and he broke a leg on a tombstone in the Salemsburg Cemetery. If you know where to look today, all these years later, you can still see where that bomber went in.

Guess I took this as a harbinger. I never took a textbook home to study again until my freshman year at K-State. Oh, yes, and I still have trouble spelling the word 'squirrel'.

Thanks, Chet for sharing your memories!

Honoring Our WWII Veterans

From every corner of our great state they came…much like they did 65 years ago when they came to fight for their country. To stand up for the freedoms for which we stand: One nation, under God, indivisible with liberty and justice for all.

For a government of the people, for the people and by the people. They were just kids then, most of them, just out of school or not quite, but with the blessings and signature of a parent, they signed up anyway. They came to fight for the freedoms which we still enjoy today in lands far away from home, to a place many called hell.

That was then.

This time they come for a different reason; to reminisce, to meet up with other veterans, but mostly, to see the memorial built in their honor. Many years late, to be sure, but no less built with great honor and humility for those who fought WWII. Men and women, soldiers, nurses, radio operators, pilots, battleship captains, engineers, infantry, chaplains…each played a key role in this terrible war, as so many have before and since, and they fought to keep the United States of America the greatest country on earth.

So, to honor these men and women of the 'greatest generation', the Honor Flight Network was formed. This non-profit organization has as its mission to fly all veterans free of charge to see the memorials built in their honor. Right now, the focus is on WWII veterans, and any veteran of any conflict who has a terminal illness. Once the WWII veterans are flown, they will begin flying Korean and Viet Nam vets to see their memorials also.

The flights are a three-day affair and completely free to the veterans including all meals, lodging, buses, and the flight. They receive an Honor Flight hat, t-shirt, WWII memorial book, and a 'tabloid' with names of all the vets on that flight and their service records. Guardians may go at a price of $650.00 and help to push wheelchairs, load and unload coolers, walkers, etc., which is a huge bargain and an incredible honor.

Accompanying veterans on these trips is a humbling and emotional journey, as they arrive at the memorial and slowly walk past all the columns engraved with all the states and all of our allies, to the wall of stars, where 4000 gold stars are mounted on a wall underneath the waterfall, each one representing 100 men or women who lost their lives in the war. The memorial has many facets, including the 24 bas reliefs depicting scenes from the war and on the home front, to the water fountains all around the center pond, which is lighted at night, to the many inscripted quotes from this period, and the majestic bronze eagles with laurel wreaths in their talons, inside the Pacific and Atlantic columns.

Then, at sunset, there is a prayer vigil at the memorial, thanking God for bringing these heroes back home, and praying for those who didn't make it, and for those who are unable to make the trip to see the memorial. This is a time of quiet reflection and emotional release for many of the veterans, many of whom have told us after the trip that they finally have closure on this part of their lives.

Speaking of emotional, the trip also includes watching the changing of the guards, and we also have four of our veterans chosen to participate in this very touching ceremony. Watching the young, tall soldier flanked by these WWII soldiers walking up and laying the wreath at the tomb of the unknown is an incredible moment for all in attendance, and a memory they never forget.

Tombs of the Unknowns at Arlington

Forgetting is something many of our veterans would like to do when it comes to the death and destruction that the war brought. One of the worst atrocities of the war was the Nazi concentration camps, and part of our trip includes going to the holocaust museum. I had the honor of accompanying two veterans who had liberated concentration camps—which we didn't know until the ticket taker there asked if anyone had liberated Dachau, and they said that they had. She came out from behind her 'station' and hugged them both, with tears in her eyes she told them that she was there, only seven

WW II Veterans and guardians surround the replicated 1775 flag, ready to be hoisted.

years old, when they came and liberated them. Words cannot capture the emotion that was in the air as the story passed through the crowd.

Going through the museum with these men—seeing it through their eyes and hearing them say "I was there—I saw this," to feel the emotion and see their eyes tear up as they walked through and relive this time in their lives was difficult. They were there, after all, seeing the bodies and breathing the stench, but also, saving those who made it thus far. And that's what they try to remember.

Ft. McHenry, the birthplace of The Star Spangled Banner was another emotional visit, as we watched the film in the theater about the Fort and the events leading up to the writing of our National Anthem. At the end of the movie, the anthem began to play and everyone rose in the darkened theater to salute and place their hands over their hearts to honor our flag on the screen. At that moment, the wall curtain opened up to reveal a glass wall, outside of which was the American flag, flying from the mast of what had been a British ship that had sunk in the harbor all those years ago. This was one of those goose bump moments, for sure.

Then, at 9:15, to commemorate the morning in the harbor when our battle-worn flag was brought down and a new flag raised, the flag was brought down by four of our veterans and folded, and the ranger brought out a 17'x25' flag which was a replica of the 1775 flag, the only one which had 15 stars and 15 stripes. This flag was unfolded and stretched out across the expanse of the yard at the Fort, with all of our veterans holding on to the edges. The rope was attached, and Lindsborg resident and WWII veteran Bob Gordon, had the honor of raising the flag into the bright morning sky. What a sight!

This is a very brief synopsis of the trips to DC. There are many other sights, stops and banquets, shopping opportunities, dinners, and the like which are part of this trip to honor our heroes for the sacrifices they made for our country.

I am proud and honored to be part of this program and to have met so many of our nation's greatest generation' and to call them friends.

About the Author

I grew up the youngest of eight children, having five older brothers, and two older sisters. Because of the age difference between the last brother and me (four years) after about age ten I was more of an only child. I loved school from kindergarten on, and I learned that I enjoyed writing nearly as much as I enjoyed reading.

Angel now.

I wrote my first report for reading to my second grade class (entitled 'Never a Dull Moment') about my family and the antics that we lived with having so many boys in the house. That story was received very well by my classmates and teacher, and reinforced in me the desire to write. From then on, I began writing poems and stories for every birthday and holiday that came about, and took English and literature classes whenever I could.

I continued to write in high school and writing has become a part of me, at least as much as my love of music. I have written a few songs, including the song I wrote for my husband for our first Christmas together, when money was scarce. To this day, we don't remember gifts we received for many other years, but we remember that Christmas when I wrote him a song and he gift-wrapped a favorite library book for me, *Watership Down*.

Libraries are one of my favorite places. I enjoy reading and discovering the various moods and styles of writing from different authors. I love that reading a good author can take you to places you've never been. My husband, TC and I have tried to instill a love for reading in our four children, Matthew, Jessica, James and Mikael, and now in our three grandchildren, Mariah, Kenzlie, and Kyla.

I decided to participate in this project because I have worked with WWII veterans through the Honor Flight program and I wanted their stories to be told. I hope that I have been able to capture some of their spirit in this book and that through it, their service to our country will not be forgotten. Thank you for reading and please, if you have the opportunity, thank these brave men and women of the 'greatest generation' before it's too late.

WORLD WAR II:
WILLARD CARLSON

by Willard Carlson

This book is dedicated to:

The memory of Willard Carlson.

Adolf Hitler, a German corporal during WWI, set himself up in 1933 as head of the German government. His army invaded Austria in 1937, and Czechoslovakia fell into the hands of the Nazis in 1938. Soon Hitler's conquest included Poland, Denmark, Norway, Holland and Belgium. President Roosevelt proclaimed the U.S. neutral. After the fall of France in the fall of 1940, U.S. declared its first peacetime draft in September, 1940. All U.S. males between 21 and 45 years of age were registered.

Millie L., me, Amy C., Maynard A., Eunice A. leaving for the service.

I turned 21 years of age on July 11, 1940, registered in October, was drafted and took my physical on January 6, 1941. I was deferred until after harvest.

I left McPherson on July 31 for Ft. Leavenworth with three other boys: Maynard Ahlstedt, Charles Cumbo and a boy from Moundridge. We

Maynard A., me, Dirks, Charles C. leaving from McPherson.

were sworn into the army on August 2, 1941. We, along with about fifty others from the Midwest were sent to Camp Wheeler, Georgia. Here we were assigned different companies for our basic training in the infantry where we were schooled in the use of the rifle, 30-caliber machine gun and the small mortar. We were also put through all the physical training to make us soldiers. I weighed 167 lbs. when I was inducted, but after thirteen weeks from being put through the rigors of hiking, calisthenics and whatever kind of hell in the heat of August in Georgia, where the humidity was at ninety percent all the time, something agreed with me, for after thirteen weeks I gained almost fifty pounds, weighing 212 lbs. Where I gained weight, everyone else lost as much as I gained. We would hike up to twenty miles a day with double timing or running half the time. It must have been the food, which was terrible, and the regular hours. Lights were turned out at ten o'clock and revelry called at 5:00 A.M. We had fifteen minutes to get outside and stand in formation for roll call, after which we made our cots then stood inspection in front of our footlockers and were ready for breakfast by 7:00 A.M. Inspection included all buttons on our uniforms, shoes shined, footlockers in order and beds neatly made according to army rules.

It didn't take long to get acquainted with the men in our platoon. I ran around with Elmer Lampe from Kingman, Kansas, Tom Hore from Missouri and Edwin Jones. Those of us who left Fort Leavenworth, Kansas, kept in touch even though we were in different parts of the camp. After a week or so we were put on guard duty a week or so at a time. Here we walked our assigned posts for two hours at a time with four hours off in between. After six weeks or so we were given passes to go into the little town of Macon, Georgia. We'd ride the old army buses, which were much to be desired in those days. Macon, being a small town compared to the size of the camp, was overrun with soldiers. You can imagine what a town of ten thousand people with a camp of soldiers nearby was like. Most all the churches had dances and bingo in their fellowship halls. The little theater in town was always packed. There was a huge beer joint called the Stage Door Canteen which was filled to the limit, standing room only, unless you were lucky to get there early enough to get a seat. It had three bars and three dance floors. The whole building, which was huge, had room for a thousand or more soldiers.

During this period of army life we received a huge amount of $212.00 a month. Out of this amount $6.60 was taken for insurance, $6.00 for laundry, leaving us $8.40 for spending money. We'd buy a bag of Bull Durham tobacco and rolled our own cigarettes.

We got pretty good at it. It seemed that 90% of the boys smoked. On payday the crap games (shooting dice) as well as poker, black jack were going strong for a few hours but a lucky few had all the money. The winners would loan the poor losers money for a $1.00 interest or one buck for two in return. I never got into those big games where they'd bet 25 to 50 dollars at a time. That was big money in those days. I'd get into a pennyanny game once in a while. I learned my lesson real fast one day when I'd won a few dollars in a pennyanny and thought I'd play blackjack with the big boys. The first time I

blackjacked and won the deal I thought I'd get rich but was I fooled! The very first hand I didn't have enough money to pay off the winners and I was only half way around the table. I learned my lesson and this was the end of my gambling.

I really didn't mind basic training too much. We had two sergeants in charge of our platoon. Sgt. Baltun was my sergeant. He made me active Corporal so I was in charge of one squad of men. We were all Midwesterners in our platoon; on the whole we were a good bunch of guys.

After thirteen weeks of basic training we were sent to Ft. Bragg, North Carolina, where we were assigned to the ninth infantry division. About fifty

Ed J., me, Elmer L.and Tom.

Me as a soldier.

or so others and I were assigned to the second battalion of the forty-seventh infantry. The ninth division was made up of the thirty ninth, forty seventh, and sixth infantry regiments. Here I was reunited with Clayton Waggoner, John Behrends and Robert Schiver who were inducted the same time I was in Ft. Leavenworth. We remained friends all through the way. Waggoner and Behrends were Nebraska boys; Schriver was from Bonner Springs, Kansas. We were assigned to the third platoon, F Co. of the second battalion of which I remain a part for

Me, Elmer L. and Tom H.

the entire military career. Waggoner and I kept in touch after the war until his death in 1996. Behrends was sent to the Pacific Theater when we went to the European Theater. Schriver was captured in Africa and spent three years in the POW camp. He came to see me after the war and told me he was moving to Limon, Ohio, and going into the tree trimming business with his brother. We soon lost contact. Behrends married and moved to Missouri after the war and we keep in touch with each other each Christmas.

Getting back to Fort Bragg – it was one of the larger camps in the U.S. with the 82nd airborne, as well as the ninth, plus a large air force and its personnel. If I remember correctly at one time there were a hundred thousand troops. Fort Bragg was approximately ten miles from the town of Fayetteville. The group I was with came up from Camp Wheeler, Georgia. The division was out on the Carolina maneuvers. We stayed in camp under the leadership of a second lieutenant who had graduated from the R.O.T.C. of Clemson University. He and I became good friends. His name was Chippy Manness. A better officer was not to be found. While at Clemson University he was quarterback of their football

team in 1941. While waiting for the troops to come back from their maneuvers we had calisthenics and a five or ten mile hike each day as well as playing touch football. This was now in November of 1941. After the maneuvers were over, we were assigned to our various companies which we remained a part of for the duration of our time in the service.

We now had more vigorous training than when we were at Camp Wheeler. We had revelry with roll call at 6:00 A.M. followed by breakfast of grits and powdered eggs, burnt toast and milk as well as coffee. We also went through inspection of our footlockers and bunks as well as the entire barracks each morning. The day of having fun was now over. Calisthenics and hiking up to twenty miles once a week besides five and ten mile hikes, bayonet training, target practice and what not was the daily routine. We'd also have a night hike whenever the company commander took a notion.

I remember so well the morning of December 7, 1941. It was a Sunday morning. We were sitting around in our barracks when it came over the loudspeaker that Pearl Harbor was under attack. We were immediately confined to our quarters. That afternoon we had orders to roll our full field pack and then we were marched over to Pope Field, which was the large air base, where we had orders to encircle the entire air base. We dug foxholes ten feet apart; two men stationed in each foxhole and were to be on the alert for saboteurs. We stayed here for a week or more. December is normally the time for Christmas leave, but not this year. We did get a week's leave starting the 28th of December. It was impossible to get rail tickets. Waggoner's brother and his new bride came to get us. We were six of us in a two-door '36 Ford. We drove straight through stopping at my place to drop me off. The Waggoners were from a little town in Nebraska north of Phillipsburg, Kansas, called Alma. As it turned out we had a telegram waiting for us when we arrived, our leaves were canceled, and we were to report back immediately. We stayed home three days and then took a train, meeting each other in Kansas City's Union Station. It took us two days to get back so by now we had been gone almost a week but we were never reprimanded.

The early part of 1942 was spent changing our outfit to a motorized division. We now had armored vehicles, half tracks, as well as tanks; such as they were back then. I don't think anyone knew for sure just what was going on. This kind of training didn't last long as they were changing us to take amphibious training. We now practiced climbing rope ladders on simulated ships. There was a small pond where we would climb these ladders into rubber rafts going to shore, making believe we were invading the foreign land. The regiment left Fort Bragg for its first real amphibious exercises in possibly June. In Norfolk, Virginia we went out to an area near Chesapeake Bay where we climbed down the rope ladders on the side of the ship into landing crafts operated by Navy personnel, and we'd attack the beaches on Chesapeake Bay. We continued doing this for a period of a month or more. This was the summer of 1942.

At this time there was a group of paratroopers of the 82nd Airborne stationed at Fort Bragg. It seemed attractive for us to join the paratroopers as they received $50.00 a month jump pay. At this time we were getting only $21.00 a month. So, with the additional $50.00 to our $21.00 it seemed attractive. A friend, Jones, and I tried to join up, but we didn't pass the physicals. One hundred and ninety pounds was the limit for paratroopers and we both were over two hundred pounds. A year later, after we'd invaded France, and saw the poor paratroopers hanging in trees shot by the enemy, we were mighty glad that we hadn't been accepted.

In the fall of 1942 we loaded transfer ships (I'd say this was in about October) and sailed for an area where a convoy was formed. This was in the Atlantic somewhere beyond Chesapeake Bay. We were not told immediately what the plans were but it turned out after sailing at sea for a few days we're on our way to invade Africa. We were really crowded on bunks four high with half of the guys getting seasick and throwing up, but I fortunately never did. I spent most of my free time up on deck at the front or bow

of the ship. We were out at sea for a week or more before our destination was announced. The convoy zigzagged across the Atlantic for three weeks. The reason for zigzagging, we were told, was to avoid German U-boats or submarines. The convoy split up the ships going each way as we were approaching Africa. On Saturday night, November 7, we were fed steak, chicken or turkey with all the trimmings, priming us for the assault the next morning. About midnight we were ready to go. If I remember correctly the night was very dark and a little misty. Our ship was about eight miles off shores where we were to land.

The destination of our battalion was the beaches near the town of Safi, about a hundred miles south of Casablanca. We were the southern most of the troops on the west shore of Africa. It was after daybreak when we started loading the landing crafts for the trip to the beach. We later found that the reason for the delay was that a vehicle had caught fire as they were unloading it from the ship. It was crawling down the net from the big ship that I saw my first fatality. One of the soldiers ahead of me on the net got caught between the boat and the ship, crushing him and he fell into the ocean. Landing on the beach we encountered very little resistance. The enemy surrendered about three days later. Our Co F lost very few men. I think our battalion had only about a dozen killed and fifty or so wounded.

We stayed around Safi for some time guarding the area. I remember in January 1943 we went to Casa Blanca as a battalion to pass in review for all the big generals and President Roosevelt. Waggoner and I happened to be chosen color guard as we passed in review. It was some time later that we received orders to leave Safi and go to a staging area near Oran, which was 482 miles. We walked or marched about half the trip before loading on freight cars for the rest of the journey. It was some time later as we reached Tunisia Border that the real fighting began. We were now near the Algerian-Tunisian border. Where we landed on the west coast of Africa we were in French Morocco. The towns of Algiers and Oran, which we passed through, were in Algeria. This was now February of 1943 and we were considered officially

Myself and Schriver in Oran.

in the Tunisian campaign. We moved forward into Casserine Pass in the mountains of Algeria where we relieved the First Division. The fighting was very fierce. It was here that I remember our ground forces being strafed by a German plane which we shot down with our rifles and small machine guns.

We moved slowly eastward toward El Guettar. Sunday March 28 we encountered the enemy in full force. Our battalion was leading the way with E Company out in front. We were caught in a trap and most of E Co. was cut off from the rest of the battalion. I still can see two big hills called Green Hill and Baldy. Here we lost our battalion Commander and about half a dozen other officers. The entire E Co. and our F Co. Commander and five men, including my friend Schriver, were captured. This fierce fighting went on for over a week; we captured hundreds of prisoners but our losses were great. Hundreds of our men were either killed, wounded or taken prisoner. I remember so clearly after we had regrouped and were ready to continue our drive to Bizerte, I was told to take two men with me and go through the enemy lines to the bridge on the main line to

Bizerte. Here we were to take cover under the bridge and see, or listen, in what direction the German troops were traveling – whether they were getting reinforcements or moving back. It was a very dark night as we found our way to the bridge. As luck would have it the enemy was retreating. We stayed under the bridge all day and when dark came we found our way back to our forces. They were already moving after the enemy and we had very little resistance and the African campaign soon came to an end. Our regiment lost 157 killed, several hundred captured and several hundred wounded.

We reorganized our units in a bivouac west of Oran. This was now in June after having marched through Bizerte on May 11. We now had hot showers for the first time in months. On the morning of July 28, 1943, we boarded on a ship heading for Sicily. We landed in the harbor of Palomo. The only troops of the enemy in Sicily were Italian. They surrendered quickly and we only lost twenty-one men. August 17 was the official ending of the Sicilian campaign. We spent the rest of our time guarding railroad bridges, etc. I had our men with me who spent a month in Caltanissetta, staying with an Italian couple who was the station manager. The first of September we were alerted to make a landing on a beach near Salerno, Italy. We were on the convoy steps ready to make the invasions when our division was told the beaches were too fortified to land. Our convoy stayed in the Mediterranean until November when we set sail for England.

We arrive in Alsford, England on Thanksgiving Day, 1943. This was really the first time we had to relax since leaving Fort Bragg in 1942. Here, we were in regular barracks with cots or bunks. We were given passes to go to London. The English received us very cordially. We spent the month of December keeping in physical condition and I think Waggoner and I went to London every weekend. London was a large city with many places of entertainment. I never will forget one dance hall, which had a revolving stage in the center with dancing all the way around.

In camp we had all kind of competitions between the different battalions of the division. I thought I was in pretty good condition, as I now weighed a trim 185 lbs. They talked me into joining the Battalion boxing team. My career as a boxer lasted about five seconds. I was against a boxer who had been a golden-glove champion in Alabama. You can guess what happened. I was knocked out cold and that was enough boxing for me. We spent Christmas of 1943 here but I don't really remember that it was much of a celebration.

In January of 1944 our vigorous training began again. We now had received replacements so our division was at full strength. Again I was lucky when a series of exchanges of soldiers with our division and the British, and I was chosen. This was to promote friendship between the British and our troops and also to develop confidence in each other's unit. I was chosen to go to the British station in Dover, which was east of London on the English Channel. You've heard of the white cliffs of Dover and it really was a beautiful place. Being the only American in a unit of British soldiers, I was treated royally. I was served tea and crumpets (crackers) in bed every morning in my own stateroom. I observed their training tactics, being with the officers in charge of the unit. At dances I was the only American, so the English lassies kept me occupied. All good things come to an end, but the month of March 1944 will always be a highlight in my military life.

When I returned to my outfit, the division was on maneuvers. The lieutenant in charge when I joined the outfit was now Battalion Commander. I accompanied him in his jeep and we acted as umpires for the war games. He was now a Major and I was a Staff Sergeant. I now had good food with the officers and a nice dry bunk to sleep in. In the field where my buddies were, it was raining most of the time. Again, all good things come to an end.

On June 6 we heard the news of the invasion. On June 8 we boarded Liberty ships and moved across the English Channel. As far as the eye could see there were ships. The channel was covered with battle ships, cruisers, destroyers, tankers and all kinds of assault and landing crafts. June 11 was D-Day plus five. We had just embarked for our assault boat; about a hundred feet from the shore we waded in water chest deep. We held our rifles over our heads landing on Utah Beach. Shells were landing all around us but there was no machine gun fire. We climbed the bluffs on the edge of the beach and went a few hundred yards to our staging area. I want to also add that as we approached the beach the water at the edge of the beach was colored with the blood of our soldiers who had lost their lives the first days invading the beach. We were now told that our objective was to seal off the Cherbourg Peninsula. The fighting was slow, one hedgerow to another. It seemed the whole area was one plot after another with hedgerows as borders. Our advance after getting started was so fast that I don't think the Germans knew what was going on.

After readying the other side of the peninsula, we were relieved by the 90th Division to seal off the peninsula so the Germans could not retreat. Our unit moved up the coast towards the city of Cherbourg. The closer we got to our objective, enemy resistance increased. The Allied bombing and artillery increased as the Germans were in concrete bunkers defending the high ground outside the city. The area was also heavily mined. Eventually we were pinned down and couldn't move. Our commander was killed as we were unable to advance. I crawled on my belly fifty yards or so and threw a hand grenade into the opening of the pillbox where they were firing on us. I no doubt killed several as their firing ceased. I saw one soldier run from behind the bunker; I raised up a little and shot. At this same time a German rifleman shot me in the neck. I passed out and I remember hearing the birdies sing. When I regained consciousness I crawled back to my men and the medics carried me off. I didn't remember much of anything until I woke up in a medical tent back on Utah Beach. I spend a week or so here as the doctors said that I had a broken neck. They wouldn't put me on a helicopter so I had to wait until the waters on the beach were cleared of mines where small craft could come in to pick up the wounded. My F Co. and E Co. got into Cherbourg three days later. The Germans on the peninsula surrendered on the 27th and the fighting at

Awarded Silver Star For Gallantry

Word has been received here that S/Sgt. Willard D. Carlson who is at present serving with the United States Army Infantry in Germany, has been awarded the Silver Star Medal for gallantry in action against the enemy on June 22 in France.

The citation which accompanied the medal stated that in advancing against heavily fortified enemy positions, Sgt. Carlson's company was subjected to heavy enemy machine gun fire, but Sgt. Carlson maneuvered his squad forward and placed his men in positions from which they could deliver effective fire on the enemy emplacements. Then with complete disregard for personal safety, he crawled forward through a mined area until he was within 20 yards of the enemy gun. Throwing a hand grenade into the position, he destroyed the gun and killed the enemy crew. "Sgt. Carlson's aggressive initiative, devotion to duty, and courageous actions enabled his company to continue its rapid advance and were a credit to himself and to the Armed Forces of the United States."

Sgt. Carlson was also awarded the Purple Heart for wounds received in France, and is entitled to wear the citation bar earned by his battalion which received a presidential citation for outstanding work in the Cherbourg campaign early last summer.

Sgt. Carlson is a son of Mr. and Mrs. William Carlson of Route 1 Lindsborg. They also have a daughter who is serving her country, Lt. Amy Marie Carlson, Army Nurse Corps, who is stationed in the Phillipines.

Normandy came to an end. My regiment lost 112 and hundreds were wounded. I was now on my way across the channel on my way to England and my fighting days in Normandy were over.

I might add here that Ernie Pyle, one of the most well known war correspondents, was with the Ninth Division during the Cherbourg campaign. He praised our division and said that we never got the credit we deserved, especially when it came to telling the folks back home about the war. Ernie Pyle was killed in the Pacific Theater after the European Theater War was over.

When I was in England I was in the hospital in Winchester. It was determined by the doctors that I had a bullet lodged in my neck. I knew enough at this time so I argued with the doctors convincing them that the bullet had entered below my right ear. The hole in the back of my neck was where the bullet came out. The doctors said that was impossible, as it would have severed my cervical spine. Due to the fact that I was firing my gun at the time, my neck was cocked so the bullet passed between the vertebrae of my cervical spine. The doctors, in order to clean my wound of the blood clot in my neck, ran a swab through the hole where the bullet had traveled cleaning out the blood clot. The pain was so terrific that I passed out. The way it turned out, I was extremely lucky as only some nerves were severed affecting the feeling and use of my right arm. It took years after the war was over for all the feeling to come back and my arm regained its normal strength. From the hospital in Winchester I was

Cpt. O. B. Larson visited me in the hospital.

sent to a hospital at Hereford on the west side of England. Here I spent July, August and September. Sometime in October I went to a rehabilitation hospital for therapy and exercising to regain strength.

Even though I couldn't carry a rifle on my right arm I was ordered to report back to my company (F Co. of the 47th infantry). The time was now November. Going back across the channel to France, I was on an Indian ship. I had a stateroom to myself and good food. Forming the convoy and going back across the twenty-mile channel, I was two weeks, or more, on this ship.

When I rejoined my own company, many of my old comrades were not there. They had fought a terrific battle at St. Lo and lost a lot of men. Paris had been liberated and the drive to the Roer River was on. I rejoined my outfit about November 23. We were in fierce fighting liberating one town after another. I'll never forget the feeling of kicking in the door and there would be a German soldier just as scared as I was. You were hoping he'd throw his arms over his head and surrender. This was a common occurrence while street fighting and liberating the villages. In the open country we crawled on the back of tanks as we were now advancing pretty fast.

At the town of Frenzenburg, there was a battalion of German soldiers barricaded in a castle, which was surrounded by a canal of water. There was a drawbridge leading to a big barricaded door of the castle. A young soldier from K Co., who had a bazooka, realizing he had the only weapon capable of blowing the door open, went up as close as he dared as we were under fire all the time from Germans in the upper story of the castle. He fired two shots but the door held. With one round left he went within a few feet and fired point blank and the door shattered. This opened the ground around the castle so we could get in. Doing this act of bravery, Pfc. Sheridan lost his life. Later he was awarded the Congressional Medal of Honor, the highest award given, posthumously.

I was ordered to take with me two men and search a barn at the rear of the castle to see if any soldiers remained. I'll never forget as the hay in the barn

caught fire from our bullets as well as the enemies. The place lit up like a Christmas tree. I don't know how we managed to get out carrying the wounded boy and getting back to our positions. I found out later that our company commander had written me up for a silver star, which was for bravery beyond the line of duty. I already had been written up for the Silver Star at the time I was wounded in June crawling up and knocking out the pillbox outside of Cherbourg. Our first sergeant, whom I never did care for, said to me, "You have already been written for a silver star so I put my name instead of yours on this document." If his conscience would allow him to live with this deception, so be it.

After capturing this area, we advanced rapidly in open country and were soon at the Roer River at Cologne. Cologne had been bombed and shelled something terrific so there was little standing. I remembered distinctly a church with a high steeple probably a hundred or so feet was untouched. We soon found out there were Germans up in the steeple and they were shooting at us like clay pigeons. We eventually cleared the steeple of the Germans. Another town nearby that was heavily bombed, was Bonn, which we liberated. We, being the northern unit of the American army, were in contact with the British north of us.

We were waiting for orders to cross the Roer River, when on December 16, we received word the Germans had counterattacked with all the strength

Co. F Officers. I am in the front row, right.

they had left south of us and driven a wedge many miles forcing our forces back. We were immediately loaded on trucks taking off for the rear. We must have traveled fifty miles or so as it was almost a day later that we took up defensive positions and stopped the rush of the Germans, we along with several other U.S. Divisions. We were now in forest-covered lands in the area of Monascha-Hafen. The Germans had been fighting with the full force of all their best divisions. We were now on the defense. I must say that the winter weather was terrible. The snow was so deep we didn't go on patrol. On Christmas Day, 1944, we encountered a patrol of Germans trying to penetrate our lines. These men were dressed in white so they were hard to detect in the heavy snow.

The last week in December our Battalion Executive officer, Lieutenant McLaughlin, and I were sent back to Brussels, Belgium, to give instructions to the new recruits who were to be replacements as all the divisions had lost a lot of men. We told them of the rigors of war and oriented them in the use of the M-1 rifle, the Browning automatic, 30-calibre machine gun and the 60MM mortar. Here we had thousands of men going through every day. Lt. McLaughlin and I stayed in a hotel. We also had a jeep for our personal use. I never will forget the first day we were to give lectures. It was a large auditorium with a stage in the front. In the back of the auditorium standing was a row of officers, including General Bradley. The General had interviewed us the day before, telling us what he wanted done. I was to disassemble the various weapons explaining each part and their functions. The Lieutenant was to speak on conditions and what to expect when they joined the units they were to be assigned to. We conducted two-hour sessions, the Lieutenant taking the first hour, then there was a twenty-minute break and I was to spend the next hour showing them the things the General had told me to do. When the General had given us the orders I told him, "Sir, I'm not a public speaker." He replied, "Sergeant, if you know your subject, you can do anything." The first day I was very nervous, but the Lt. was a real nice fellow and even though I was but a Staff Sergeant we

got along real well and were very compatible. Thousand of men went through this place in the three weeks we were here.

When we rejoined our battalion they had been relieved on the line of defense and were in a rest area for a few days. The orders came to pull out and the push was on to close the Bulge. The going was tough in the deep snow and also the mud as the snow melted. We captured thousands of prisoners which slowed us down. The Germans had used all their best divisions during this counter attack and now their morale was down as we were defeating them, so they surrendered easily. This drive took place in January 1945. We reached the Roer River at a point miles south of where we had been in Cologne. The Roer was a river not much over a hundred feet wide but had a very swift current. Time and again we had orders to cross but the swift current prevented the boat from crossing. Finally, several days later, the last days of February, the engineers built a bridge upstream and we marched across.

The drive to the Rhine was now on. We encountered small pockets of resistance but one day we ran into a bunch of German tanks which slowed us up. After about a week of steady fighting and moving forward we were all tired and cold and wet. On March 7, we reached the Rhine that night where the 9th Armored Division had seized the bridge at Remagen. I remember so clearly being one of the first on this railroad bridge while our company crossed. I filled in at Company Headquarters when a platoon leader or whatever else was needed. In other words, I was an extra officer. On returning after being wounded, I'd had the opportunity to receive a Field Commission as a First Lieutenant but I refused as I didn't want to make the army a career.

After crossing the bridge we were now entering the town of Remagen. There were Germans in the town as we had made such a swift crossing of the Rhine they didn't know what hit them. They even hid our vehicles so it was hard to distinguish at night who the enemy was. Orders came over the radio, if worse comes to worse, destroy your weapons before you surrender. We held the town that night, the next morning moving to high ground to the east of the town. A few minutes of silence from all the artillery and guns firing, I was making rounds checking to see how many men we had left. Steitz, Harvey and I, were the only original men left from the days in the states. As we were shooting the breeze, an artillery barrage came in on us, killing both Steitz and Harvey. My face was all bloody from flying rock and mortar as the shells struck the wall near us. At this time the old railroad bridge which we had crossed the night before was destroyed by the enemy so we had no reinforcements to help the few of us who were left. In less than a day the engineers had built a pontoon, or floating bridge, across the Rhine. That evening the Regimental Commander, Colonel Maness, who was a Second Lieutenant when I had joined the unit at Fort Bragg, came over to our unit and told me I was going home.

The army had established a rotation system based on points which we received from time overseas, different campaigns we'd been in and also in major battles. I had been in five campaigns, namely the African, Sicilian, Normandy, Northern France and German campaigns, besides all the major battles we had been in. I had way more than enough points to go home for a 45-day furlough. I could add at this time; he had a bottle of Scotch and we shared a few drinks.

I went with Col. Maness back across the River to Regimental Headquarters where we joined sixteen other men all ready to go home. I was put in charge, but I'm sure I was not the most capable. We were all Tech Sergeants and Staff Sergeants. I had been Tech Sergeant for some time now. I was given all the papers in charge of our group and we loaded in trucks for our trip back to Paris. Here, we boarded the train for Amsterdam, Holland. Holland was a beautiful country, having been spared from the destruction of the war. The wooden Dutch windmills were pumping water for irrigation. The brick streets and old buildings were a sight for our eyes after having seen all the destruction of the cities and villages where we had gone through in France.

Our orders were to go to the dock where, before

On board the ship we took home.

loading on ship we picked up five hundred prisoners to take to the States. A medical doctor, who was a Major, was to take care of the sick. I was still in charge of the entire group, including the prisoners. We loaded the prisoners below and conditions were not very good. We called it "the hole". We gave each one a cot and blanket. For eating all they had was the bottom half of a gallon can to serve as a plate. No utensils were available so they had to eat with their fingers and as they went through the chow line everything was thrown into that bucket so it didn't look very appetizing. The expression of their bewilderment was something to behold. We seventeen soldiers had staterooms; I had one of my own. We

Arival in New York.

took turns standing guard to see that the prisoners stayed down below where they belonged. The crew on this ship was Swedish. I can talk a little Swedish, which I had learned when I was a child from my grandpa, which was paying off.

It having been March 8 when we crossed the Rhine, it was now the latter part of March when we set sail for the U.S.A. Again, it took a week or more to form a convoy as this was still wartime. We had destroyers and cruisers on our flanks for protection. We were sailing the North Atlantic and it was very rough. Most of the prisoners were older men and were very seasick. The poor doctor, who was a Major, spent a lot of time down in the "hole" taking care of the sick. The smell was horrendous. We lost a few who died, who we placed in mattress covers and buried at sea. I, being in charge, had to keep the records of these men who died. We also had a few of Hitler's SS troops who were fanatics. We caught two of them trying to crawl through the ventilator shaft which was about two feet in diameter and led to the engine room. Their intention was to sabotage or cause trouble in some way. We were waiting for them as they came out of the shaft and the rest of the trip they were locked in confinement. Outside of this incident everything went pretty smoothly. We were on our way back to the States when President Roosevelt died on April 12, 1945.

As we approached New York City, we paraded all the men above deck to see the Statue of Liberty and the lights of the city of New York in the harbor. We sailed right down a channel, which I believe was Fifth Street, to Fort Hamilton. The prisoners stood amazed at the sight before them. They'd been led to believe that New York and the Statue of Liberty had been totally destroyed. When we docked in Fort Hamilton, a detail of men including a Major came aboard and I turned over the records and papers of the prisoners to him. Was I ever relieved and happy to get rid of the responsibility of them.

We soldiers (17 of us) were taken to another part of the camp, processed and given two-day passes. We'd have much rather been on our way to our various camps to receive our forty-five day

Happy soldiers.

leave. I remember another boy and I from Lincoln, Nebraska, were invited into a Jewish home where we stayed. They showed us around New York but we were more interested in going home.

When the time came for us to depart for the camp closest to our home, a young soldier from Lincoln, Nebraska, and one from Ponca City, Oklahoma, and I boarded a train for Leavenworth, Kansas. When we arrived at Ft. Leavenworth we were given physicals and had to stay there a day or so while our records were being processed. We were then issued 45-day leaves.

I remember being in Marquette on VE Day which was the end of the European Campaign on May 8, 1945. After I reported back to Fort Leavenworth at the end of my leave I must have stayed there a month or more. I was discharged the 28th of July, 1945. I lacked four days in having four years. I had spent three Christmases overseas – one in Africa, one in England and one during the Battle of the Bulge.

This was the end of my years in the service. I'd been a Corporal when we left the States, made Sergeant in Africa, Staff Sergeant in England and Tech Sergeant after Normandy. As I stated earlier, I had several opportunities to receive a battlefield commission as a Captain but I turned it down. I never will forget Captain Smith; he'd gone through West Point in order to receive a commission and I could have received the same rank as he immediately. He thought I was NUTS. I was just waiting to get home to be a civilian again.

I must say that I was fortunate to come through the war like I did. My regiment, the 47th Infantry, had one-hundred-fifty-six men killed in Africa, twenty-one in Sicily, three-hundred-thirty-eight in Normandy, two-hundred thirteen in Northern France and five-hundred and six in Germany. We'd lost a large number the first day on the other side of the Rhine River. My company alone had lost fifty or more in Africa. Twenty of these were killed in a mine field. We also had about a hundred taken prisoner. As for the number of the wounded, the history of our regiment said that we had over seven thousand wounded.

In closing this part of my life I want to copy an article, which was sent to me after the war. Quote: "A lot has been said about the Remagen Bridgehead in W.W. II. It is common knowledge that the capture and the winning of the fight on the east side of the Rhine shortened the war by several months. It's also known that the battle waged in that tiny sector was one of the fiercest in the history of warfare, and that the 47th Infantry was right in the thick of it. Although it has not officially been awarded at this time, the Raider Regiment has been recommended for a Presidential Citation for saving the Bridgehead. The Germans threw everything they had at the doughboys, trying to get them the hell back across the river. Capture of the bridge had upset the plans for a stubborn defense of the Rhine, and the Krauts were plenty sore. The losses of the 47th Infantry in the Remagen Bridgehead were appalling, and none but a veteran organization could have taken these losses and gone on fighting. Platoon leaders saw entire platoons annihilated in pushing up the high ground on the east bank. Company Commanders saw entire companies dissolved right before their eyes. Battalion commanders considered themselves lucky if they could muster one company out of an entire Battalion."

After being discharged from the service I came back to the farm. I was very foolish for not going

```
                    HEADQUARTERS 47TH INFANTRY
                    A P O # 9, c/o POSTMASTER
                    NEW YORK, N. Y.

                                        25 March 1945


                         C E R T I F I C A T E

         I certify that the following named Enlisted Man is entitled to wear
    the military awards and decorations as listed below:

         NAME:  T/Sgt Willard D. Carlson      37012219

         AWARDS AND DECORATIONS:

              A.D.S.M. Ribbon per WD Cir #44 1942
              Good Conduct Medal per Ltr Hq 47th Inf dtd 1 Sept 1943
              E.A.M.E. Ribbon per WD Cir #1 1943
              Five (5) Bronze Campaign Stars (Algerian-French Moroccan,
              Tunisian, Sicilian, Normandy, and Germany Campaigns)
              Combat Infantryman Badge per GO #5 Hq 47th Inf dtd 18·
              May 1944
              Silver Star per GO #97 Hq 9th Inf Div dtd 13 Nov 1944
              Distinguished Unit Badge per GO #88 Hq 9th Inf Div dtd
              13 Oct 1944
              Oak Leaf Cluster to Distinguished Unit Badge per GO #22
              Hq 9th Inf Div dtd 3 Feb 1945
              Purple Heart (Eligible, but has not been awarded.  WIA 22
              June 1944 in Normandy, France)

    For the Commanding Officer:

                                JOHN W. FITZPATRICK,
                                1st Lt., 47th Infantry,
                                Ass't Personnel Adjutant.
```

Back at home.

to college on the GI Bill. We don't known where I would have been now or what kind of a career I would have had. One thing I'm sure of is that I wouldn't have been around Marquette at this time. I probably wouldn't have met my dear wife, Vada, and I can't imagine what life would have been like or be like today without her. One thing for sure; I wouldn't have all the grandchildren and great-grands around today to call me "Grandpa." They have all been a great blessing to me, and in my younger days I could not have imagined this scenario.

I worked for a construction company in Salina, Busboom and Rauh, for about three years. At that time, after the war, old army camps and air bases were being dismantled. This construction company had contracts with the government to dismantle these bases all over the state. I worked at Camp Phillips, south of Salina, the air base at Victoria, Kansas, Herington Airbase, and Coffeyville, Kansas.

It seems that I had taken up bowling when I met this gal, Vada, in Salina. At the time I met her, I was bowling with a league in Salina, one in Lindsborg, and one in McPherson. I bowled on Monday,

Tuesday, and Thursday evenings. On Wednedays I had choir practie at church after which occasionally I'd go to Lindsborg to watch the ladies bowl. Don't know how I missed her as long as I did, until this night when I saw this gorgeous person I didn't recognize. I stood behind the lanes on which she bowled and then I offered my services as a score-keeper. I think either Joan Wickstrom or LaRuth Lindh introduced us, and the past and present life that I'd been living was history. Joan, LaRuth, Vada, and I went to the cafe for coffee after bowling so I got better acquainted. I'd go back down every evening after choir to watch the ladies bowl, but never saw Vada again for weeks. Joan and LaRuth told me she had back trouble and couldn't bowl. They talked me into calling her, but just as I figured, I got this news that her back was bad. After weeks, I finally got her to go out with me and I guess she really did have back trouble. This was the fall of 1965, and we were married in February 1967. I might add here that on our first date in going to Salina, I offered her a cigarette. She politely said, "No thanks. I don't smoke." Believe it or not, I put the cigarettes back in my pocket and from that moment on, I never smoked another cigarette.

One of the richest blessings of my life was marrying a Christian woman like Vada. The good Lord has blessed me continually, and I am grateful for all the ways my life has been blessed.

My sweetheart and me.

THE DAHLSTENS' STORY

by Edna Dahlsten

THIS BOOK IS DEDICATED TO:

The loving memory of my husband,

Lambert Dahlsten.

I, Edna Swenson Dahlsten, was born August 27, 1912 in Kansas City. My family and I attended Kansas City's First Lutheran Church where Lambert Dahlsten, a Kansas City resident and a Bethany College graduate, served as organist and choir director while he taught at the Kansas City Conservatory. After graduating from Bethany College in Lindsborg, Kansas, with two degrees—piano performance and organ performance—he had taught in Michigan before coming to Kansas City.

I expressed an interest in music at an early age—about six, if I recall correctly. My mother finally relented with piano lessons which lasted as long as she was willing to put up with my infrequent and inattentive practice schedule. Before long, I knew that singing—vocal music—was my passion, and I studied privately until I had completed Kansas City Conservatory of Music.

War remained a bit of a mystery for me. I had heard on my radio about the attack on Pearl Harbor and United States' new involvement, but I wasn't affected much by it and I didn't hear much more.

As a member of the Kansas City church choir, I had admired Lambert from afar at first, and soon we began to date. We talked about marriage. Then

Lambert Dahlsten in England.

Lambert was drafted. He didn't know what would be required of him, although his chances of being required to serve were slim, given his near-sightedness. And when he was to be sent to war, he expressed his hesitation to marry me and run off, not knowing whether he would return or what his condition might be. He was stationed at an Air Force base north of London, where he daily witnessed fellow comrades leaving the base, many never to return. He told me about a life-threatening experience, being rocked out of bed by a nearby bomb. I knew only part of what was going on in Europe and with Lambert, and I was worried at times.

Lambert with children north of London.

One of Lambert's assignments was to work with English children in makeshift schools. Many were taken north of London to protect them from the raids and bombings going on in London. During leaves, he and friends often went into London to attend theater productions. He lived a life of contrasts from heavy danger to musical diversions for pleasure.

My Kansas City neighbor and good friend, Mary Edith Thomas, had moved to New York City to earn her doctoral degree in Medieval Literature. She began a career teaching college and continually urged me to come visit her, saying that New York City offered great exposure to music experiences, both training and performance opportunities. I relented, gave up my job in Kansas City, and traveled for the long overdue visit in 1943. I extended my visit. Mary Edith and I rented an apartment. I found clerical employment and studied voice privately after office hours.

Within a few weeks of my arrival in New York City, I had a desire to sing in the Riverside Church's salaried choir. By chance, I met the organist/director of the 56-voice choir. He allowed me to schedule an audition, I was accepted, and I became one of their sopranos. But for the good fortune of meeting him, I would have had to wait a year of more to get into the famous group. Music was my goal always. My office job paid rent and bought food.

During the one and one-half years I lived with Mary Edith, my voice teacher from Kansas City, Frances Van Duzee, wanted to return to New York City following her husband's death. I welcomed the chance to share music with her again. We rented an apartment together and enjoyed attending concerts and performance venues around the city, often with additional musicians from Kansas City who lived in New York. From where we lived in the Columbia University area around 125th Street, we boarded the Fifth Avenue bus which took us close to the Theater District, Times Square, and large churches where performances took place. I remember noting bus

Lambert while stationed in London.

and train passengers engrossed in newspapers, reading about the war.

Experiencing the war in New York City was different than elsewhere. With its location on the coast, troop ships sailed the Hudson River every night, loaded with soldiers and equipment. It was a dramatic sight, ships going out, blacked out because of the troops on them. Everything in those days for us was about the war, even though we treated it as our normal life, even though it was a whole new life for me.

While Lambert was stationed at an air base near London and I in New York City, all residents of New York were directed to have blackout curtains on all windows. New York was a coastal city and a potential target for Germany. When the evening sun set, windows were to be covered, no light visible from the outside. Volunteers, known as monitors, roamed the streets, checking for light that showed through the windows to the outside. One night I heard a knock at the door. The monitor announced that a slit of light showed from one of our windows. We had a blackout curtain on the window, but light had seeped around one side of the curtain. We were directed to fix it. Vehicles on the street, which were mostly public transportation—taxicabs and buses—had their headlights three-fourths blacked out, keeping them nearly invisible from the air. Blackouts were a part of the culture from the time I moved to New York City. I wasn't alarmed and accepted the practice as normal and routine.

Riverside Church, New York City.

Marble Collegiate Church, New York City.

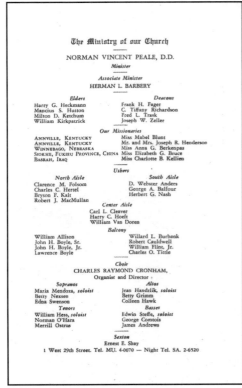

I admired the illustrious career of Germany's famous operatic soprano Lotte Lehmann. Her brother, Fritz, was an equally famous actor and musician in Germany and Austria. As the war hardened in Europe and Austria was annexed by Germany, Lotte, in a panic, contacted Fritz in Vienna and told him to leave his apartment immediately—no clothes packed, no treasures taken—and enter the car she had arranged to pick him up. Hitler had heard her sing and ordered that she sing only for Germany. She declared that her voice was for the world and quickly choreographed a rapid escape for herself and for Fritz and his wife to London and then New York. They came to New York where Fritz opened a vocal studio. By this time, I had a job in the offices of the Julliard School of Music. With limited connections in the musical world, I was able to audition for Fritz Lehmann and studied private voice with him for two years.

I auditioned for the choir at Marble Collegiate Church. There were twelve in the group and we sang for two services on Sundays. I sang with them for nearly three years and was paid a salary of $100 per month.

Like elsewhere in the nation, stores in New York couldn't get or sell meats, butter, sugar, and other foods. I knew about rationing and learned not to expect much. It was hard to buy many things. Nylon hose had been replaced with patterned cotton stockings. I knew these times were unusual, yet my friends and I eventually accepted such limitations as normal. When I visited family in Kansas City, I was surprised to see very little evidence of change because of the war, compared to New York City. They had access to butter, meats, and of course, no blackouts at night.

My friends and I celebrated the end of the war, May 1945, as did the city of New York. Mobs collected in the streets, shouting and screaming, an exciting time.

When Lambert was discharged, he was still held in Europe until he could be returned to the United States. He was sent to the French Riviera, Poulx, where he studied with a piano coach at the American University, waiting to come home.

The Kansas City Conservatory held his position as choir director and organist for him. But he went first to his family in St. Louis, then came to New York City where I waited for him. I paved the way for him to begin studying and teaching at the Julliard School of Music where I still worked. Emory Lindquist, future president of Bethany College held an office in New York City. Emory made connections for him to serve as organist at the Bethlehem Lutheran Church in Brooklyn. Lambert did not return to Kansas City. Within a few days, we arranged a small wedding party of five and

Mr. and Mrs. Lambert Dahlsten

were married in the Gustavus Adolphus Lutheran Church at 22nd Street and Fifth Avenue. He later attended Columbia University during the five and one-half years he was in New York. Our daughter, Linda, was born in New York.

In the meantime, Emory Lindquist became president of Bethany College in Lindsborg, Kansas. He contacted Lambert, asking him to come to Bethany's music department. I hesitated. So did Lambert. He liked what he was doing. He said, "No." Emory asked again. Again, we both expressed our delight in being part of the music world in New York City—me, a total of eight years in New York, Lambert five and one-half. Lambert declined again. Emory asked a third time. Lambert asked me if I would agree to two years in Lindsborg, thinking the teaching experience would enhance his resume

Lambert in Paris before returning home.

Gustavus Adolphus Church
151 East 22nd Street
New York City

1946

ENGLISH SERVICE at 11 a. m.

PRELUDE: "In Dulci Jubilo" .... Edmundson
"Pastorale" .... Clokey
Lambert Dahlsten
HYMN No. 34: "Hark! the Herald Angels Sing"
LITURGY.
THE EPISTLE: Hebrews 1: 1-3
HYMN No. 33: 1-2 "Come Hither, Ye Faithful"
THE GOSPEL: John 1: 1-14
SOLO: "Rejoice Greatly" .... Händel
Edna Swenson-Dahlsten
HYMN No. 32: 1-2 "Joy to the World"
SERMON: "We Haven't Forgotten Bethlehem Yet"
Dr. Evald B. Lawson
OFFERTORY SOLO: "What of That Midnight Long Ago" .... Eakin
Edna Swenson-Dahlsten
HYMN No. 46: "Silent Night! Holy Night!"
CLOSING LITURGY.
POSTLUDE: Toccata on "O Sons and Daughters" .... Farnam
Lambert Dahlsten

NÄSTA SÖNDAG, DEN 29 DECEMBER:

Svensk högmässa kl. 9.45, Söndagsskola kl. 9.45.
Högmässa på engelska kl. 11.

NYÅRSAFTON, den 31 december
FÖRSAMLINGSAFTON MED PROGRAM kl. 9 e. m.

Vår kyrkofamilj samlas till samkväm kl. 9 i kyrkans nedre våning. Intressant program med filmförevisning. Kaffe med dopp och tillfälle för närmare bekantskap. Alla välkomna! Samkvämet varar till 11.30. Därefter följer:

Nyårets Midnattsgudstjänst kl. 11.30 e. m.
(slutas kl. 12 på slaget)

Den samlande tanken i denna andaktsstund blir "Kristus, Världens Ljus". Det blir en ljuständningsgudstjänst som blir både stämningsfull och inspirerande. Om vårt hopp för nyåret skall bli verklighet, så måste Kristus i sanning bli "Världens Ljus" även för massorna. Kom med och börja det nya året med bön och andakt.

NYÅRSDAGEN — inga gudstjänster

OTTO H. BOSTROM, Ph. D., Pastor
Anders Emile, Mus. D., Minister of Music
Beatrice M. Kluenter, Organist

for future work. We moved to Lindsborg, a location where Lambert's family had originated. His grandfather, Dr. A.W. Dahlsten, one of his family's original Swedish immigrants, organized many

Edna now.

Swedish Lutheran churches, among them Freemont Lutheran Church and Salemsborg Lutheran Church in this area.

I liked Lindsborg. I liked the response of the college community, the welcome we experienced, and the musical opportunities were enough for me. I had sung in the New York Oratorio Society and welcomed Bethany's traditional performance of the Messiah. I taught voice at a Central College in McPherson for two years before beginning at Bethany as a private voice coach from 1959-1979. Lambert taught nearly forty years at Bethany before he succumbed to a short, fatal illness.

After Lambert's death, I considered returning to Kansas City. My family continued to live there, I liked city life, but my connection to Bethany would be different with Lambert gone. I stayed, and I'm glad I did.

V-MAIL TO E-MAIL:
PERSONAL EXPERIENCES
OF DON FERGUSON

by Don Ferguson

This book is dedicated to:

All who served their country during war time.

INTRODUCTION

Shortly after my mother passed away in 1972, my sisters, while sorting through her belongings, found that she had saved all the letters I had sent her while I was serving overseas in the military. They finally convinced me that I should write a story of my experiences.

Those letters and records I had kept are the basis for this story. I chose the title V-mail to E-mail because V-mail was a system they used to photograph our letters, condense our letters on negatives to save space, and enlarge them before final delivery. E-mail was chosen because at that time I had just bought my first computer, and I was still amazed at things it was possible to do with it.

August 1942

Early in the morning of August 4, 1942, about thirty other more or less bewildered 'draftees' and I reported to the courthouse in McPherson, Kansas, to begin the process of becoming members of the United States Army. Although I was acquainted with several others, only one really good friend, Orville Rawson, was among the group. After an uneventful bus trip, we arrived in Fort Leavenworth in the afternoon. We were assigned to a barrack for the night. After leaving our belongings on our bunks, we were assembled for our first indoctrination into army life.

A sergeant spent several minutes making us aware of our lowly status in the scheme of things, very profanely, and of the unpleasant things that would happen to us if we even thought of questioning any part of the procedure that would get us through the next day. After that, we were assured that no matter what, we would be made into soldiers.

We marched to a mess hall and were fed in an assembly hall along with several hundred others who were going through the same process. There, an officer using much gentler language explained what we should be prepared for and even answered a few questions. After all of this, we marched back to our quarters for the night.

Early the next day, we were marched to the mess hall for breakfast and spent the rest of the day going from one long line to another for all the examinations, both physical and mental, to see if we were fit for service. At this stage of the war effort, it was almost impossible not to pass.

Late that afternoon, all the men who had passed were assembled for the swearing-in ceremony. My estimate is that over two hundred of us repeated the oath and became members of the United States Army at that time. We were then allowed to board the buses and go back to our homes for a two-week furlough to get our affairs in order for a long absence.

It was on August 19, 1942, that I reported back to Fort Leavenworth for active duty. August 20 was spent receiving all the supplies and clothing we would need for army life, and start a series of tests designed to place us where we would fit in best. After we were in our quarters for the night, we were given paper and pencil and told to write letters home so that our folks would know we had safely returned. The next day, I finished the testing process, and was placed on KP duty for the rest of my stay at Fort Leavenworth. I think that was my only KP duty during my army career.

About noon on August 23, I was called to gather my belongings and report to a staging area for shipping out. We were not told where we were going. After an all night train ride, we arrived at Camp Crowder, Missouri, on the morning of August 24. I was assigned to the 232 Signal Operations Company. I belonged to this company while in the army, but spent very little time with them while overseas. The 232 'Sig Op Co' was just being formed and the Radio Platoon to which I was assigned consisted of one first lieutenant, one master sergeant, one technical sergeant and about twenty of us recruits. The company was made up of the Radio Platoon, the Installation and Maintenance Platoon, the Message Center Platoon, the Telephone Switchboard Platoon, the Telegraph Printer Platoon, and the Headquarters Platoon. For the first three or four weeks, about all we did was learn to march and study the rules and regulations peculiar to army life.

About this time, our platoon received around forty new recruits, and as help was needed for our original non-coms, four of our original group were promoted to Technician Fifth Class or T/5, the same rank as corporal. From then on, we were the primary trainers for the new recruits. We each had our squads and had quite a lot of debates over who was the best drillmaster and so forth. By being fortunate enough to go right into a regular company, we received very little of the strict regulation and training required of most recruits. In fact, I was issued a pass the first Saturday night. There and after my promotion, I had a permanent pass for when I was not on duty. For the recruits, however, they were not allowed to go off camp for the first six weeks, and even had to get special permission to go to the PX on camp.

At this time, we were living in two-story barracks with a large squad room on each floor. Bath and toilet facilities were on the first floor, and on the end of the second floor were two main rooms for us new non-coms. Part of our responsibilities was to see that the barracks were always clean and neat, especially for our regular Saturday morning inspections. My job, on the first Saturday, was to meet the inspection team at the door and make notes of any infractions.

Always as before, when the two senior non-coms lived in our barracks, these rooms were never inspected. After the rest of the tour, as the officer in charge walked past our rooms, he stopped and said, "Let's take a look in here today."

Radio Platoon.

The beds were not made; things were scattered about, and so forth. He took one look, shut the door and said, "I will be back in half an hour."

Things were very neat by then, and as he was our platoon officer, he did not want to write an unfavorable report on his own group.

Now that our company was about at its full strength, our training switched to the jobs we were supposed to be able to do, should we become more involved in the active part of the war. Our radio platoon was composed equally between repair and maintenance sections and radio operators. We even had three truck drivers. We had no equipment, yet, so we went to other parts of camp for most of that.

I spent several weeks learning Morse code and the procedure for sending and receiving messages by radio signals. Of about thirty of us that were supposed to train as operators, only a few were able to administer it at all, and I was the only one who became good enough to be classified as a high speed radio operator. Many of the others were switched to other departments after we were overseas.

As far as our training, things now became pretty much routine: going to classes, an occasional march, and enough exercise to keep us in shape. About the middle of November, we were moved out of our permanent type barracks to what some called 'tar-paper shacks' in a different part of camp. They were not nearly as nice: one stove in the middle of each barrack; hot if you were nearer the stove, cold if you were at the ends. I think we were displaced by the first contingent of WACs to come to camp. Needless to say, we were not allowed to come near our old area.

December 1942

About the middle of December, I was promoted to T/4, the same rank as sergeant, and a few more responsibilities came along with the title. I was allowed a ten-day furlough at Christmas time. I had been home on a weekend pass at Thanksgiving time, and one some time in the spring.

Each trip involved catching a bus to Joplin, from there to Wichita, then to McPherson. Brother George lived in McPherson at that time, so transportation from there was taken care of. Also, Mom and Dad, Marge, Betty, and Doris made a trip to Camp Crowder in the fall, and George and Erlene, a little later while I was still in Missouri.

Things were pretty quiet around camp until the rest of the company returned from their furloughs. However, we did start receiving some of our equipment at this time. Some of the larger things I remember were two large vans, equipped with radio transmitters, and pulling trailers equipped with 100 horsepower generators to power the transmitters. On the other end of the scale, we also received several small hand-powered transmitters that could be carried by a two-man team. I assume we were set up to be a mobile communications unit, as our telephone, construction and maintenance platoons had all sorts of large equipment. We had truck-mounted posthole diggers, and trucks equipped to haul long telephone poles. I doubt the radio equipment was ever used by any of our company; some of the construction equipment probably was.

About the first of February, we were sent on a three-week training bivouac in the hills not too far from camp. We were called out in the middle of the night and given about twenty minutes to gather the personal things we needed, and then load up in our trucks and start out. We had prepared for something like this for some time, but were surprised that it started in the middle of the night.

We drove about thirty miles, without lights, to where we were to camp. There we set up our two-man pup tents and settled in. The weather was very warm for that time of year so we were not too uncomfortable. This changed about the third day with a foot of snow and extremely cold temperatures. I was in charge of one of the radio trucks, and they were equipped with small hot plates, a small refrigerator and heaters, so I was fairly comfortable most of the time. After a few days, it turned warm

again, and mud became the problem. We hauled supplies and conducted our training exercises, as all our trucks were four-wheel drive. Our tracks should still be visible.

Back in camp, we were again trying to learn more about our equipment and how to use it. One Saturday afternoon, I happened to be outside our barracks and saw a girl walking by, which was very unusual. All at once I recognized her. She was a classmate of mine from Marquette, and her name was Lola Grub Cox, whose husband was in a company just across the street. We had a short visit, as I was leaving for some other duty. I did visit with her husband often after that.

In March, we started getting all our equipment crated. Everything that we could leave in our radio trucks had to be secured to stand a lot of rough handling. Early in April, we started loading all the big trucks and equipment on flat cars and getting everything in shape for shipment. The camp had a special company that took charge of seeing that we got everything loaded and fastened down properly. It turned out to be quite a lot of work. We got everything loaded, but the personal things we could carry. Deciding what was necessary and how much we could carry was difficult. Every time we moved, we carried less stuff. On the fifteenth of April, I was promoted to Staff Sergeant, which made me responsible for most of the day-to-day working of the radio platoon.

April 1943

By the twentieth of April, we had all our packing and loading done, and on the twenty-first, started a three-day train ride. We arrived at Camp Stoneman in California on the twenty-fourth of April. It seemed every other train had priority over ours, as we sat on sidings waiting for other trains to pass a good deal of the time.

Our route took us through Kansas, I think through Salina, but at three or four o-clock in the morning, I was not aware of where we were. I know we crossed the Great Salt Lake on a beautiful moonlit night. Just before we left Camp Crowder, all the original non-coms who were long time regular army members, were transferred out of our company. That was probably one of the reasons I received the promotion to Staff Sergeant.

At Camp Stoneman, we had very little to do, as everything we had crated and loaded on flat cars went directly to the ship we were to be sailing on. Early on the first of May, we took a large ferry from Oakland to the dock area of San Francisco where the ship we would spend the next thirty-five days on was waiting.

Loading all the supplies and equipment for the fifteen thousand troops the ship was to carry took all day. The troops were the last to load, and this was accomplished very smoothly. Each unit was called in turn, marched down the dock, up the gangplanks, and were sent to their areas of the ship. I cannot recall the name of the ship. It was named after one of our presidents and had been out of service for years before being re-commissioned as a troop ship.

At daylight the next morning, all sorts of activity started, and we soldiers soon learned to stay out of the way while the crew was doing their work. The lines were cast off, a couple of tugs shoved us away from the dock and we were on our way. Quite an exciting time for most of us who had never seen a large ship or an ocean.

We sailed out of San Francisco Bay under the Golden Gate Bridge, onto the Pacific Ocean, but still had no idea where we were headed. It took a day or two to learn our way around the shop, but after that, things were pretty much the same routine every day. Our meals consisted of breakfast, a sandwich and some fruit for lunch, and a regular army type meal for supper.

About three weeks on our way, we must have received something at our noon lunch that put the whole fifteen thousand troops out of commission; the worst kind of diarrhea hit almost everyone in the middle of the night. Bathroom facilities were barely adequate when everyone was healthy, but not for this situation, and many were unable to make it that far anyway. It was a mighty unpleasant ship to be on for about thirty-six hours. The only ones escaping this had skipped the noon lunch that day. Most of us escaped any lasting ill effects for the time being, but quite a few developed some problems later, and I will have more on that subject later on in this story.

After leaving San Francisco, we saw no other ships for two days, but after that, we started seeing a small ship in the distance occasionally, which turned out to be our escort for the rest of the trip. It was smaller than a Destroyer and was called a Corvette, and was very fast. It seldom got close enough for us to get a good look, but when it did, it seemed to have a lot of guns for such a small ship.

We crossed the equator on May 12th and the International Date Line on May 16th, 1943. The members of the ship's crew, crossing the equator for the first time, were subjected to a very rough, and I thought, unnecessarily rough initiation ceremony. However, all troops received cards showing we had crossed the equator, which saved me from going through the ceremony on a couple of other occasions.

On May 26th we arrived at Brisbane, Australia. We unloaded the belongings we had carried onto the ship and were assigned quarters at Camp Doombue. I was looking forward to spending some time in Australia, but early the next morning, we were called out and marched right back and boarded the ship again. At least I had one breakfast in Australia.

The port of Brisbane was quite a ways up the river, and a very busy port at this time. We saw submarines, cruisers, and one small aircraft carrier. Very shortly, we were on the Pacific Ocean again and still had no idea where we were headed.

June 1943

June 5th, we arrived at Post Moresby, New Guinea, and this turned out to be my home for several months. The first evening, after unloading the ship, we were trucked to a large grass-covered hillside and set up camp for the night. Two-man pup tents got up pretty fast, so by dark, mostly everyone had a place to sleep for what turned out to be several nights. All went well until eleven o'clock.

Everybody was pretty settled for the night, and the air raid alarm went off; we heard a few anti-aircraft guns go off, and after about half an hour, the all clear was sounded. We were quite a bunch of worried and homesick boys about that time. It took a couple of hours for things to settle down after that, and just as everybody was getting back to sleep, we were sure we were being attacked again. To us it sounded like a lot of small guns firing. We all had guns and were hunting for shells which had not been issued yet. It turned out to be some sort of birds that wake up every morning about that time and made that sort of racket. Hard to tell what might have happened if shells had been available.

The next day, we started clearing an area for a more permanent camp. There was not much equipment to work with, but some of the older residents gave us some ideas. In the bay close to where we were to set up camp, several drums of 100-octane aviation fuel were floating, so we salvaged several and put them to good use. We would soak an area with gas, then make a trail of gas about 100 yards or so, light it and duck. We suffered a few singed eyebrows, but it made the work a lot easier.

We were to set up eight-man tents for more permanent quarters. I never had a chance to live there, as most of the radio platoon were sent to the 415th Communications Company of the Fifth Air Force. We soon learned that no matter how good we had been in training exercises, actual working conditions in the field were much different.

Two-man tents where we slept for our first ten days in New Guinea.

The last air raid at Port Moresby came on June 13th, and though no bombs had been dropped, it was a relief not to be awakened every night. When we got to the 415th, tents were ready for us, so all we had to do was move in. Mosquitoes were a problem; we had netting suspended over our bunks, and soon learned to tuck it in securely. Also, we were required to take an atibrine pill every day to prevent malaria; it gave us a yellow complexion but must have worked as not one of our group contacted malaria.

The first morning, I developed the same symptoms so many of us had on the boat, and as a result, spent the next two weeks in the hospital. About thirty others from the boat were also in the hospital, some of them very sick. I recovered quickly, but it took two weeks before 'stool' tests allowed me to be discharged. While in the hospital, we were kept isolated from other patients, as they feared the problem could spread.

Now, I was back in camp and about to find out if my radio training had been adequate. As I had the highest rank of our group, and higher than almost all of the old timers there, I felt that I was sort of on a hot seat. They started me out on one of the Morse Code slower circuits after warning the operator on the other end that a greenhorn was taking over. Of course, the shift chief stayed close by to straighten out any problems. I had my share of problems at first, but soon learned to relax and did not cause any serious trouble.

It was almost a month before I could handle the fastest circuits, but was told I picked it up faster than most. As soon as I was good enough to handle any of the circuits, they made me take over as shift chief, which made me earn a larger salary.

The radio station had about fifteen different circuits; the two to Brisbane were very busy and always had a stack of messages waiting to be sent. At the other extreme were several that had very little traffic and several stations that would break in at any time with some very urgent messages. Several times I copied messages for our planes or our guns to stop hitting certain areas as our troops were being hit. It probably happened because they had advanced faster than thought possible.

The messages we handled were sent and received from 5th Air Force headquarters over teletype, not much like the equipment we had trained on in the States. On the Brisbane circuits, we always had changed frequencies twice a day as atmospheric conditions would make us lose contact. Most of the time we could tell when our signals were getting weak, but occasionally it would change so quickly that we would lose contact and the search would begin until contact was made on one of our other assigned frequencies. Our transmitters were remote-controlled and would take a telephone call, and then after a few minutes, they would get a frequency changed. Once in a while we would even have to send a message through some other channel to get back to operating. We controlled our receivers at workstations and would search for a signal so we could tell the transmitter station what frequency to change to.

About a month after getting to the 415th, we heard that one of our remote teams was coming in. They had been up in the mountains with native guides to keep us informed of Japanese troop move-

My tentmates.

ments. They were a pretty rough looking bunch as they had not shaved for the three months they had been out. The evening after they were back, I walked by their tent and heard someone yell, "Hey, Fergie!" Barney Hanson from Marquette was a member of the group. We visited often after that, and a couple of times looked up Amy Marie Carlson from the Freemont area who was a nurse at one of the hospitals in the area.

February 1944

Everything settled into a regular routine until February 19, 1944, when the 415th company moved to the Lae-Nadzab area of New Guinea. The new radio station had already been built and had new transmitters and some new receivers. We radio operators flew up on two different days, so there was very little interruption of radio operation. However, we were busier than we had been. Many nights, if I could get a fast operator in Brisbane to agree, we would set up a third circuit and work all night to clear some of the piled up messages. It seemed that, at night, the signals were a little clearer, and with fewer interruptions, we could really get a lot of work done. Of course, we still had to work our regular shifts. I was promoted to technical sergeant on February 22, 1944.

Our radio station was located on the top of a large flat-topped hill. The station walls were con-

structed with about a foot of hail screen at the bottom, then a four foot section of heavy tar paper roofing and another foot of hail screen at the top. This kept things reasonably comfortable most of the time, except if the wind was blowing. Then, we had to keep weights on all messages and other paper work. Below the hill on one side was a bomb storage area, probably a half-mile away from our station.

One morning as I was leaving the station, I noticed a fire in the area. I thought it was a little strange; our camp was across a gully on the other side of the hill. I ate breakfast and went to bed, as I had to be back to work my regular shift at four that afternoon. When I got back to work, we could see that the fire was burning in the bomb storage area. Just as we completed the shift change, bombs started exploding. About all the damage done at the station was that it knocked all the tarpaper off our walls. We were pretty shook up, but were told that there were no bombs stored in that area big enough to cause us any serious damage.

Our transmitter station was a little closer, and occasionally one of the transmitters would be knocked off the air and have to be reset. For two days, every so often an explosion would shake us up, but not any serious damage done to any of our equipment. As far as we could find out, there were no injuries to anybody in any of the other units in the area. I never did learn what started the fire.

In April, we learned that thirteen other 232nd company members and I were to be sent back to our own company. After going to the airstrip and boarding a plane three mornings in a row, only to have something go wrong with the plane, we were ready to seek some other means of transportation. But, finally, on April 24, 1944, the plane took off, and we rejoined the 232nd Sig Op Co at Finchafen, New Guinea.

It turned out that my stay with my home company would be very short. I don't know exactly what they had been doing, but were in the process of getting ready to move. On May 3, 1944, I found myself on a landing craft on our way to Hollandia in the Dutch part of New Guinea. Although I always had

a gun, this was the only time that I carried ammunition and kept it with me all the time. The landing craft I was on was not the open type that is always shown when troops are trying to establish a beachhead, but the front end did open up and could get into very shallow water, and we had to wade ashore. I do not believe that there was any Japanese resistance, as we were close behind the first landing party and never heard a shot being fired. By evening of the first day, May 5th, mountains of supplies were piled on the beach, and available to anybody that had a need for anything. Two weeks later, much of it was still there and going to waste, but if there had been any resistance, it would have been very bad not to have been well prepared.

The group I was assigned to was no regular unit, but made up of men from many different organizations. I was the only one from my company. The day after the landing, we moved about a mile or so inland, up a twisting road just being bulldozed up the side of a hill, to a large level area, where we were to get a radio station operating as soon as possible. Some small units we got going almost at once, but it took about three weeks to build the antennas and buildings needed for some of the large units.

My job was to get them operating as soon as they were set up, and as I knew very little of the ability of the operators assigned to the group, this was a challenge. Some of them were very good and some had to have a lot of help. It took a few days, but I was able to have a couple of good operators on each shift that could straighten out any trouble the poorer ones got into.

Up until this time, I had no trouble at all getting along with the officers in charge of the different places I had been, but that was not to be the case here. The first problem arose when the captain in charge insisted on putting both the transmitters and receivers in remote locations. I was just sure that it would not work since each operator liked a different sound, and receivers had to be retuned constantly as conditions changed. However, the transmitters and receivers were placed in a remote location, and more time was spent calling for the receivers to be tuned than anything else. After about three days of this, the receivers were moved to the operating stations so each one could tune his own and things worked as they should. This would not have caused too much of a problem, but another incident did.

This unit had no central headquarters, so I, and the ones in charge of the other departments, had to schedule necessary details such as other clean-up operations. After about six weeks, a few men were transferred into our group that had worked with the captain before. They were set up as a headquarters platoon with an acting first sergeant and clerks to take care of the paperwork for the group. There were more than two hundred of us now, so that was good, except that I had trouble with the sergeant right from the start.

The problem was that when they took over the schedule for KP, they placed two of my men on duty that had just served on KP two days before. I thought there would be no problem for this to get changed, but when I brought it to the acting first sergeant's attention, he informed me that this was his department now, and he was not making any changes just because someone was complaining about too much KP duty. Naturally, I took this up with the captain and was told that he had worked with this man before, and that he was very capable, and he would not interfere with the way he ran his office. I was unhappy. I had two very unhappy men that I could not get treated fairly, and from then on, I am afraid I was more interested in making life miserable for the captain than helping to win the war.

Things did settle into a regular routine, finally. The other thing I couldn't do anything about came up in the first part of August. This, I couldn't blame on the captain. Somewhere in the chain of command, they decided to monitor some of our own operations to see if proper procedures were being used, and I ended up being in charge of that operation, also.

All of the older operators had ways of identifying each other, which was not according to the book, but sure helped when, as trick chief, you were matching your operators with the ones on the other end. There were other little shortcuts that were in

general use that also did not fit into the strict interpretation of the rules, but sped things up a lot as long as both operators understood them. In the time I was there we came up with no serious violations, for which I was glad, as a lot of the operators were ones I was familiar with even though I had never met them except on the radio circuits.

September 1944

Towards the end of September, thirteen others and I received orders to report to a small radio ship for some unknown mission, and it turned out to be my home until the middle of June of 1945.

T.P. 249 was the army name for the ship; Geoanna was its civilian name. The ship had belonged to the Seven-Up Bottling Company president, or so we were told, and had raced between California and the Hawaiian Islands. The ship was 112 feet long, 32 feet wide, had two masts over 100 feet tall and had over 40 tons of lead for ballast in the bottom of the hull. The army had raised the booms about six feet and shortened the sails so there was room for a deck house with room for twelve men to bunk.

The ship's crew consisted of the captain, and first and second mates; first, second and third engineers, who were civilians; and twelve sailors from a

small boat company. This made thirty-two of us in pretty close quarters, but, surprisingly, very little friction developed. The Signal Corps group was made up of one lieutenant and myself in charge, one T/3 technician to keep our equipment in working order, and eleven others to carry out the tasks we were sent to do. Two of the sailors were cooks for the whole bunch, and the other ten were kept busy keeping the ship in shape.

We sailed away from New Guinea on October 4th, 1944, and arrived at Morita Island on October 9th. The ship had two fifty-caliber machine guns mounted on the bow, and one forty-millimeter cannon on the stern. About the most exciting event of the trip was when the crew was learning to fire the guns. We crossed the equator on October 6th, 1944.

The ship had one 100-horsepower engine, and could make only about four knots by itself, but with full sails and a strong wind, we would at times get going up to fifteen knots. The first time another ship tried to contact us by visual signals, we learned none of the crew could take Morse code, so I ended up being the signalman for the rest of the time on the boat. That was quite a challenge since that was new to me, but I turned out to be the best of the radio operators. Also, our signal light was so poor, ships very far away could not read our signals. For our radio transmitters to work, we had to use the mast guy wires for antennas, and they had to be re-turned for every frequency change. As this took place at least twice a day, our technician had to train several of us to do this, or he would never have gotten any sleep.

We were supposed to be a relay station, if needed, while the Philippine campaign was taking place. It turned out we were not needed, as we sat in harbor at Morita for over four months and handled only one message, and that was after the fighting was almost over in that area. However, we manned two stations, twenty-four hours a day while we were there, as those were our orders when sent on this mission. I have always thought, because our group was made up of men from many different companies, we were more or less forgotten. Also, we could

have left Morita much sooner even if we had been needed to relay messages. Even at the time we left, I received no orders to leave, but the captain of the ship managed to get permission to leave as the ship's engine needed some repairs.

Morita was a small island, only twenty-six square miles where the Air Force had built a large base that was in striking distance of many targets still on the list that needed to be hit, and out of range of most Japanese planes at that time. However, for fifty-six nights after we got there, we experienced air raids.

There was a large island a short distance away, and the story was that one hundred thousand Japanese had been bypassed there, and we assumed the planes came from there. The harbor here was home base for many ongoing activities; there was one submarine tender in port, one ship to take care of PT boats, and all sorts of supply ships in and out. Many small ships were anchored there for a lot of the time; many of them we never did find out why they were there.

The Japanese planes making the bombing runs were small planes, and would try to get in and out without being detected. The main target was the airbase, and at times they managed to do a lot of damage. In one raid, twenty-six of our planes were destroyed on the ground. Only one night did they drop bombs in the harbor, and we got shook up pretty good. Six of the crew had cots on top of the deckhouse, rather than sleeping below deck, to get away from the heat. Many times we ignored the alerts, but for some reason, all of us were out of our bunks that night.

Shrapnel riddled the bunks on top of the deckhouse. No one on our ship was hurt, but we hauled four men from a small boat next to us, who were cut up pretty badly, to the hospital on shore.

The air raids continued until the air force sent in a group of P-61 Night Fighters, planes with radar that could hone in on enemy planes. With our radio equipment, we were able to track our planes and hear them talking, and as soon as they made contact, we would see a string of tracer bullets and almost always, the enemy plane would explode.

After few nights of this, the air raids stopped. The air raid alert was three shots from a cannon, which we had been ignoring, but after our near-miss, most of us would be out of our bunks, flat on the deck and only remember hearing the last two shots. The captain, the two mates, and three engineers, being civilians, received one-hundred dollar bonuses for each raid that took place. This seemed a little unfair as everybody was subject to the same risks.

Finding things to do to keep from getting bored was a problem. I learned to play chess (very poorly) and cribbage, which I was better at. We had a small boat with an outboard motor to get to shore and back, which we used to get mail and small supplies. Supply boats would bring bigger items and water. Water was very limited; our supply tanks held about forty gallons per person and it had to last between delivery dates and anytime we spent traveling. We were allowed about a carton of cigarettes a week, and about this time, we started getting a small beer allowance, occasionally. As senior non-com on board, I had to sign for all the recreational items, which was no problem, except any traveling on shore was by hitching rides. The Negro truck drivers would almost always stop for us, but it sometimes took most of a day. It took at least three of us for each trip, as one person had to stay with our small boat at all times or it would disappear. We had to go to one place for the necessary paperwork, then to a warehouse to pick up the items, then find a truck driver kind enough to haul everything back to our boat.

February 1945

On February 14, 1945, we left Morita Island. They were unable to start the ship's engine and were being towed by a Liberty ship back to Hollandia, New Guinea. All the Signal Corp Group, but me, were transferred to the Liberty Ship for the trip. I was needed on our ship to handle communications between the two ships. The only bad part of this was that the five-hundred yards of tow cable made our ship roll a lot more than normal, and that was the only time I ever came close to being seasick. How-

ever, we arrived back in New Guinea in good shape on February 19th.

We were in Hollandia until May 23, 1945, and I have no memory of anything that took place during that time. I know I lived on the ship all this time and had no work. As there was nothing on shore to interest us, I have to assume that we spent all the time loafing. I was able to find out that my company was in Manila, and that was where we were headed when the engine was in running order and sailing orders were received.

We left Hollandia on May 23, 1945, and arrived at Tacloban Bay and Leyte Island in the Philippines on June 4, 1945. On this trip, some things took place, which took some figuring out. After about two days out of Hollandia, our boat started receiving challenges from planes, and I would send back the recognition code we had been given; if it was a PBY sea plane, they would turn and circle so closely, we could wave to men looking out the windows of the plane. This happened several times. We thought it a little odd, but even when the challenging plane was a B-25, which was too fast to circle so closely, we would turn and make one very close pass so they could get a good look at us.

After about three days of this, we were approached by a small warship with sailors manning their guns, pointed at us, and signaling for us to send over a small boat to bring back a boarding party. After some negotiating, they did use their own boat and sent a boarding party over. It turned out that the recognition signal we had been given was not the correct one for the dates we were using them. We felt fortunate the planes had taken time to look us over, as a sailboat in that part of the ocean was probably very odd. Also, our signal light was so poor they probably could not read it. The crew that boarded our boat would not give us the correct code, but we sailed four more days and right into Tacloban Bay without being challenged again.

June 1945

We were there until June 10th, but the only one

ashore was the captain to get authority for us to go to Manila using an inter-island channel that was much shorter than going back out into the ocean and sailing around the other islands. In places, this waterway was barely deep enough for the ship, but we made it in good shape. At times, we had men out in front to measure depth to tell us where we could get through. We left Tacloban on June 10th and arrived at Manila on June 13th. It would have taken at least twice that long to go the other way.

I think all the Signal Corp members of our group found their outfits. I was lucky that the 232nd company was located in a bombed-out warehouse only about two blocks from the dock where they unloaded us. They were now working in McArthur's headquarters in the communications department. I reported in to company headquarters and found out they had no idea where I had been for these last nine months. They were aware I had been assigned to the ship, but their records showed me as being somewhere in the Philippines for ten days before the first invasion took place. This would not have bothered me, but now the army had come up with a point system as they were starting to rotate some of the men with the longest overseas time home. When we checked my points, I would have lost five points, so we took time to trace everywhere I had been to get my five points back.

As I was not on any work schedule for the company, I wondered where I would go next. I had never spent more than ten days at one time with the company since being overseas; however, it was soon made clear. We were informed that the whole company was to be relieved of their duties and moved to the outskirts of Manila to a staging area. Here, we were to start getting equipment crated up and ready to move. This involved some mobile radio equipment, trucks and construction equipment for the telephone platoon. Everyone was sure this was to prepare for the invasions of the Japanese mainland, and nobody was looking forward to that. I am sorry, but I do not have the exact dates for what took place in early August. It all started when the two atomic bombs were dropped on Japan.

A few days after the bombs were dropped, I was called to get three or four other radio operators from the company and report to an office in Manila where they had set up a couple of transmitters and receivers. Our job was to monitor a couple of frequencies. The second day of this, in about the middle of the afternoon, we started getting some signals, using procedures that the Army had not used since about the first month we were in Port Moresby. I was the only one who had been around long enough to remember them. We were able to establish a way to communicate, and I got to copy a message from the Japanese agreeing to the unconditional surrender demanded by the Americans and the other Allied Forces.

There were only about six of us there at the time, but as soon as we started relaying the messages to headquarters, I think every high-ranking officer in Manila showed up, except MacArthur. We had to be very careful. We had to be sure every word was correct. The message was addressed to 'The High Command of the Allied Forces' and we acknowledged receipt and said, "An answer would be returned as soon as possible."

I maintained contact, but the only messages the rest of the afternoon were to try to make arrangements for meetings to work out all details. Most of the time was spent waiting for answers to come back from headquarters on both ends of the system. Later, I learned that the Japanese had put information on some of their news broadcasts for us to be watching for messages on these particular frequencies.

The next morning, when I reported to the station, some special intelligence force personnel were trying to operate the station, but not understanding the procedure the Japanese were using. I was standing behind the operator, trying to tell him what the signals meant, which helped a little, but was soon told I did not have the proper clearance to be there, and I was ushered out of the station. I think that other means of communication had been set up, and at least the fighting stopped.

One other odd coincidence was when I reported to the station the first time, the officer in charge was the very same one that I had all the trouble with the first time while I was in Hollandia. He said, "Oh, no! You again!" And I thought the same thing, but this time we had no disagreements, and he was told to leave the station the same time I was.

That I was involved in the original contact in the surrender negotiations is one of the things that I have always been rather proud of. During the celebration place, when word got around that the war was over, the 232ⁿᵈ Signal Operations Company suffered their only casualty of the war. Everyone that had a gun was firing them into the air, and a friend of mine, sitting on his bunk, was struck by a thirty caliber bullet that fell through the tent roof. He was hit in the shoulder but not too seriously, and he was out of the hospital in time to go to Japan with us.

September 1945

Things moved rather quickly after that, and on the 22ⁿᵈ of August, we were on a ship headed for Japan. We sailed through the harbor at Tokyo while the surrender ceremonies were taking pace on the Battleship Missouri, and landed at Yokohama that same evening. I had been promoted to Master Sergeant on September 1ˢᵗ while on the ship. We moved into Tokyo on September 6ᵗʰ, and were stationed in what had been a large office building, only about two blocks from the Emperor's Palace, and stayed there all the time we were in Japan.

Signing surrender.

The area of Tokyo around the place was not hit by the bombers as so much of the city had been. The industrial area from Yokohama into Tokyo had been completely flattened, and the only sign of life were people that had gathered a few pieces of tin together and were living in the middle of all the rubble. We were among the first troops to land, and were the first to move into Tokyo. A week or so later, at a movie, watching the news reels, they were shooting what was supposed to be the Big Red First Infantry Division moving into Tokyo, and the pictures they were showing were of our trucks. I never saw any sign of infantry troops in Tokyo, but they had made the pictures fit the story they wanted to tell. We were a little worried the first couple of days, but the Japanese people did just as their Emperor had commanded, and anything we wanted was given without question.

Our company was once again working out of MacArthur's headquarters, and I was still not on any schedule, so I had a lot of free time to explore and felt perfectly safe any place I went. If any of us got lost and could make someone understand that we wanted to see the Emperor's Palace, and if they could not make directions clear, they would guide us back personally. The first sergeant soon realized I was not on any regular duty, and then he had plenty of details that I could take care of for him. There was a shrine across the street from our quarters and we got so we could communicate a little with some of the young people that visited there. A couple of my friends even managed to get invited into one of their homes, but I never got quite that friendly.

Toyko

Early in October, some of us became aware that some men in other outfits were being sent home who had fewer points than many of us. Our company officers could do nothing about this, but we did get permission to bring our concerns to the office of the Inspector General. There were five of us master sergeants, one from each platoon, and we dressed as neatly as we could and represented the

Toyko

whole company. It must have done some good, because on October 21, 1945, about one hundred of us with the most points received our orders to return to the United States. As happy as we were about this, we were a little sad that we, the whole company, could not go home together.

A couple of other things are worth mentioning: I had not been paid for over a year and received all my back pay in Japanese Yen at an exchange rate of about 120 to 1. You always got your pay and then you had to count it back to be sure there were no mistakes. It took quite a while to count over 150,000 Yen when the biggest note was 100 Yen. I bought money orders and sent most of it home the next day. I did have payroll records and statements from my company commanding officer to show where the money came from. There was a flourishing black market going on now, and this was one way of catching those involved.

One other thing: soon, after moving into Tokyo, we received a new company table of organization which authorized enough new promotions so that almost everyone received one. One member of our platoon was about ten years older than most of us, and could have transferred out before we went overseas. He had always turned down promotions before, and as I had to leave, two men off the list were to be promoted, and he was one of them. At this time, he was ready to accept, and as

he deserved it more than many of the others, he was very unhappy and I was also. I had not asked how he felt about it. After some discussion with the company commander, we were able to work out a special promotion for him so that he got to go home as a sergeant instead of a private.

November 1945

On October 27th, we left Tokyo on a train to Yokohama and boarded a ship for our trip home. It was a very cold, snowy day, and we saw many Japanese women standing in rice paddies up to their waists in water, trying to salvage what rice they could before winter really set in.

We arrived in Seattle, Washington, on November 5, 1945, and left there on a troop train on November 8th for Denver, Colorado, where I received my discharge from the United States Army. I am not sure of the date, but I think I made it home about the 14th of November in 1945.

The time I spent with the 5th Air Force, I feel, was the only time I really was accomplishing a lot of

Japenese street scenes.

good for the war effort. The first time I was in Hollandia, I had more responsibility and was able to get the job done. But when doing something so very distasteful as trying to catch some of your fellow radio operators making mistakes, and trying to work with the only officer I could not get along with, made this the most unpleasant time I had in the army. The assignment on the radio ship would have been great, except it turned out we were not needed, and then just left sitting with nothing to do. At least it was an easy bunch of men to get along with, which is worth a lot. After catching up with my company in Manila, the work I did there, and the two months spent in Japan made for a very interesting finish to my Army career. And as bad as the atom bombs were, everybody that I know was glad we were in Japan as peace keepers and not as invaders.

Money the Japanese had printed for use in territories or countries they had taken over. One was printed in preparation for invading Australia (which, of course, they never did).

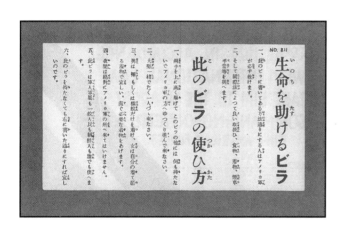

Leaflets dropped before I arrived in Japan. They were to tell the Japanese how to surrender. A Japanese friend of mine remembered when they were dropped. They were told not to pick them up.

FOLLOW UP

I wrote this story about thirty years ago and didn't make any changes for this book. I was discharged from the Army November 12, 1945, and settled back into the farming operation with my brother and dad. My dad's health was not good, and my brother went to work for a grain company shortly after that, and I ended up with the whole farming and cattle feeding operation. I farmed and had a cattle feeding operation until a few years ago.

The Army must have needed radio operators at the time I was inducted because my friend, who was inducted at the same time, also ended up as a radio operator, but for the 40th Infantry Division. A lot of my friends served in the same time period as I did, and could probably write very interesting stories of their experiences, and all of them would be quite different. Two of my friends suffered very serious injuries, and one classmate was killed in a bombing raid somewhere in the European Theatre.

I certainly wish the countries of this world could, somehow, settle their differences some other way than going to war.

Donald P. Ferguson
Ex-Master Sergeant
U.S. Army.

THE ONE
WE CALL HERO

by Kathryn Frantz

THIS BOOK IS DEDICATED TO:

35th Infantry Division, U.S. Army.

The Normandy Countryside

July 10, 1944 6:00 p.m.

A staff meeting revealed the plan of attack. The following morning, on the crest of a rise at Normandy, France, Carl Frantz's platoon would be ready to advance down the gentle slope of the hill ahead. A grove of hedgerows north of St. Lo, hiding the enemy, would be obscured by heavy artillery fire and a smoke screen.

July 11, 1944 6:00 a.m.

At dawn the platoon was ready, waiting for the support systems (heavy artillery and smoke screen) which had not yet arrived. The day was misty and there had been rains earlier. When the order came over his radio to advance, Carl said, "That would be pure suicide." The Master Sgt. said, "That is an order!" Preparing to obey the direct order, Carl told him, "My scout and BAR (Browning Automatic Rifle) machine gunner and I will go first. My men will follow."

Carl and the two went over with the rest following on their bellies, crawling through the wheat field. The enemy waited until the three got half way down the hill headed toward the woods below when bursts of machine guns hit their targets. The scout and BAR man were killed instantly and Carl was strafed across the abdomen. The official report reads, "Holding his intestines in with one hand, S/Sgt. Frantz got to the BAR machine gun and fired until it was quiet while his forty-two men retreated safely."

Carl's Army Career

Carl Frantz's 35th Division had been mobilized on December 23, 1940. It was a National Guard unit and had previously been activated during World War I. In conjunction with the Selective Service Act, the National Guard of the United States had been ordered into active military service for one year of preparedness training to ensure its viability should the nation enter World War II.

It was in the spring of 1941 that fifty-four draftees met at the courthouse in McPherson, Kansas. Mothers, fathers, brothers, sisters, sweethearts and wives were there to wish the fellows well and say goodbye. There were men from all walks of life—farmers, merchants, city employees, postal workers, mechanics, hotel employees, police, and many more. It wasn't a happy bunch even though there was lots of laughter. Most of the conversation with the draftees was about what to expect when they got to camp. They didn't know to which camp they'd be going.

This was the largest group of draftees (56) to leave McPherson County.

They loaded onto two buses, and waved goodbye to the crowd outside. They were on their way to the induction center in Wichita where buses came in from every direction. After their ten-minute physicals, there was an indoctrination which lasted another ten minutes, and then they were sworn in. By that time they'd joined some of the fellows from the other buses and they were loaded on a train to their unknown destination.

The following day they arrived in Little Rock, Arkansas, where they were loaded on trucks and taken to Camp Robinson for basic training. At some point they were assigned to their designated companies—Carl was in Company E, 137th Infantry, 35th Division. As "selectees," these men had to take thirteen weeks of basic training. In order to catch up with the Guardsmen, they worked hard to learn to keep in step when they marched. They were issued

General George C. Marshall arrives to review 35th Division Troops.

rifles and learned to take them apart and put them back together.

It was during basic training that Carl's proficiency with firearms was noticed. One of his instructors told him one day, "You're not so rusty with a gun!" and the nickname of Rusty became his.

Later that year they participated in the Louisiana Maneuvers (August - September 1941) which were a prelude to the greatest war the world has ever seen, World War II, and led to the birth of Camp Polk. The maneuvers were called the "Big One" because it involved more than a half million men in simulated combat. It included nineteen Divisions and was the largest such military exercise ever held on the U.S. Continent.

In October 1941. Carl and three buddies borrowed another buddy's car and on leave, drove home to Lindsborg for the inaugural Swedish Hyllningsfest celebration. While home, he walked through Stockenberg Drug Store each evening on his way

downstairs to practice in the shooting gallery which was located in the store's basement. An "A-Smile A-Minute" photo studio was located at the front of the store, operated by a high school girl, Kathryn Keding. On the first evening, she asked him if he'd like his photograph taken, but he shyly declined. The second evening he was a little more interested and the third time he succumbed to her charms. So began the romance which would grow greater over the next sixty-two years—more than fifty-nine as husband and wife.

After the bombing of Pearl Harbor December 7, 1941, the 35th Division was loaded on a troop train, destination unknown. Given the fact they had been issued lightweight uniforms, it was assumed they would be heading to the Pacific Ocean Theatre. The direction of the train gave credence to that suspicion and when it stopped near Kansas City, Carl had a chance to call his sister who was in nursing school there. As the train continued on west, he asked an officer if he could have permission to write a note to his sweetheart and tack it to a board which he would kick off the train when they passed through Lindsborg. Permission was granted but, as it happened, Carl's train stopped in Lindsborg on a siding to allow a Navy train to pass through, and he was able to give the note to someone. He asked the person to please deliver it to Kathryn Keding at the high school. He also asked someone nearby to call the family farm since the railroad tracks crossed their land less than a mile from the house to let them

35th Division in the Rose Bowl Parade, 1942.

Carl on furlough in Lindsborg, 1942.

your other letter Sunday night. I have to work all day Sunday." All my love, Carl.

Two months before going overseas, the 35th Division participated in mountain training in West Virginia. A tragic incident occurred immediately after Carl's platoon had safely crossed a treacherous mountain stream in Blackwater Canyon by way of a rope bridge. He followed his platoon over and waiting behind him to cross were two medics carrying another soldier strapped to a litter. Carl thought to himself that with the ever increasing melted snow runoff cascading down against the moving rope bridge, those three would not be able to make it across. At that time the floor of the bridge was partly covered by water. Just as Carl reached the other side, he turned and watched in horror as the bridge broke loose carrying the three victims downstream. An area newspaper reported the very sad story.

There was another message delivered to Kathryn at her classroom just days after the Blackwater tragedy. This time it was a telegram from Carl, "Come as soon as you get this. My parents will meet you at the Lindsborg City Bakery after school today." They were there when she arrived at work. They handed her a small leather purse with currency enough to purchase a ticket on the Colorado Eagle, a streamliner on its eastbound route, coming through town at 2 a.m. The Barretts, an elderly couple, were providing a home for her while she worked her way through high school. When Mr. Barrett heard her plan, he offered, "You can use my suitcase Kathryn. It does not have a clasp on it, but we can put my belt around it." At Durham, North Carolina, Carl came in from Camp Butner. It was the evening before Palm Sunday. The city was teeming with family members of the 35th who were spending precious time with their loved ones that would soon leave. Lodging was impossible to secure without aid from the Red Cross who called citizens to open their homes to the large amount of visitors. A call came in from a lady, "If the soldier would sleep with my brother, his fiancée may sleep on a cot in the bedroom occupied by my mother and me."

know he would be passing. His twin brother, Paul, drove their parents to the crossing and they waited there to wave to their beloved son and brother as he and his division headed to California.

After performing coastal defense duties in the Los Angeles area as part of the Western Defense Command, they were sent farther north to San Luis Obispo, California, where the division received further training. While there the division was re-designated as the 35th Infantry Division.

Rather than heading into the Pacific Ocean Theatre, the division was assigned to Camp Rucker, Alabama, in April 1943 for advanced divisional training and participated in the Tennessee Maneuvers in November and December of that year. In January 1944, the 35th went to Camp Butner, North Carolina, to undergo final training prior to overseas embarkation. During that time at Camp Butner Carl wrote to Kathryn:

"They've got me on the go night and day now. I'm over at Regimental in the daytime and working in the company supply room at night. Next week when the movement order comes down…I'll stop now as it's after one o'clock I've got to get up at 6. I'll try and answer

Kathryn and Carl were very thankful for this kind offer. They were married the next day, Wednesday, April 5, 1944, complying with North Carolina's three-day waiting period, which gave them time to secure lodging. Their first home in North Carolina was an enclosed porch. With Division orders, leaves were cancelled after Sunday, April 9, Easter Sunday. The next day, Kathryn started back to Kansas on the bus, a four-day trip, with one chance to lie down at a U.S.O. in Knoxville, Tennessee.

In May, the Division was sent to Camp Kilmer, New Jersey, to await orders for Europe. The S. S. Wallace Berry was the ship designated to transport the 35th Division to Europe. As Carl and others boarded, they saw the ship's captain, whose back was to them, speaking with some of the division officers. Carl thought he recognized that voice! On board, he inquired about the name of the captain, and a little later heard himself paged to come to Captain Larson's quarters. Dunward Larson and Carl had been high school classmates and hunting buddies. In trapping season the boys set traps every evening and checked them each morning before school. Lots of reminiscing took place as they crossed the Atlantic. Dunward showed Carl the repaired smokestacks which had been damaged by German gunfire in an attack off of the North African coast. The two friends eventually reconnected in Lindsborg after the war.

The month of June was spent in England, training and waiting for battle orders. Between July 5-7, 1944, the 35th Infantry Division was shipped across the English Channel and landed on Omaha Beach, Normandy, France. It entered combat on July 11 and fought in the Normandy hedgerows north of St. Lo., where Carl's severe injury occurred. The area had been occupied by the enemy for several years. The following description of the battle near La Meauffe is taken from Chapter 3 of the unit history book *Presenting the 35th Infantry Division in World War II, 1941 - 1945.*

"At La Meauffe every house and shop had been converted by the Germans into individual pillboxes. From behind hastily constructed barricades they poured forth streams of hot bullets and flesh-ripping grenades. But the Infantry did not falter. With full confidence in the precision of their artillery fire, they advanced steadily behind each well-placed salvo and wiped out nests of resistance."

After the fatal attack on his scout machine gunner and emptying the BAR automatic rifle, Carl lay in the field, trying unsuccessfully with his free hand to get his intestines contained so he could move. It perhaps was assumed he did not live as no one tried to come for him. But in the afternoon, a unit from B Company came near enough to hear Carl's call for help. One of the men, Al Shock, left his platoon to give aid, and he helped Carl by sprinkling sulfa powder from his medical kit onto the gaping wound. Shock then used some pins and wire to enclose Carl's right hand and guts within his shirt. Shock helped him to stand and then hurried to catch up with his own unit. This location was in the La Meauffe area where an attempt was being made to take the strong point of Le Carillon, so Carl headed back north. He walked into the direction of the highest firepower, knowing it would lead him away from the enemy where he could receive help.

He came to an empty farmhouse but did not lie down on the cot as it might have been mined, so instead he used a bread table to rest upon. Perhaps it would have been easier to arise from the table since it would have been higher than the cot. When it started to get light in the morning of July 12, he continued to walk alongside the hedgerows which were on very high embankments. Some of them were waist to shoulder high with thick, tangled root systems.

Carl kept his M-1 on his left shoulder as he walked. This was an example of a time in Carl's life where God's hand was on him. When a first grader in his one room country school, his teacher required him to write with his right hand, although he was naturally left-handed. As a result he became equally proficient in shooting with both hands. As a very young boy, he grew up using his hunting rifle to kill game for furs he could sell. He entered the service, qualifying with both his right and left hands on the rifle range. When Carl was in his mid-twenties, he was a member of the National Rifle Association and was listed in their National Achievement Awards booklet.

Carl had walked some distance when a bullet whizzed by his head. He knew exactly from which direction it had come. He stopped dead still and waited about two hours before the fellow who shot at him lifted his head above the base of the hedgerow across the way. Carl had to take him out. He mentioned more than once the regret of seeing this very young German kid lying there, dead from the bullet.

He continued making his way until he saw the field hospital with its red cross on the tent. A chaplain was walking around the tent and heard Carl's call for help. Carl learned later that another person nearby was a man from his company, Ralph Cortese from Michigan. He was taken into the tent with many other wounded. He recognized the voice of another who was in distress as a fellow E Company guy. In the surgical area they removed nine feet of Carl's exposed intestines and cleaned away as best they could the grit and twigs in his abdominal cavity.

Three days after his arrival at the field hospital, Carl was evacuated to England where a severe infection was treated. That was followed by more surgeries and months of attempts to get liquid through the passage way narrowed by adhesions and other intestinal problems. At one point before the infection was under control, Carl recalled a chaplain and a nurse staying by his bedside for many hours because it appeared he would not survive. His suggestion to the nurse to go get some rest was ignored. During that time, also, 35th Division officers were checking with the medical personnel to determine which of the soldiers would be able to eventually return to the front line. When they asked about Carl they were told, "No, he's not making it." For Carl, one of the most difficult aspects of his injury was not being able to rejoin his men. It grieved him greatly that he was not able to finish the job to which he was called.

Five months after arriving in England, Carl returned home to the U.S. on the Queen Mary, a luxury liner which had been converted into a troop/

Carl, recovering at Baxter General Hospital, Spokane, Washington, more than sixty pounds lighter than before being wounded.

hospital ship during the war. He was taken first to Halloran General Hospital in New Jersey. Carl made that important phone call home to his wife informing her that he would be sent to a hospital closer to home. That hospital was Baxter General Hospital in Spokane, Washington—not exactly close to home! Kathryn joined him there, getting a room and a job so she could be close to her husband. More surgeries and convalescence took place in Spokane, and at long last Carl returned to Lindsborg nearly a year after being wounded. They returned to the homestead. Kathryn had been living there with Carl's parents since her high school graduation.

Post war

It had been Carl's dream to come back from the war and farm the homestead. That dream could not be realized due to the extent of his injuries. In years to come his agricultural interest would be satisfied by growing vegetable and flower gardens in which no weed in sight lived long. Left without any abdominal muscles, lifting was restricted and excess activity at times would cause a condition that left Carl faint and nauseous. His heart was strong and the doctors said not to worry, and although he would continue to have those spells, each would pass. He was a very *patient* patient and would never complain, but his loved ones soon recognized signs of intense discomfort.

Carl spent Thanksgiving and Christmas 1945 in the V. A. Hospital in Wichita away from his wife and newborn son who remained on the family farm in Lindsborg. During that hospital stay, in a ceremony covered by local press, the mayor of Wichita on behalf of Philco presented Carl with one of the first radios produced after the war. On Christmas morning Carl knew his intestinal situation had become very serious and advised medical personnel, "If you don't operate now, you can just forget about it," and he was rushed to surgery right away.

Throughout the rest of his life Carl suffered after effects of his war injuries. There were frequent gastrointestinal problems and more surgeries to endure but God blessed him with a long productive life. Thankfully, there were also periods when the problems abated somewhat. He and Kathryn had six children: Carl Daniel, Judy, Shirley, Peggy, Richard and Susan. In addition, they were blessed with dozens of grandchildren and great-grandchildren.

Carl received a number of awards for heroism including the Distinguished Service Cross, the Bronze Star and a Purple Heart. In addition, he received several awards for firearms expertise as well as campaign ribbons and others awards.

While he was recovering from his injuries after returning from Spokane, he received a call from the Defense Department. Carl was told they wanted to present his Distinguished Service Cross in a ceremony at a nearby military base, but he declined. He truly did not want to draw attention to himself in light of the fact that so many of his fellow soldiers had remained on the front lines until the war's end and many didn't return home alive.

Some years after the war, there was a meeting of Army officers in Texas. Colonel O'Connell from Topeka was speaking with the doctor who had treated Carl upon arrival at the field hospital. The doctor said to Col. O'Connell, "I'll never forget that soldier who came in with his intestines in his hand," to which Col. O'Connell replied, "Oh, yes, I see him and his wife at 35th Division reunions." The astounded doctor said, "Oh, no! Don't tell me he is alive!!" The doctor obtained Carl's address from Col. O'Connell and wrote a letter to him describing his amazement in learning that he had survived his injuries.

Following the war, the 35th Division Association worked hard to ensure that the close bonds which had developed between these brave soldiers during their time together could be maintained and the memory of those in their number who made the "ultimate sacrifice" would be honored. The 35th Division Association holds an annual reunion for the veterans and their families.

These men treasured their annual 35th Division reunions and many still do, although the numbers of World War II veterans have decreased dramatically. Often, at earlier reunions, there would be fellows attending for the first time who had not known Carl survived due to that initial report from the hospital in England. At one reunion, Carl and Kathryn were on a hotel elevator. She noticed a captain take a quick look at Carl. Realizing who he had just seen, he turned and hugged him in an

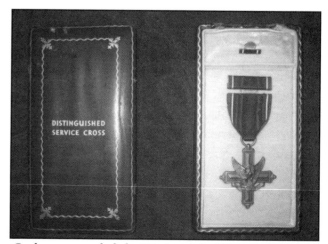

Carl was awarded the Distinguished Service Cross.

emotional embrace. On another occasion, two men entered the reunion hospitality room, took a look around for a familiar face and then left through the same door in which they had entered. They came right back in exclaiming, "Rusty! We thought you were dead!!" These two men, Ralph Cortese and Lt. Bondie, maintained contact with Carl in the years to come. Al Shock, the man who tended to Carl's injuries in the field, also learned of Carl's survival.

In the early 1950's, a young neighbor boy used to follow Carl around the garden. Decades later, grown up Ken Beauchamp came back into Carl's life, traveling from Washington state with his wife Andee to be reunited with the Frantz family. There was much reminiscing, but Ken also told of learning of his own need for a Savior. Romans 3:23 says "for all have sinned and fallen short of the glory of God." Ken had recognized the necessity of accepting the free gift of salvation. The Lord Jesus paid for this gift on the cross where he bore the sins of the world. "But if we walk in the light, as he is in the light, we have fellowship with one another, and the blood of Jesus, his Son, purifies us from all sin" (1 John 1:7). Ken shared his personal testimony with Carl who listened intently.

Two years later, Ken and Andee returned for another longer visit and spent three wonderful days. At one point during their visit, he and Carl were having a spiritual discussion and he asked, "Carl, have you ever invited the Lord Jesus into your heart?" Carl answered, "No, I never have." Ken then asked him if he wanted to and Carl did. After Carl finished his prayer asking the Lord to forgive his sins and acknowledging his acceptance of Christ as his Savior, he said "I should have done that a long time ago!" With this burden gone, Carl was a changed person, confident and happy with his citizenship now in Heaven and his name written in the "Lamb's Book of Life" (Rev 21:27). "In the same way, I tell you, there is rejoicing in the presence of the angels of God over one sinner who repents." Luke 15:10. There was certainly rejoicing among his family as well!

He is my Grandpa Frantz

Two very special events took place in 2009. Members of Carl's family were invited to be present at a number of ceremonies in France in July of that year commemorating the liberation of St. Lo sixty-five years earlier. Representing the family were Kathryn Frantz, Ed and Judy Pilewski, Peggy Weddle and Susan Achenbach. A relative from Sweden, Larsa Eriksson and his friend Gerd Mattsson, attended also. The family was deeply touched by the sincere gratitude expressed by the people of Normandy. Even after all the time that had passed since their liberation, the people there remain profoundly thankful for the price that was paid for their freedom. "You did not have conflict in your own land, but America sent her young people to bring us the freedom we still enjoy sixty-five years later," one of our hosts, André Chan, commented.

In addition to participating in the many ceremonies, the family had the incredible opportunity to actually visit the field where Carl received his wounds. Thanks to the availability of military maps, the historical research performed by young World War II re-enactors, the assistance of their hosts and permission from the current land owners, they realized a dream come true. Thankfully the land remains a farm so the area is preserved much like it would have been in 1944.

In September most of the members of Carl's family were present at the 35th Division Reunion in Topeka, Kansas, when he was honored as a member of the initial class of inductees into the 35th Division Hall of Fame. It was an event the family will always remember as they honored this very special and much loved man, their husband, father, grandfather and great-grandfather.

Carl went to be with the Lord on January 13, 2004, just five days after his 90th birthday. Although he is greatly missed by a family who treasured him, a poem written by his granddaughter, Emily Weddle (now Emily Handke) on the day Carl died summed up their feelings.

My Hero

A hero of mine has fallen today
A hero, brave and strong
He was valiant and courageous
All of his life long

My hero is beyond mere words
For words cannot explain
How he fought with purpose
No matter how great the pain

His love, vast as the oceans,
Was not expressed in word
But he, by thoughtful actions
His love to us assured

A hero, yet still one of us
In need of Christ the same
And so, one day in humble faith
Christ's blood, my hero claimed

A man of character, my hero was
A man who feared not death
But lived steadfast moving onward,
Until his final breath

So many things I'll miss about him
So much that I hold dear
His smile, his hug, his little chuckle,
His squeeze, which was sincere

Who was my hero, you may ask?
This one of sweet romance?
My hero, whom I'll never forget,
He is my Grandpa Frantz.

AUTHOR PAGE

Kathryn Frantz was born on a New Gottland farm in McPherson County, Kansas, June 16, 1926. She was eight years old, the third of five daughters, when her father was killed in an accident in McPherson. Her mother rallied as best she could and, with Kathryn and three older daughters' help, started a

Kathryn now.

dairy. They put their herd on a 4 a.m.-4 p.m. schedule so the two oldest could milk the cows and deliver milk before going to school each day, only to repeat the process when they arrived home. When she was ready for high school, she and her sister moved to Lindsborg, where they worked and completed high school with vital and life-saving encouragement from teachers, including Kathryn's being employed in the school superintendent's office.

One of Kathryn's jobs was at the old drug store where Carl Frantz, on leave from the Army to attend Lindsborg's first Hyllningsfest, came to do target practice in the basement gallery. Kathryn, in charge of A-Smile-A-Minute photo booth, asked, "Soldier, could I take your picture?" He shyly declined. The second night he returned with friends for more target practice. He again skirted her request, but the third night, he allowed her to photograph him, and sent a friend back to ask if she would accept his invitation to have a date with her the next evening. Thus began a long distance courtship by mail. He sent her a diamond when she was a junior in high school, and they were married April 5, 1944. She had received a telegram at school asking her to hurry to the drugstore where his parents would have a message for her. She was given a small leather pouch with enough money for a one-way ticket to North Carolina where Carl was stationed. When she arrived, they arranged to be married, she returned home and graduated from high school while Carl was sent overseas.

Carl's twin brother Paul appeared with a serious look on his face and a telegram in his hand, stating that Carl had been "seriously wounded." It was a form letter with no details. Kathryn learned the nature of his injury when a Kansas City Star reporter who was following the 35th Division wrote an article about his condition. Carl described his injury in his first V-mail correspondence to Kathryn, "I got scratched up a little."

Doctors and military personnel did not expect Carl to survive. He spent months recovering enough to be brought to the States where he received more rehabilitation. His life was one of multiple surgeries, hospital visits, and constant attention from Kathryn. Nevertheless, they raised a family of six

children, and he lived as full a life as possible. Five days following his 90th birthday, January 8, 2004, he took his final breath.

Kathryn is certain Carl would not have married her after he was so badly wounded. Therefore, she has lived a lifetime of gratitude that they married when he had leave before shipping overseas. Together, they enjoyed family and extended family of dozens of grandchildren and great-grandchildren. She honors his dedication to his country and his loyalty to her by participating in 35th Division reunions several times a year, writing articles for their newspaper, and keeping in touch with veterans and their families.

She thanks and credits her children for all their help in writing this, Carl's story, *The One They Call Hero*.

Greater love has no one than this, than to lay down his life for his friends.

REBUILDING:
DEBRIS AND RUBBLE

by Emery Frost

THIS BOOK IS DEDICATED TO:

All the veterans of World War II.

I'm not a writer, but I have heard things over the years that I think are worth telling. When you take time to look around you, you realize what a beautiful world God has created for us. Then on the other hand you think about man and what he has done with this world. There are a lot of good and outstanding people in this world. Then you also have the other kind.

One of the other kind of person was Adolf Hitler. He was a very smart person and then started going in the wrong direction. I have never studied about him, but I know he had a way of collecting top people like engineers, scientists, and outstanding men in their fields. Hitler had a plan to go to war and conquer all of Europe.

Germany didn't have a lot of oil or oil fields in the late 30's so Hitler had Germany making ethanol and alcohol out of grain and other things. They were making rockets in the early 40's and were firing them at London randomly. The rockets weren't too accurate but when they hit the city of London, they caused a lot of damage. The people of London couldn't hear the rockets coming like they would the motor of an airplane until the rocket was right on them. England finally hung down long cables from balloons hoping the rockets would hit the cables and they would explode in the sky harmlessly.

After Germany surrendered it was divided into three parts. America, Russia, and I believe England, hurried in and picked out the top German scientists and engineers and they were brought to the U.S. and Russia. These scientists and engineers were a big part of the U.S. Space program.

Hitler had built large rail yards and had put double tracks between nearly all the large cities so supplies could be moved at night without making stops between towns. When I was in Germany in 1946, Russia was taking up one set of tracks which were in the Russian sector and bringing the tracks back into Russia. Germany also had a huge highway called the Autobahn. It consisted of roads where you could travel any speed you wanted and this was where Eisenhower got the ideas for our highway system.

I think we all remember Pearl Harbor on December 7, 1941. I know my folks and I were in Church and we all heard about the bombing of all the ships and the fires and of all the service men that were killed. I was only 14 at that time so didn't worry about getting drafted or put in service. I remember the gas rationing that was put on at that time. With us living on a farm, we had to go and apply for so many gallons to last us for a few months. I remember the old kind of metal tube of toothpaste. We had to save the used tubes and turn them in when they were empty. To buy a new tube of toothpaste was about $.30 to $.40. We had stamps to get sugar, meat and a lot of food supplies. Months later the government came by and told my folks they would give us some money and we had so long a time to move out.

In that time there was no negotiating with the government. They told you something and you had to take what they offered you and get out. The Beck family that had a neighboring farm was given only two weeks to move out. Another family, the Gustafsons, was given a week or two to move out. The land where these farms were located was going to be used for an army base called Camp Phillips. Young men would work as survey crew and they came out to survey the land to figure out where the various military buildings would be built. At the base they had a Prisoner of War camp. They had various P.O.W.s from different European countries that included Italy and Germany. Imprisoned, the men were allowed to work on local farms.

Several years later after the end of WWII, I was drafted into the service and was put on a bus to Fort Leavenworth for my physical. Less than a month later, I got notice to go to Ft. Leavenworth again and get sworn into the service. Many others and myself were put on a train and were sent to Fort Bliss, Texas, for basic training. I had never ridden on a train so that was a new experience.

While at Ft. Leavenworth I took six weeks of basic training that would end up including six weeks of training in different areas. Those areas were: truck driving, anti-aircraft, gunnery, field lineman, artillery, and a few others. After we had been in the

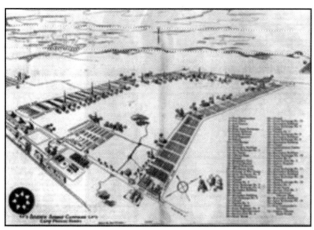

A map of Camp Phillips from documents prepared by the post public relations department.

classes about three weeks, they were closed out and they had other officers come and talk. They wanted us to enlist for three years and get into a field we wanted. One speaker was a paratrooper. He was a sharp looking officer that showed pictures and talked about how the training would be. He said, "We would run till our tongues hung out, wait for them to go back in, then would start running again!" I was not happy to be drafted and couldn't wait until I could get out and go home. I had only been in the army for eight or nine weeks and already wanted to leave!

We had other schools we could choose to go to but we would have had to enlist for three or four years to go to those and I wanted to go home, or get a furlough and go home for ten days. So most of us left, took furlough, and went home instead of signing up for the additional schools. When our time was up we had to report to Fort Ord, California, and we were there about a week taking more tests.

After all the tests, we were put on a troop train and went to Camp Kilmer, New Jersey. Our trip took nearly a week as all the other trains had priority and we had to be put on sidetracks. We had to ride in old coach cars that had been taken out of mothballs somewhere. Several places we stopped, the Salvation Army was there with coffee and doughnuts. We were in New Jersey nearly a week and got a weekend pass and went to New York City. While in

New York City I got to see many major attractions that included the Statue of Liberty.

During the war the Allied countries had performed a huge campaign of bombing. They conducted raids with several thousand planes loaded with bombs on nearly every major city in Germany. I saw this first hand during my service. Many of the cities were reduced to nothing but piles of debris and rubble. I heard stories that many people chose to have barrels of water in each room of their house and during an air raid, if a fire started in their house or apartment, they had the water to put out fires and save the building where they lived. When the Allies came with the thousand planes, they kept on for 24 hours and the whole city was reduced to rubble. Many people were killed trying to save their houses. Even in the summer of 1946 if you walked down a street and walked into a foul-smelling area, you knew a human being had been killed and buried under the rubble. Some days if you went down the street and saw a wreath of flowers on a pile of rubble, it probably was a birthday or anniversary of some person that was still buried there.

I don't remember when the Marshall Plan was started, but it was a large-scale plan developed by the United States for rebuilding the countries of Europe. I started to see old people sitting by tall buildings early in 1946. They were buildings that had been reduced to a pile of rubble maybe 10 to 12 feet high. The people would start at the bottom of a rubble pile if it was by a street that had been

Supply ship at the port at Bremerhaven unloading food to feed the army.

We took this ferry to pick up rail cars. When the tide was out, the ferry would be six feet lower.

This is like the cars we rode in guarding food. When it got too cold we got up in the steam engine and rode where it was warm.

Street in Bremerhaven after the Allied bombs hit Germany.

A German citizen separating bricks from trash. When the large cars were filled with bricks they would be dumped at a central place.

dozed out. They had small four-wheeled carts on a narrow set of rails and as they cleaned the mortar off of the bricks, the bricks were put in a neat pile or stack. The concrete dust and dirt was placed in the carts and a person would push it down the street and dump it in a pile.

In looking at the crude way of working, we had to think that people had to move a lot of earth that way if they were going to clean the whole city. We were told that the people were still alive but had no home and no money. The U.S. would give them two meals a day if they worked.

Germany had done a lot of preparation for air raids. We stayed in one large shelter that was maybe 25 feet wide and maybe a hundred feet long and had three to four feet of dirt on top. When the air raid warning sounded the people had just so many min-

Results of 1,000 planes bombing Germany.

The Bremen rail yard. People would come and clean bricks so they could rebuild their town.

Raising a sunken barge.

The main street in Bremerhaven.

Rubble on a street in Bremerhaven.

Mass destruction of a town.

The Bremen rail yard.

Someone had dug through the rubble and was living here.

Three GI friends in Germany. We couldn't believe the damage.

This the backside of the building we lived in while stationed in Bremerhaven.

One of Germany's cobblestone country roads.

Reading the newspaper.

Typical European toilet.

utes to get there before two massive doors closed. If you were late, you were left out.

I didn't think too much more about it until we were in Norway in 1987 and we were in Vegeland Park. We had been in most of the park when we heard music way over in the corner of the park. This park had more than 600 statues of people carved out of stone or marble. We decided to walk over to see what it was and we could hear the music. When we got closer, we saw a lot of red, white, and blue banners

Armistice Day in Norway, 1987.

Civil War re-enactment in Norway, 1987.

and Pepsi, Coke, and Pizza Hut and other American signs and flags were hung up and displayed.

A young, pretty girl was handing out programs and we asked her what was going on. She told us it was their Armistice Day that they celebrated every year always the closest weekend to our 4th of July. This was to honor the United States for the Marshall Plan because without it maybe a million Norwegians would have starved to death. The Germans had deprived the country of everything and there was nothing left for the Norwegians to live on or eat. For the Armistice Day celebration Norway had brought people from America to perform for them. They had a group of teenaged girls from a Norwegian settlement in the state of Washington that sang Norwegian songs and American songs. They had real attractive black and white outfits on. They had several other acts also. The most popular group was a number of young people from Texas that wore jeans, western shirts, and straw hats. They were doing line dances and teaching the Norwegian kids the western music and the step. They were selling a lot of Pepsi and pizzas.

Then they had a reenactment of the American Civil War. They had a battlefield at two ends of the field and they were dressed in authentic looking uniforms of the Civil War. Then the South started advancing and the North started shooting the black powder guns and muskets and the smoke nearly

overshadowed the soldiers. When the smoke had cleared some of the southern soldiers were wounded and lying on the battlefield and the north then won the Civil war.

It sure gave us a warm feeling that a country was still thanking us for helping them out more than 50 years later. I have heard that Norway's people are still celebrating 4th of July in honor of the U.S.

When you take time to look around, you realize what a beautiful world God has created for us. There are a lot of good and outstanding people in this world and then you have the other kind.

It seems a lot of men can only think about fighting and shooting if they don't get their ways, then it's go to war. When countries start wars, there is no limit to the damage that they can inflict on their neighbors, or other countries and the number of people that will be killed, wounded, or property that gets destroyed. When you look around, every country has spent themselves broke in preparation for war or defense of war.

When you think of it we all send the very best young men (that's our breeding stock) to go out and get killed, or get their arms and legs shot off. What we should do is take all the men lying in prisons and put them in training and send them off to battle and some of them, if they make men of themselves, could get freedom. Each war we send off our best men and that leaves a lot of the undesirables to have more children like them and our society goes downhill after each war. If all the money we spent on wars was used to build more and better schools, roads, parks and churches, we could really have a beautiful world to live in like God would want us to.

Author Page

Emery Luther Frost was born on March 27, 1927 in the Saline County area. He attended school in Smolan, Kansas. He met his wife Doris Ostenberg of Smolan, Kansas, before he was drafted into the service. They were married on Sunday, March 30th 1947. When Emery's tour of service ended he returned to the farm. He raised cattle, hogs, and chickens and worked in construction that included pouring concrete for a grain elevator and building houses. He is very active and still farms. He helped harvest the wheat last year, and is planning to help this year as well. Emery and Doris had four boys all born a year apart, they have eight grandchildren (all girls), and four great-grandchildren (all girls).

Emery and Doris now.

I WAS A POW

by Glenferd Funk

THIS BOOK IS DEDICATED TO:

Emily Jones.

In my childhood, a person hardly saw an airplane, and yet at five years old, I knew that one day I would fly one. It was my goal, my dream, and my highest aspiration to be a pilot when I grew up. And because of December 7, 1941, when the Japanese attacked Pearl Harbor and the U.S. declared war, my dream was closer to becoming a reality.

In February 1942, after attending McPherson College, I was drafted as a private into the United States Army. Everywhere I went from then on I advocated to be a pilot. My first post was in Missouri, then on to Scott Field, Illinois, for radio school. While I was on kitchen police peeling potatoes, I got word that I was to enlist in pilot training. I was on my way.

My first six weeks of Aviation Cadet Training started in April in Santa Ana, California. Dos Palos was my next stop for Primary Flying School for the next two months. At the time, I was already engaged to the May Queen of McPherson, Edythe Howard. I wired her to join me in California so we could be married. She was studying at Wichita State at the time, and she left without graduating to be with me.

My Edythe and me.

Basic training, September-October, 1942, Chico, California.

When she arrived, I had the seven other men that I shared the barracks with draw "straws" using pencils to see who would be my best man. The base commander gave Edythe away when we were married on July 11th; our life together had only begun.

Advanced training followed in Chico, then Stockton, California. Finally, on January 4, 1943, I got my commission as 2nd Lt. and my pilot wings. My parents came by train from Wichita to see my boyhood dream become a reality. During the war years, a military wife was allowed one free trip; Edythe's was from California to Florida. It was the first of our 49 moves. My orders sent me to Tampa, and we lived in St. Petersburg. On base, we had a little saying, "A plane a day in Tampa Bay." We tested two-engine B-26s. Due to the hot temperature, we usually lost an engine, and pulling back on the good engine to belly in for a safe landing was difficult. The plane would flip over on account of all the power and would crash into the water. I lost many classmates that way. My first paycheck as an officer was a whopping 300 dollars, all in cold, hard cash. Edythe and I flung it in the air and let it settle like snow. We bought our first car with that money-a Club Coupe Oldsmobile. St. Petersburg was the next location for further training, but we weren't there long. We found ourselves in Smyrna, Tennessee, for my next post. Once again, we just got settled and then were on our way to another base, this time to Arizona to log more flight time. I was waiting for an outfit to be put together that I could join. A partial crew was formed and I was sent to McCook, Nebraska, in October to join up with the 465th Bomb Group, a unit for B-24s.

By now, Edythe and I had our first baby. Glenda was born November 9, 1943. Because of gas rationing, the doctor had to be picked up on the way to the hospital. Sadly, I didn't have much time with Glenda and Edythe before I left. My next orders were for overseas, leaving on the 17th of February, 1944. I was to enter the action in Italy, stopping first in Fortalaza, Brazil, for refueling, and then flying 11 hours to Djedeida, North Africa, where we had practice missions, ground school, and waited and waited on a plane for our crew. We stayed there until April 20th before we got to Italy, anxious to get into action so we could have our 50 missions and return to the states.

In the 16 missions I was involved with out of Pantanelle air base in Italy I flew 7 different aircraft, since something was always going wrong with them or parts were needed for other aircraft. The crew

My crew. I'm left, back row.

was made up of ten men, me the pilot, a copilot, navigator, a bombardier, and six enlisted men. I was the oldest at 25. Usually, our missions lasted anywhere from two to twelve hours. As the Americans bombed the Ploiesti oil fields during the day, our British allies would do the same at night. We were flying a B24 four engine plane when our orders were given to bomb the oil fields on D-Day, June 6, 1944. That was when we decided to "visit" Romania.

We had already disposed of the bombs and were on our way back when we were shot down. Our wing was in a fiery blaze and I saw a bullet streak between me and the flames. As the pilot, I was to be the last to jump. At first, I couldn't find my chute. I thought maybe someone had borrowed it without asking. Finally, I found it behind my seat. With all the smoke from the fire, I couldn't go back to check on my men. And it was so dark one guy stepped on another's back. Bail out time came and the warning bell sounded. On the second ring, the copilot, radio operator, and I went through the bomb bay when we couldn't stay on board any longer. It was the first time we had parachuted out. (Only paratroopers get to practice.)

When I exited the plane, I counted nine other chutes; we all had made it out, although it might not have been the smoothest jump! The lemonade I had had the night before made a reappearance when I was making my way down, dancing its way back and forth in front of me. During our descent from 20,000 feet, we could see the enemy moving in to position themselves where we would be landing. I watched as the plane came down on its belly in a landing better than any I had ever done. The fire had gotten so hot by the time it crashed that the .50 caliber bullets on board began to explode. The Germans thought that there was someone else still in the plane shooting at them when they showed up. We never told them otherwise.

My chute got hung up in a grove of trees and I had to climb down the tree. Once I was back on the ground, I saw a path nearby. I didn't get too far on it when suddenly I heard someone yell, "Halt!" A German soldier then asked if I had any guns on

HELD PRISONER BY ROMANIANS

First Lieut. Glenferd Earl Funk of Wichita, who was reported missing in action June 6, is a prisoner of war of the Romanion government, according to information received here Saturday.

Lieutenant Funk, who was first pilot on a B-24, was forced down in Romania while on a flight from Italy to Russia. At the time he was reported missing in action his rank was second lieutenant, but since that time the war department has advised relatives of his promotion to first lieutenant.

Glenferd Funk

His parents are Mr. and Mrs. Melvin Funk, 3952 Cleveland. His wife now is living in McPherson, Kas.

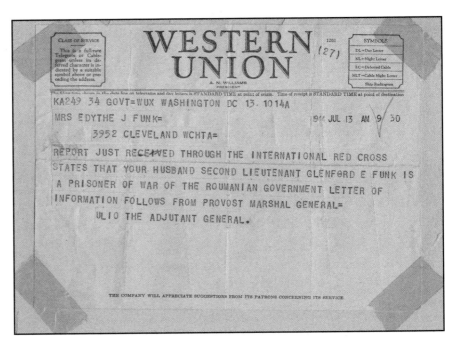

me and proceeded to take me to camp. Our copilot, Mickey Hoffman, was the only one of the crew that wasn't caught immediately. He was from Hollywood and quite the character. When he landed, he stayed in the brush until dark in hopes that he would be able to make his way back to Italy. The escape plan was that we should cross into Bulgaria and make our way to Turkey, which had by then had capitulated, where we would turn ourselves in and be returned to our forces in Italy. Well, Mickey saw a bridge and made his way towards it. He tossed his heavy flight boots over his shoulder and strolled across whistling. He was about halfway over when the Romanian guards stopped him. They brought him into our camp the next day.

During my interrogation, I was asked in English why I was fighting the Germans. Funk was a common German name and my interrogator thought that it was wrong that Germans were fighting Germans. I simply responded, "Why don't you give up?" All he could do was laugh. I just acted dumb, as were our orders, when they asked specific questions about bombs and other locations. All I was allowed to give was my name, rank, and serial number, and, at my own risk, some sass. Yet that wasn't the first time I encountered an unfriendly when I was captured. On the truck taking me to the POW camp, an old gentleman took a swing at me with his cane. The 465th had been bombing railroad yards in Bucharest, as well as the oil fields, and the bombardiers weren't always spot on. Sometimes the bombs were too short or too long off their targets and I suppose that his swinging at me was his way of getting back at us for the excess damage.

I did get to send a postcard back home on the day I was captured, but Edythe did not receive it until after she had gotten the telegram saying I was missing in action and the one saying I was a POW. My brief note on the postcard was: "Am OK. Was knocked down by flak and the whole crew bailed out when the plane caught fire. The food seems to be good; quarters are adequate. All in all we are treated swell. Nick and I are here together in Bucharest. From what I saw of it, the town reminds me more of the states than any I've been in. That is about all I can say except I plan to get much sack time." We were allowed to write one letter per month and 4 postcards. Edythe received only 2 of my letters and

2 of my postcards from me during that time, but I did not receive any letters from the States. It usually took about 4 ½ months before POWs started receiving their mail.

The officers and the enlisted men were divided into two groups. The enlisted men were placed in a camp located inside a hospital and the officers were sent to a schoolhouse. Hospitals weren't supposed to be targets, so the enlisted men were safe from bombing. I'm not sure what kind of message they were sending us when they put us officers in the schoolhouse. I spent the rest of June, July, and August as a prisoner. The camp probably had a name, but I never remember hearing it. We ate the same kind of food the Romanian civilians ate, the most memorable being sheep head soup. You can imagine how hungry it made us when we saw the eyeballs floating around. But like I said, we shouldn't have complained, since we were getting just what the Romanians were having, we just weren't accustomed to the diet. There were no hot fudge sundaes for us!

Breakfast consisted of some stuff they called coffee, a sort of rye bread, a marmalade or jam, sometimes berry, sometimes apricot, but most of the time we had a brown marmalade that did not remind you of any kind of fruit. For dinner (lunch) we had watery soup-soy bean, navy bean, cabbage or some sort of vegetable and for the next course, we were served meat-beef or mutton-or more macaroni, or just beans. Then for supper we had potato salad with a vegetable stew or cottage cheese with onions and some peas or beans. We had onions every day. They were in practically everything-soup, stew or just plain, raw onions.

We spent a lot of time talking about the good things we enjoyed eating. That would be the first thing we would do when we hit the States and we planned and dreamed about our meals at home. In a postcard I sent to Edythe July 20, I laid out the tentative plans, "Dick said he would pay for the first meal. He doesn't know what he is in for." On August 4, I wrote "We are receiving cakes with our chow and besides that receiving things they call turnovers, and a sort of Divinity candy. These turnovers are

Delousing

something like pie crust with jam between them. We are supposed to receive some Red Cross packages before long. They contain many things that remind you of the good old USA. By the way, I have shaved off my beard and mustache. It got in the way of my soup. I was planning on leaving the mustache there till you saw it but it was too much trouble."

Our camp was bombed all day and all night. By day, the Americans bombed Bucharest and the surrounding oil fields and railroad yards. Once, a stray bomb landed in the prison yard, but luckily it was a dud. The British air force bombed at night. They put screamers on their bombs. The screamers scared you worse than the actual bombs. You could hear their shrill screeching all over town. We spent a lot of time hiding in the basement for shelter. When we weren't hiding or gorging ourselves on sheep head soup and onions, we made our own entertainment. We fashioned playing cards out of cardboard, one man even made a monopoly set, and we put on plays. Some of the guys had to play the girl parts because there obviously weren't any women.

At another prisoner of war camp, a Romanian princess was a frequent visitor. Princess Catherine Caradja snuck food to the prisoners. I found this out

Princess Catherine Caradja

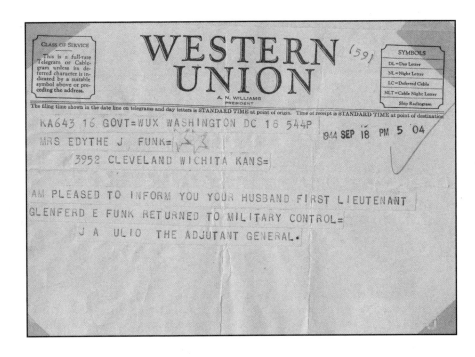

many years later when I had the opportunity to meet her in Denver, Colorado, at a Former Prisoners of War of Romania meeting. She relinquished her title and came to the United States for safety after the war. Her land was confiscated in 1949 by the Communists, which had taken over after the war. The Princess helped arrange the meetings to get all 2000 of the former prisoners together. She always called us "her boys." She told us at our first meeting that maybe Americans should be ruled by another country as her people had been for years so that we would know the true value of freedom.

On August 23, 1944, King Michael of Romania ordered the German commander to leave his country. The Russian army then came through its borders. The Romanian guards simply opened the gates and said we were free. Our POW commander allowed us to walk around the city. We were fortu-

American air force men, back in Italy following their liberation from Romanian prison camps, hear Maj. Gen. Nathan F. Twining, commanding general of the 15th air force, foreground. Men were flown back from Romania.

nate that there weren't many anti-American people around. There was a chocolate factory down the street. The owners became my friends forever when they offered me some because chocolate is my absolute favorite candy. One family invited a couple of us in and we spent the night with them. I think back wondering how many bed bugs and lice we left them. In the meantime, the Russians were entering Bucharest. I saw several Russian women driving big trucks, but they weren't too friendly looking. After we toured the city for a day or two, we headed back to the schoolhouse. We were about to start our journey home, or what was officially deemed as Operation Reunion.

In order to get a message to Italy to let our forces know the POWs in Romania had been freed, a Romanian pilot flying a ME 109 took Col. Jim Gunn, who was bolted into the fuselage since the plane was so small, to the base in Italy. The airlift began. B17s would transport us to Italy on August 31 and September 1. The planes would stay on the ground for only so many minutes and they would squeeze about 20 of us on board. All those trips and not one single casualty. In my camp alone there were 1,109 men to be airlifted. I was so excited that I got to go on the first day of the rescue. From Bucharest we flew to Italy.

Back with our own forces in Naples, we removed the grime we had collected from our months as prisoners. After we stripped, our flea and lice infested clothes were burned. We took hot showers in makeshift tents between the trees and deloused with DDT powder. Afterwards, we were given brand-new clothes and fed a turkey dinner with all the trimmings, which was a good start for all the tasty eating we had planned. That night, we slept on Army blankets, the softest wool you ever felt after sleeping on horse hair blankets as we had in Romania. With DDT applied, our bellies full, and a good night's sleep under our belts, we began our next phase of returning home.

Next, we boarded a ship that would take us to New York. The ship was a French frigate, the *Athos 2*, and it was a 13 day cruise to the land of the free and the home of the brave. As we passed the Statue of Liberty, that beautiful sight that was the first glimpse of America for so many immigrants, I couldn't help but think, "Home at last!" After our arrival, I went on to Fort Leavenworth to meet my beautiful wife and daughter that I hadn't seen in what seemed like an eternity.

Home at last.

A Note from Emily Jones, writer of this story as told to her by Glen and Edythe:

With this project, that I was so graciously allowed to be a part of, certain ideas of mine were proven to be absolute. The most important of these being that history isn't made up of distant, abstract figures and events that are locked up in dusty books and atlases. History is sitting right next to you in church, your next-door neighbor, or even that crotchety man ahead of you in the checkout line. History has gnarled hands and peppermints in its pockets, and occasionally blue hair. By grasping those hands, one can discover that history isn't solely made up of radical figures. It is made up of everyone. Every individual has a part to play. And while we are looking for the next Napoleon, Washington, or Churchill, we are overlooking the ordinary men

Emily Jones

Glenferd Funk now.

and women who cheered or jeered them into existence. And they are slipping away from us faster than we can learn to appreciate them...

I cannot thank Ann, Glen, Edythe, and the rest of those who shared their stories for allowing me to witness and have a hand in the moment when they were given the spotlight to share the history they helped create.

Glenferd Funk

Glen was born and raised in Conway Springs, Kansas, and attended McPherson College before being drafted by the Army Air Corps. In 1946, he finished his degree at McPherson College and taught in Canton, Kansas, schools for two years while staying in the Reserves. He missed flying and went active military again, where he had a most interesting and varied Air Force career before retiring in 1972, after which he worked security at a new occupational school in Denver. The Denver location of Lockheed Corporation approached him about serving as chief of supply, which he did before being sent to Iran by Lockheed in the same capacity. While in Iran during the early 1980s, the Funks were caught in the Iran conflict and were shut in and isolated for days on end. The conditions worsened until they were sent back to the States. They returned to their home in Denver and lived there until 2005 when they moved to McPherson.

A MILITARY EXPERIENCE

by Don Heline

THIS BOOK IS DEDICATED TO:

Military and veterans of the past.

I was not involved in the service during WWII. I was in the home front workforce, taking care of a farm. Being in the service at another time was very different from now.

The service we know today is a far cry from the military of long ago. Today, our soldiers are much more humanitarian, helping people by helping them learn discipline, order, and giving purpose to their lives.

Yes, we traveled to Kansas City and I was assigned to Fort Riley for sixteen weeks of basic training in the dead of winter at old Camp Funston, which no longer exists. We learned the discipline and fitness the service requires, as does civilian life. Rise early to make the twenty-mile hike over the hills to fire the weapons of war, to do kitchen police (KP) and housekeeping, etc. Through the drifts and cold, we made good friends during those weeks of basic training. This was in 1950 when the Korean conflict was going on and Viet Nam was starting.

More than 50,000 men trained at Camp Funston in WWI. The camp was named for Brigadier General Frederick L. Funston IIII, a native Kansan who distinguished himself during the Philippine Insurrection in the early years of the 20th century.

The camp was one of sixteen division-sized training sites established across the nation as we entered World War I in the spring of 1917. Approximately 1,400 buildings and twenty-nine miles of paved streets were built at a cost of $10 million. The camp also included fourteen infirmaries, fifteen YMCAs and four large theaters. Soldiers from the Great Plains came here for training. These soldiers initially carried wooden rifles. Eventually, the 89th and elements of the 92nd Divisions deployed from here for the battlefields of France. The 10th Division trained here but the war came to an end before they were shipped overseas.

Major General Leonard Wood commanded the camp. Camp Funston has the dubious distinction of being the site where the great flu epidemic first broke out in the spring and fall of 1918. The lives of more than a thousand soldiers were eventually claimed during these outbreaks.

In the early 1920s, the camp was torn down and the lumber sold at public auction. The campsite became maneuver area.

As war clouds gathered in the late 1930s, Camp Funston was rebuilt and again used for training. In the early years of the war, it was the home of the 2nd Cavalry Division. In the decades following the war, the camp was used by the 10th Infantry Division and 1st Infantry Division. The buildings of the second Camp Funston have been replaced and today this area is used as a maintenance equipment site for the

Camp Funston

Kansas National Guard and Army Reserve as well as a rail shipment point for the Army.

After completing basic training, I went to Fort Benning, Georgia, to Communications in the Headquarters Company. John Eisenhower, son of President Dwight D. Eisenhower, was our battalion commander for a time.

I was in the communications platoon. In those days, telephones and radios were used a lot. Scripts and codes were used. I was in Headquarters Company of our battalion. I was a field lineman with our telephones.

Down there we had a big building on the hill called Harmony Church. We would go up there and set up 150 telephones for all of the departments of a command center. Then all the officers would come in and run their problems. They would run conflicts to train their people and afterwards we would go in and tear it all down again. One of our duties was to set up mock war exercises for troops, generals, major, captains, and lieutenants.

I had the privilege of going to communications school at Fort Jackson, South Carolina, for about twelve weeks to learn wire communications, as opposed to the radio side. All of that was to learn more about communications in general, so important in all our daily lives. It was winter time when I was in South Carolina, too. The camp burned coal to keep the buildings heated, and with the heavy air, walking outside was like trudging through a black snow storm. The coal dust particles made the place

I saw these planes and paratroppers training at Fort Benning, Georgia.

The U.S.O. Club in downtown Columbus, Georgia. This building opened in May 1942. It was one of the five largest of such clubs constructed in the United States.

look like stormy winter time. I was never without the service of a chaplain and the worship services that we attended.

When I came back, I went from the squad room to the cadre room. I earned a stripe so I got to move into the cadre room. We had to have a jeep and a trainer so there was time to spend in the motor pool, getting it washed and taken care of.

After completing communications school, I went back to my company at Fort Benning to work. I never was assigned foreign duty, and was stationed at Fort Benning next to Columbus, Georgia, the rest of my time.

We continued to set up mock war exercises for troops, generals, majors, captains, and lieutenants. Some of them were South Korean personnel, as well as our own company and battalion workforce. We set up telephone communications, strung wire throughout the nearby woods, and set up radios, etc.

We often had inspections, time to meet the generals who visited. Everyone was to dress up and be sharp. I had been issued rough-out, combat-type boots. I was assigned to be on a one-day exercise for the generals' visit, where we had to look sharp with spit and polish (a term about spitting on your boots to polish and shine them). But there was no way I could shine those combat boots. I didn't have the "right" look, so I was taken off the detail.

A typical day for me at Fort Benning was to rise early, go to breakfast, and find out my day's assignment. It might have been to set up a problem for students (one of those exercises) or go somewhere in the battalion to do repair work. And of course, there was never-ending cleaning and repair of the equipment.

Every piece of equipment we had was recorded, written down—we had so many telephones, so many flashlights, etc., and they always had to be ready for inspections. If we needed any additional tools, etc. we had to requisition them from higher-up, and that took time to get them. So we always managed to have extras in case we needed them. When we got word that inspectors were on the way, we put the extras in an old truck that we sent to the woods on a problem. When the inspectors were gone, we got the old truck back and put the extras back on the shelf. We had to figure out how to keep ourselves equipped and able.

To repair, our typical day might include "police call," which meant cleaning up the grounds, keeping them spiffy. Every hour, we were granted a ten-minute break, which meant lots of candy bars and cigarettes.

My service was from 1953 to 1955, which was a time of "declared conflict" even though I never left the States or saw action in Korea. That made me eligible for the America Legion, which offers membership only to those who have served during a time of declared conflict.

After a brief history of my service time, I take time to reflect on the broader military life. Since time began, warriors, soldiers, dictators and such have been with us. Of course, the prime mission of our service is to make fighting people for an army for protection from enemies, but we do not all storm the beaches or take the hill under fire. Then the job of support is unbelievable and many of us were in that group.

Before we learn the tactics of battle, strong discipline is learned, as Paul Harvey stated. Self-government will not work without self-discipline. Our lives depend on the person next to us. We have to work and depend on our neighbors, have self-discipline to work with other people.

And a sense of patriotism becomes a driving force in our lives. We should be so thankful that we live in this country. The service is a strong teacher of patriotism, which we need to teach in the schools.

There were many job opportunities and professions to think about for later when you chose not make the service your career. Opportunities to train and go to school, being helped as people watched you at your work or play, encouragement to travel the country and world, led us to see that we all have the same problems and concerns to think about, regardless what we do.

I like to think of the humane things, the positive things that came from my military experience. When I was in, I was with people who had never had sheets on their bed at home, things like that. We cultivated the discipline of knowing that you have to work and live and look out for other people because your life depends on those people. The opportunities that it brings educationally and otherwise are great.

It bothers me just a little that everyone likes the exciting stories and may have horrible stories to tell, but my experience lacked that kind of excitement. I can't say I regret my service time or anything like that. Look at the support that it takes to keep a few men on the battlefield. I was part of that.

I met a lot of good people, like my company commander. He helped screen the people who came in pretty hard, so we had good people.

I maybe should have stayed in the service. A lot of people do that. A military is something we have to have. We cannot let our guard down. We have to protect ourselves.

The service experience has turned the lives of many people around, even though the end reason for the military is to do battle. But in our free time, we were allowed to take advantage of educational opportunities in other fields of work or helping with the education of others that it takes to support fighting groups. The discipline we learned, we took into our civilian lives. The working with your neighbor is a must wherever we are, with patience and understanding.

Yes, I have experiences of service, but you didn't get much but a few thoughts of service advantages. I am not concentrating on war stories. My idea is to tell about service life. A lot of good things come out of the military. We go to study the ways of war, but we hope it never happens.

I wouldn't discourage anyone from the military experience. Like life, what you put into it can come out for the good. We should thank God for America and do what we can to keep our country free and God-strengthened.

AUTHOR PAGE

Don Heline was born on a farm in McPherson County, Kansas July 19, 1925. He completed all but one year of his elementary education in three different one-room country schools; Johnston, Swedesburg, and Harper. His family moved to Lindsborg for his last year, where his mother taught school.

Mom needed a way to support her family. Dad died in 1936, and Don's youngest brother had fallen from a swing at age five, broken his neck and died before Dad's death. Don had one more younger brother, John, who died September 2007.

Don attended Lindsborg High School and enjoys the company of a few classmates in this area to this day. Following graduation, he farmed with his uncle before obtaining a farm of his own. He was drafted in 1953.

Following his military duty, Don returned to

Don now.

Lindsborg and worked at the Lindsborg Hospital in Environmental Services (Don says that's a fancy term for janitor) for fourteen years before retiring, but stayed busy with odd jobs.

Don and wife Betty were married in the chapel at the Old Mill in 1984, a lovely setting for their wedding. They shared a life together until she died in 1996.

Don has the honor of being the first user of Bethany Home's rehabilitation for broken hips program. He returned home for one year before he tired of cooking and doing his own dishes. He became a full-time Bethany Home resident in 2010, a status he shares with Virgil Sandoll, who was drafted with Don in 1953. They share "war stories."

BEING A NAVY WAVE:
DURING WORLD WAR II

by Jo Holmquist

THIS BOOK IS DEDICATED TO:

My children, Terry and Paula.

I enlisted in the Navy WAVES in 1943. I went to Oklahoma City for a physical and a mental test where I met with other women recruits for the journey to New York City Hunter College.

On March 10, we went from Oklahoma City with twenty others to be WAVES. Our troop train went on to Little Rock, Arkansas, where we obtained many more women to become future WAVES. At least ten or more railroad cars pulled by two steam engines traveled over the hills, valleys, and mountains enroute to New York City.

When we arrived in New York, we went by subway to Hunter College where we were assigned our quarters. Usually four girls were assigned to a room where we were to sleep on bunk beds. After good food at the Mess Hall and a good night's sleep, we were ready to learn all we could about the Navy. We learned the art of marching, the Navy protocol and etiquette of whom to salute and how, how to react when boarding a Navy ship and also leaving that facility. We learned the workings of the Navy—the knowledge of ships and personnel. Also learned about the different departments and their functions. We learned about the officers of the Navy, the function of enlisted personnel, etc. When the weather was inclement, we marched in a large armory. We took swimming lessons. My instructor was a young woman who was an Olympic participant. We wore

Left to Right: Jo, Bette Lazich, Wyline Lazich and Adele Clinton.

our civilian clothes for two weeks before we were given $200 to buy uniforms from the "WAVES" store which was located on base. New WAVE recruits were classified as "Seamen."

The next week, we were each given $20 and allowed to on "liberty" in New York City. We caught the subway to go uptown New York. We passed Ebbets Field enroute (baseball field). The cost of riding the subway was five cents.

As we dressed in our uniforms and went on our journey in New York, we got lots of comments and stares from civilian spectators. We visited Rockefeller Center, the Waldorf Astoria, St. Patrick's Cathedral, and went to the top of the Empire State Building to gaze all over New York. We went to Staten Island to see the Statue of Liberty, etc. Needless to say, we were exhausted by the end of the day and so took the subway back to our barracks at Hunter College.

The next two weeks were much of the same in learning and training. We each finally found out where we were to be stationed or where we would go for further training.

Since I had worked as a PBX operator part time during my high school years, I got orders for the "Naval Training Center" in San Diego. I was delighted as that was where I really wanted to go anyway! We had a short time to visit our family in our home town. Much to my delight I went to spend a few days with mother and dad in Red Rock, Oklahoma.

We left from the train station in Newton, Kansas for our journey on a troop train for San Diego. After two days of travel, we arrived in Los Angeles. What a delight—I had never seen a palm tree, needless to say there were many in Los Angeles.

Before catching our train for San Diego that evening, my friend Ruth Sandmeir and I went to the Hollywood Palladium in Los Angeles to hear Woody Herman's Big Band. Since I'm a huge jazz fan, that was a highlight. Ruth had a brother-in-law who was a trombone player in the band. Ruth introduced me to her brother-in-law and also to Woody Herman. I was thrilled!

After a short time at the Palladium, we caught the troop train for San Diego, about one hundred miles south of Los Angeles. There were no lights on the train (blackout) for safety reasons. We arrived in San Diego and were taken to the US Naval Training Center where we were to be a part of "Ships Company." A brand new barracks had been built for a new WAVE contingent. We were the first naval women to arrive in San Diego. The barracks were beautiful. We were very happy with our new surroundings and quickly fit right in.

My role was in communications. Ten of us women replaced twelve sailors at the PBX board, which consisted of three positions thus giving each operator access to all calls incoming and also those calls going off base if they were restricted lines. Since we were all accomplished PBX operators, we fit right in.

Our "duty" was a shift of four hours on and four hours off for the day or night. Being in communications, one of our duties was to be on watch every four days and nights with the "Officer of the Day" at the communications building. We were to assist the Officer of the Day with his duties such as decoding messages coming in on the teletype. This part of being on "duty" was my favorite—which was helping the sailors to "make colors." This means lowering of the flag every evening and the raising of the flag the next morning. It was quite a process—solemn and awe-inspiring. The WAVE was to give a

Being hostesses to the Navy seamen.

Having Cokes and pie with the GI's.

signal to the man holding "Old Glory" to lower or raise the flag at the appropriate time. What a thrill!

While standing on the tower to give the signals, we had access to San Diego Bay, viewing the ships going out to sea, planes flying, and from the "Naval Air" which was right across the bay. I loved seeing the pontoon planes, Catalinas and Coronados take off or light on the San Diego Bay.

San Diego Naval Training area consisted of seven bases. First was where the recruits (men) started their training. They were in training in each area for a few weeks, then graduated to another area for further training until the training was completed and each was sent to his next base, shop, or "duty."

Celebration of the WAVES second birthday.

Dancing with the guys.

Hoist newspaper, our base weekly paper telling what the USO did and why.

Our base was beautiful—very large area. Lots of beautiful flowers and vegetation. Over the entrance to our office was a beautiful Bougainvillea vine—blooming all the time. I loved that. Also, more flowers and plants in our courtyard. I don't remember their names. We walked a few blocks to the WAVE "mess."

The food was exceptional since we were in California and had access to the wonderful fruits and vegetables raised there. One thing which was on the menu every morning was a huge vat of Navy beans.

On Saturday mornings was barracks inspection. We each were dressed in full uniform and stood at attention by our perfectly made bunks, totally clean

Having Cokes with the sailors.

rooms! Some Saturdays we had field inspection of all personnel on base—marching and personal inspection. On Sundays, we usually attended services at our Base Chapel, which was small, but quite beautiful.

On base was a "Ships Stores" for WAVES only. We could have our white shirts laundered at the base laundry for ten or twenty cents each. We could attend movies at the Luce movie theater free of charge any time we wanted—usually, first run movies. We were allowed to attend movies at the next door Marine Base free of charge or at any Navy facility. If we went to the Army Base at Point Loma, we paid fifteen cents. We had access to the nearby tennis courts and the golf course next to our barracks, where I saw Bing Crosby play golf!

On "liberty" we often went to the famous San Diego Zoo, the largest in the world. We could attend, which I often did, concerts at the huge Russ Auditorium off base where I saw Frank Sinatra, Lionel Hampton's Jazz Band, and many more.

There was a ballroom in downtown San Diego, where every two weeks we could go to listen or dance to the Big Bands. I saw many big bands—Woody Herman, Artie Shaw (Ava Gardner, his wife-to-be sat to one side of the bandstand). I saw many other bands and personnel.

One of the most enjoyable concerts was Bob Hope. It was a huge outdoor show, attended by

Memorial to the women who served, located at the gate of the Arlington Cemetery in Washington, D.C. Jo is a charter member of this Memorial, honoring all women who served.

members of all the armed services. What fun! It was special for all of us. We had access to many beaches in the San Diego area—Ocean Beach, Mission Beach, LaJolla, etc. We were frequent visitors to "Old Town" where the Mexican food was superb. "Ramona's Home" is there—lots to see.

I studied hard and finally made 2nd Class Petty Officer (S.P.X.). I got to go home on leave a few times on the Scout Train. My best friend in the WAVES was Wyline Lazich, who was from North Hollywood. We often went to Wyline's home by train, and I was welcomed as their own to the family.

The U.S.O. (United Service Organization) was created in 1942. Many of the women of the WAVES spent the time at the U.S.O. talking with service men, serving them coffee, donuts, etc. Having good conversation, dancing, just giving these men good fellowship, showing them we cared. These men were due to be sent to a "basc" or on a ship to serve our nation.

I would say my time in the Navy was perhaps equal to at least two years of college. What a privilege to serve our country. I received much more than I ever gave. I loved the Navy and feel it would be good training in many ways for young people. I came from a family where we all had chores at an early age, studied hard in school, and made good grades, so the Navy fit me very well.

There would be much more to my story, but I don't want to bore you. I'm thankful to my country for letting me have the "Navy Experience," which I would describe as worth at least of couple of years of college.

Thelma Josephine (Bilbrey) Holmquist.

Jo celebrated her 90th birthday, hosted by Terry and his wife Becky and Paula Allman, Jo's daughter.

AUTHOR PAGE:

Jo Holmquist was born in Arkansas, near Springfield, February 23, 1920. She and her family soon moved to Oklahoma, where her father had homesteaded before their stay in Arkansas. She heard stories about her father staying up all night, shotgun at the ready, watching for Indians. She remembers him playing the banjo; Mom, the guitar. She thinks she remembers hearing that the family

Jo now.

WAVES. They both enlisted; the friend did not pass her physical, so Jo became the first WAVE from Ponca City.

Following her Navy career, Jo married Evan Holmquist who served in the 187th field artillery during World War II. On June 6, 1944, plus four days, he landed on the shores of Omaha Beach in the invasion of France. Evan was injured, spent some of his time in the hospital, and was awarded a "Purple Heart" award for valor. They married soon after he was discharged from the Army and lived in Smolan. He managed the grain elevator in Smolan.

Evan died at age 61 when Jo was 59. She remained in Smolan and joined the Bethany College staff as operator for their new PBX system. She then joined St. John's hospital staff as PBX operator and as admittance clerk. She stayed with St. John's until her retirement at age 65 in 1985. She traveled to Oklahoma often to visit family, to Topeka to visit her son, and had been active in her church. She moved from Smolan to a Bethany Home cottage in 1998.

may have traveled between Arkansas and Oklahoma in a covered wagon. She graduated from Red Rock, Oklahoma, high school.

She worked in a defense factory in Ponca City for a while when a friend suggested they join the

ALL ABOARD

by Mary Holmquist

This book is dedicated to:

My son Tom and daughter Kristin.

I was born in Garfield, Kansas, a small town of less than four hundred people. It is located about half way between Larned and Kinsley. My birth date is September 8, 1919.

My parents were John and Minnie Olson. I had an older sister and brother, Tureda and Lennart and a younger brother, John. The older ones are now deceased, but Johnnie still lives there with his wife, Emma. I attended grade school and high school there and graduated in 1937.

I went to Bethany College from 1937-38 and received a 30 hour teacher's certificate. I had no trouble fitting into the college routine. I had a job working in the library. I received 25cents an hour which went directly to the college to put on my tuition. I enjoyed all the aspects of college life.

I went back to Garfield when school was out and started looking for a job. I was hired by District 38, a one room school in Edwards County. My sister had taught there the year I was at Bethany. The memorable thing that happened at that

My younger brother, Johnnie.

school was that we got caught in a blizzard. I was staying at the home of my first grader's parents and it was snowing lightly. We didn't think much about it and went on to school, but by 10:00 it was snowing very hard and the wind became very strong and we knew we were in for it. All the parents had come for their children except the parents of a pair of twins in the sixth grade that lived about a quarter of a mile from the school and my first grader's parents. It soon became apparent that they couldn't come to get their children. We decided to try to get to the home of the twins so we started out. We had to carry our first grader and we made it to their house luckily, but I gave credit to the twins. They had walked to school and knew how to get home. We spent the night there and were able to get back to my first grader's house the next day.

I was awfully proud of my 8th grade girl who got second place in the county exams that were given at that time. She graduated from K-State with a degree in home economics.

They closed District 38 that year so I had to look for another school to teach. I found one close to Rozel, Kansas. I was not happy there.

My older brother Lennart, 1943, U.S. Navy.

This was a school with many windows. We had an oil-burning heating stove, but it didn't keep the school warm, so I had to let them sit around the stove which was not conducive to much learning. It was there that I decided to go back to Bethany another year to get a sixty-hour certificate.

I returned to Bethany and had another good year. I had a wonderful roommate, Billy Johnson. She lived in Spearville and was a freshman at Bethany. I also met my future husband, Darrel Holmquist, there. We dated most of that year, but he went home a lot to help with farm work. He was only about fourteen miles from home.

When the school year ended, I was eligible for a 60 hour certificate, so I started hunting for a job. I got a job teaching sixth grade in Lewis, Kansas.

I enjoyed teaching in Lewis very much. I usually went home on weekends, but for some reasons I had decided to spend the weekend in Lewis. Sunday I had gone to church. I do remember that it was not cold and the sun was shining brightly. I walked back

Darrel and I, college age.

to the home where I stayed and found everyone crowded around the radio. In one voice they said, "Pearl Harbor has been bombed by the Japanese." I couldn't believe my ears, but I immediately thought about my brother who was in the Pacific on the ship named the Saratoga, an aircraft carrier. I learned later they were in the New Hebrides. They came into Pearl Harbor a few days later to help where help was needed to restore the area.

Life resumed near normalcy for a while. I had to finish the school year. I thought I would be back the following year as I had been offered a contract. I began to think that I might like working in an aircraft factory. It would be a change and I would be contributing to the war effort. A Boeing representative came to my parent's home and asked if I would be interested in working at their plant. I went to Wichita to see if I could find a job soon after school was out.

I applied at Cessna because I wouldn't have to go through a training period that I would have to do at Boeing. I was hired that first day. They told me I would be in woodworking. I would help build window frames for a small five-passenger trainer. I admitted I wasn't very talented with a hammer and nails. They said it wasn't hard to learn. "Put the nails in your mouth, spit them on the hammer and start nailing." They did tell me later that I was the first person they had that could put a curve in an 1/8th inch nail!

The day I got my job at Cessna I ran into Jimmy Bruce, an old friend of both Darrel's and mine from Galva. He said he ran into Darrel in Sioux City, Iowa where they were both stationed for a while. He said he would give Darrel my address and he would write to me. I began to hear from Darrel so we kept in touch all during the war.

We started our jobs at Cessna for a dollar an hour. I worked there for two years and when I quit I was getting $1.05 cents an hour.

I enjoyed working at Cessna very much. They did everything they could to bolster our morale. They played music a half hour before lunch and a half hour before closing time. They rented a building

Darrel, Tech Sergeant, in uniform.

downtown where employees could dance and visit. It was kept open for all shifts. We really didn't go very often because we were too tired and there were very few young men to dance with. They also had contests for writing safety jingles. They would give you a book of war stamps if you won. It took about five books of war stamps to trade it in for a war bond. War bonds were sold to raise money for the war effort. They cost about $25.00 apiece. They accumulated interest. You could cash them anytime you needed money. I won this contest several times. The only jingle I can remember is:

> "Rings on your fingers, bells on your toes, are safety hazards most everyone knows."

We were also fed very well. They brought a cart around every noon with full meals on them. We had to pay for these. You could bring your lunch, if you wanted to.

One day they brought in a woman who had been a prisoner of the Japanese. She was an American woman about 35 years old and maybe she just looked that old because of her experience as a prisoner. I'm sure life was tough for them, but she didn't say they were tortured. I don't know why she was

released. She showed us a pair of sandals that she had made. They were made of scraps that she found. They were pretty nice. She made us feel how lucky we were.

My friends were my fellow co-workers. There was Vermo who hated her name. She said they took the first three letters of her mother's name and the last two letters of her dad's name and put them together.

Joyce and I lived in a small apartment together. Her dad owned a ranch in southeastern Kansas. I went to church with an older lady about 40, once in a while. She was Catholic and I was Lutheran. I was so impressed with her because she rented an apartment close to her church. She was very devout.

We worked seven days a week, but we did get some weekends off if we were caught up with our work. Sometimes we worked overtime if they needed more trainer airplanes. We received time and a half for overtime.

Some of us girls decided we were tired of our blue and white checked coveralls and would like to have something a little more attractive to wear. We chose about three girls to go before the powers-that-be and present our case to them. They furnished us with catalogs and we picked our new overalls and shirts. They were made of a sort of rayon material so we ordered what we wanted and were thrilled when they arrived. But, in woodworking we worked with glue and these new clothes were ruined by the glue so we quickly returned to our blue and white checked coveralls. We got glue on those too, but it didn't matter. We washed them and wore them again and again.

Orders for five-passenger trainers evidently came to an end and Cessna sub-contracted parts of the B-29 to be constructed at Cessna.

The B-29 was the largest bomber ever built up until that time. We were completely awed at its enormity and very proud that we had a part in constructing it. I left my woodworking tools behind and became "Rosie the Riveter." Incidentally, we were all called Rosie.

The B-29 dropped the bomb on Hiroshima. The devastation was so great that the Japanese capitulated and the war in the Pacific was over.

B-29 Bomber produced by Boeing with parts made by Cessna. I worked on this plane.

Once in a while we had a weekend off, so I would go home to Garfield. I rode the train. Sometimes, there were troops on the train. They were really tired and I would give my seat to them and sit on my suitcase in the aisle.

We shopped, went to movies and went ice skating a few times on a rink there for entertainment.

I had been in Wichita about two years when I received a letter from my lifelong friend, Peggy. She was working at Curtiss Wright Aircraft Company in Columbus, Ohio. She had been sent to school by them to become an engineer. She asked me if I would come to Columbus and get a job so we could be together. I thought it would be a nice change, so I quit my job at Cessna and boarded a train for Columbus. I applied for a job at Curtiss Wright and was hired immediately.

I was to work in the blueprint department. I received about a nickel less an hour than I received at Cessna. My job was to put changes on the original blueprints. In other words if they changed a part on an airplane it also had to be changed on the blueprint. There weren't changes to be made at all times, so I would file blueprint in the blueprint cabinets. They were always getting out of place. They trained us how to put the changes on the blueprints. The training period lasted several weeks. Peggy was working not too far from where I was designing a brake system for some plane.

I made a lot of new friends there. Most of the people in the office were young women, but some were officers' (Air Force) wives and there were a few men. Our boss was a man, and he tried to date every new girl who came to work at the plant.

Peggy, a girl friend of hers named Mary Lyn, and I lived in an apartment in a section of Columbus called Bexly. There were several other older women living in apartments there also. They were not happy that we had moved there. I think they thought we would be too noisy. There was a cherry tree in the backyard. They wanted those cherries very badly. I picked their cherries for them because I was the only one who could climb a tree. They still didn't like us. We didn't stay there very long.

In the meantime, Darrel and his flight crew had finished their 50 missions and were on their way to Walla Walla, Washington, where they would be stationed for a while. He decided he would stop in Columbus to see me on his way to Walla Walla. Peggy, Darrel and I went out to dinner and Darrel and I had a good long visit before he went to bed on our living room floor. He had to leave the next morning. I was very happy to see him. We continued our correspondence.

Peggy and I rode to work in a carpool just as I

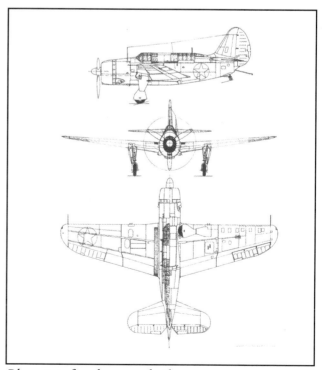

Blueprints for planes we built.

SB2c Helldiver. I worked on the blueprints for this plane at Curtiss Wright in Columbus, Ohio.

had done in Wichita. I can't remember how much it cost us, but it wasn't very much.

One of the men who rode in our car was investigated by the FBI, but they found nothing to incriminate him.

Mary Lyn left us and moved to another apartment. Peggy and I moved into a private home. The master of the house was a retired Colonel who had served with General Pershing in World War I. His wife was very nice. Her sister had lived with them for many years. They travelled the world over after he retired. The sister had since died.

The Colonel and his wife were very nice to us and were happy to have some young people around. They would probably have had a housekeeper, but there was none to be had. Peggy and I went to the Presbyterian Church with the Colonel and his wife

went to the Catholic Church. We dropped her off on the way to the Colonel's Church and picked her up on the way home.

Peggy's dad came to visit us for a day and night. It was great to see him. Peggy had a great dad. He was in the service. He taught math to the guys in pilot training in Texas. We had a little sun porch off of our room and we fixed it up for him to sleep in.

Both Peggy and I worked the day shift. Peggy was the most unathletic person I had ever known. I joined a softball team with girls from my office and went swimming at the Y. We also went shopping a lot. Columbus was such a football town that they let off workers to go to one football game. Peggy and I saw Ohio State and Navy play. It was so much fun. If I remember correctly, Navy won.

We went out to eat dinner quite often with some of the girls from our workplace. The seafood there was out of this world.

The one thing that was bad about Columbus was soot from the steel mills. If you went to downtown Columbus you would have black flakes of soot on your clothes. I'm sure it isn't that way anymore.

President Roosevelt died while I was in Columbus, and the nation grieved. Truman took over the reins of the presidency and did a wonderful job.

Shopping in Wichita.

This was my team at Curtiss Wright in Columbus, Ohio.

My brother, Lennart, had become ill and he was diagnosed with tuberculosis. He thought he contracted it in China. They put him in a hospital in California and they put him in the terminal ward, but he didn't die and they transferred him to Leavenworth. He married the nurse that took care of him. They moved to Garfield and were doing all right. Lennart was working for my Dad when he was in a serious accident involving some machinery that he was hauling.

Lennart never was able to work much after that. He died at the age of 69.

My brother Johnnie was still in the Pacific with his group. They were the 909th bomb group. It is probably group 134 Air Force. They were stationed at Fort Morrisby in the Philippines. Each mission lasted 15 hours.

The European war came to an end. The very day it ended we were all fired. There was one girl in our office that was not fired. She might have worked there before the war began.

Peggy and I said goodbye. I took a train from Columbus and headed to Garfield. I wasn't there very long when Darrel called me and asked me if I wouldn't come to Walla Walla for a visit. It sounded good to me, so I packed my bag again. Someone took me to Newton and I think it was the "El Capitan" train that I rode to California. This trip was quite uneventful, but when I got on the Portland Rose train heading for Washington it was more interesting. There was a Jewish couple that was very nice to me. They seemed to think I needed to be taken care of. There always were troops on the trains. There was also a girl who was going to marry a soldier and she was going to wherever he was stationed. I don't know if he was in Walla Walla or some other place. She didn't marry him because she met a soldier on this trip and decided to marry him instead!

I had to change trains when I was not too far from Walla Walla. This train had been in mothballs for many years. It looked like the trains we saw in old western movies. There was a potbellied stove toward the front of the car that burned wood. There were some rugs on the floor and the seats were sort of ornate. I thought it was real fun to ride in that old train.

Darrel was at the station to meet me. He took me to the Marcus Whitman Hotel where he had reserved a room for me.

He took me out to the base. I was shocked to see how beautiful it was. It looked like a place where you would love to spend your vacation. The lawns were beautifully green, lots of trees. I can't remember if there was a lake there or not, but I kind of think so. There is also a Whitman College in Walla Walla

I was fortunate to get to eat some meals on the base with Darrel. The food was super delicious.

We sat on the ground by a pond in Walla Walla and planned our wedding. Darrel asked if I wanted to wait till the war was over completely, which we knew would be soon. We could get married in the Lutheran Church in Garfield.

I thought about it, but I knew no one would be able to help me. My mother was nearly blind and my Dad had been sick since early in the war; my sister was working in a munitions plant in eastern Kansas; Lennart was still in the hospital and Johnnie was still in the Pacific theater flying missions. I told him I wanted to get married in Walla Walla.

We were married in the base chapel by Pastor Helland on the 12th of July, which also was Darrel's 24th birthday. One of Darrel's buddies sang two songs, "I Love You Truly" and "Oh, Promise Me." I wore a gold suit, white blouse, hat and gloves. Darrel wore his service uniform. It was a simple wedding, but very nice. We had no flowers, but we had gone to a jewelry store and bought a ring. It was a simple white gold band. It had a pattern on it but over the years the pattern faded. It cost $40.00. The ring now would cost several hundred dollars, probably. We had a pretty big celebration for our 50th anniversary and Darrel bought both a gold wedding band and a diamond for me. I still have the first ring. I loved it.

Darrel's friend, Pryor Adskim and his wife were our only attendants. We went out to dinner after the wedding. There were about ten or twelve of us. We sat down at the table and Darrel cried, "Where's the cake? I never thought about a cake!"

Wedding Day, July 12, 1944.

We moved into a private home after we were married, but we had no cooking privileges or any place to wash clothes, so we ate out in the evenings and washed clothes in the bathtub.

One Sunday our landlord and his wife took us on a long ride down the beautiful Oregon coast. We both enjoyed that a lot.

I started looking for a job. I was hired by Montgomery Wards to sell baby furniture. It was much in demand.

I didn't work there very long because they were going to send Darrel to New York City to a school to teach their soldiers how to find how many points they had so they could go home.

I boarded a train and headed for Garfield. I told my mother that I needed to learn how to cook so I bought a cookbook, "The Household Search Light." I still use it.

Darrel wasn't in New York very long because he found out he had enough points to get out of the service. Darrel was soon honorably discharged and on his way to Smolan. He soon came to Garfield to get me. When we arrived at the farm, his mother told us that his Aunt Ida, her sister, had dressed up and went outside and sat in a chair and pretended to be at our wedding, on the 12th of July. WHAT A NICE THING TO DO!

Darrel's folks soon left the farm and moved into Smolan. We raised our two children, Tom and Kristin, on the farm. We lived there for thirty-six years.

AUTHOR PAGE

Mary Holmquist enjoyed her early teaching career, and when her children were in school, she returned to Bethany College to complete her teaching degree at age 50. She taught sixth grade in Smolan for twelve years, moved to Salina, and continued teaching another two years before retiring at age 64. Her son Tom and wife Marlysue moved to the Smolan farm, which was homesteaded by Darrel's grandfather in 1860 when he came to the States from Sweden.

Mary and Darrel traveled for many years after their retirement—Sweden, Africa, Italy, Egypt, and Israel. Her friend Peggy Pihlblad, granddaughter of Bethany College's second president, Dr. Ernst Pihlblad, accompanied them on many of the trips. Darrel died in June, 2010, one month before their 65th wedding anniversary.

Mary was an early member of Lindsborg Lioness Club and continues to work in her church, maintaining her keen interest in Lindsborg community affairs.

Mary now.

STORIES OF
WORLD WAR II

by Wilma Larson

THIS BOOK IS DEDICATED TO:

My husband, Hiram Larson, in memory of the years he served in the Armed Forces during World War II.

I'm so new at this and I can't seem to get anything to work right, including this computer. But it is better now, so I'll try to get a few things written.

I remember a Sunday morning when we heard over the radio that Japan had attacked Pearl Harbor with no warning at all. The United States was not prepared, but I know there were troops stationed in Hawaii and many of them remember the attack very clearly.

Communication was not as good as it is today, and I'm not sure about the time of the attack, but I think it was around noon, Lindsborg time, when I heard the news. This was December 7, 1941, and I was dating my future husband at that time—Hiram Larson—and I remember he called me that Sunday evening and asked if I had heard the news. Of course he was real concerned as he just turned 21 on November 28 and already had registered for the draft. So he said, "It will not be long before I'll be in the army."

It was a real scary feeling, but we went to Salina to a movie and enjoyed our evening. But we were very concerned about what would be ahead for us and our country. President Franklin D. Roosevelt declared all-out war on Japan and Germany. Germany was already at war with England and Russia and was also fighting with France, I think. Some things are not too clear to me.

As I said, Hiram was worried about when the time would come when he would receive his notice to report or be inducted in the army. I know he soon got the letter congratulating him about being in the U.S. Army. Actually, there was no choice, unless one had a very good reason why he could not serve—being a farmer or helping one's parents with farming, bad health, etc. But they took everyone else unless maybe you had flat feet. In other words, you would serve your country, and back then we were all ready to save our country. I remember Hiram left on March 1, 1942, from Ellsworth to go to Leavenworth where he was inducted into the U.S. Army.

Getting back to the time before he went into the service: It was very difficult. We were in love and I wanted to get married, but he felt with his being in the service, marriage wasn't a good idea. So I promised I would wait for him to return, but it was very hard. Nothing was a guarantee that a serviceman would come back. Many were killed or wounded in action, so he thought it best to wait.

Before I go any further about the war, I want to tell a little about the times before the day that Japan attacked Pearl Harbor. The country was just recovering from the Great Depression of the 1930's. I was a very young girl when the Depression started, so I can't remember too much. But speaking what I know about my parents, I know they struggled to keep the farm which they owned. The banks were going broke and the whole country was in financial trouble. My Dad would go to the bank to ask for help, to loan him some money to pay the taxes on the farm or maybe buy some cattle, but the banks would refuse many farmers. It was very difficult to keep from going broke, which a lot of the farmers did. They lost their farms and had to move off the farms and try to find something else to do.

My Dad was able to save his farm, but it was not easy. Besides, it was hard to raise the crops for your income because there was a great drought and the dust bowl. The "Dirty 30's". Rain didn't come very often and with the very dry ground, the wind would blow and cause the dirt to blow. It would get so bad you couldn't see two feet in front of you. Western Kansas was the worst as there was more bare ground and when the dirt would blow, it would pick up momentum. It would get so bad it was like nighttime. Many people got sick and their lungs would fill up with dust and they would die.

I could tell more stories about those years, but I need to get back to the stories of World War II. Franklin D. Roosevelt became President and he started a lot of programs like W.P.A., which was a program for building highways and many more tasks that I can't remember. But things were starting to get a little better. They also started to build dams to help prevent flooding along the rivers. That's when Kanopolis Lake was built. This was above the Smoky Hill River and when big rains would come, it would really flood. I think the work started sometime in 1941. The start was building the tunnel which today lets the water out into the river when the lake gets too full.

Hiram was working on building the tunnel along with many others as that was the start of better times. He was very happy to have a job, and I think the pay was about sixty cents an hour. That was working the night shift, so he worked there until he left for the army. I'll try to get more information about the dam but I'll get back to what happened when Hiram was in Leavenworth.

They were issued their army clothes. The civilian clothes they were wearing were sent back to their homes. Can you imagine how their parents felt when that package of their son's clothes came back to them?

Hiram was assigned to the 53rd. Infantry and then sent to Camp Callan in Alburn, California, to guard railroad tunnels. Two men would walk from one end of the tunnel to the other. The tunnels were about two miles or more. They did their eight-

Service Club at Camp Callan.

Partial view of Camp Callan.

Hiram in front of barracks at Camp Callan.

hour shift and then were relieved by the next shift. He said it was real scary because sometimes trains would come when they were walking through, and they would have to hug against the side of tunnel. Most of the time they knew the schedule and times the trains were coming, but once in a while an extra train would come through and that is when they would have to hug the side of the tunnel for their safety. He enjoyed it there and sometimes they would get a weekend pass to go into Alburn. He said the people were nice and friendly to the all the service men and invited them to their homes for a meal. There was the U.S.O. where the service men went for entertainment. There were always a lot of girls there. They could talk or play cards, also there was dancing, and everyone had a good time. Hiram became friends with many other servicemen and they remained friends for years after the war ended.

Cecil Jacobs from Langley, a small town west of Marquette, went to Leavenworth the same day with Hiram so they were buddies and in the same Infantry throughout the war. He also met Alfred Larventz from Nashville, Kansas, and many more that I will not name. Alfred was married so Hiram sent me her name—Margaret—and address to get in touch with her, which I did, and we became very good friends. I'll tell more about that later.

I'm not sure where they were stationed in California, and I think they were there for about two months when they were put on a boat and sent to Alaska, still in the 53rd Infantry. I know I received a letter from him telling me I wouldn't be getting any letters from him for awhile, but he couldn't tell me why or where he would be going. I can't remember how long it was before I heard from him and the letter didn't say much because they were not allowed to give out any information that might get to the enemy. All his letters were censored before they were sent and if anything was said that was not allowed it would be cut out, so it wasn't fun writing or reading them, but he would send me letters often anyway. I sent him a letter about every other day telling him what was going on at home.

I do not remember this happening, but Japan's intent was brought to light June 3, 1942, when Japanese carrier-borne aircraft flew out and bombed the American installations at Dutch Harbor near the town of Unalaska. I'm getting this information from the Internet, and like I said, I don't remember any of this, and the servicemen were not allowed to tell anyone where they were or what was going on. Now that I read this I guess that was why his unit was sent to Alaska and later to the Aleutians. I can't find any information that the 53rd Infantry was at Attu and Kiska, but I know they were there to be on guard if Japan attacked. I know the troops were sent to Alaska in June, 1942, and they were stationed there till 1944. According to this information, there was more going on there than Hiram ever talked about. He did say it was bitter cold with very little daylight, and I understood not too many people lived there. The troops lived in huts and slept in sleeping bags

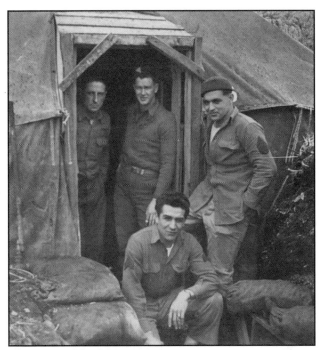
Hiram and buddies at their tent.

Alaska

or maybe cots, but it was very hard to keep warm. I guess they had some kind of wood stove, but they would have to keep the stove going all the time. Hiram didn't talk about his days in the service.

I have pictures where they were fishing for salmon and also some pictures of their huts where

Alaska

Alaska

helping England fight the Germans. We at home did all we could for the war effort. Many things were rationed and hard to get. The farmers were allowed more than anyone so they could keep farming. Gas and tires were the main items rationed and sugar and cigarettes, items that everyone thought they needed. If you didn't smoke before you went into the army, it wasn't long until you did. Very stressful, these times. Many more things were rationed, but I can't remember all of them. I stayed home with my parents for awhile after Hiram left and helped my dad with the farming.

I had a cousin and her husband who lived in Wichita as he was working at the Beechcraft factory. She was expecting a baby in the fall of 1942, so she asked me to come to Wichita to help her. I did, and we always had so much fun.

The Boeing Aircraft Company was just starting the plant in Wichita, building the big B29 planes. They were asking for workers, and this was the time when the women started to work, as all the men were in the army. They advertised for help and would pay one to go to a school where they would teach the trade of building planes.

I applied, and within a few days, I started school to learn how to rivet and put or make differ-

they lived. Their time was spent playing cards and reading when they were not on duty. A very lonely time for all of them. They were stationed there to guard our country from Japan. The information the internet tells is more than we ever heard at that time. News was not very good then and probably a week old when we did hear it on the radio. I could put in what the internet has, but I think I'll just continue what I remember.

The time was very lonely and so uncertain. It was hard on everyone as the country was at war

Wilma in her work clothes.

ent parts hold together. I think I went to school for a couple of weeks and then we went to the Boeing Aircraft plant to start work on the B29s. It was a little scary at first. The women were not accepted by the men at first, but they soon got used to it and found out we could do the job as well as anyone, and besides, we were at war, and everyone wanted to help. Most of the men working were married with children, so they didn't go to the army. That was not the case for all married men, because many were in the army. Also some men didn't pass their physicals, so they were called 4' Fers, but they were good guys and doing their part by working in the plant.

I was assigned to a section called the bombbay section where we installed different parts. This was the section where the bombs were placed. I worked the second shift which was from 4pm to 3am.—a 10 hour shift. We would get two fifteen minute breaks and one half hour lunch break. Each shift would put out two or three planes a day. I'm not sure on that number but I know there was a schedule that was met. It is so many years ago I can't remember everything. Gas was rationed so we would pool rides to work. I didn't have a car so I rode with some one and I would pay him so much a week to help pay for the gas. I think he would get a ration book to get extra gas. A farmer or anyone needing extra gas or anything else that was rationed would be issued a ration book. It was really hard, but everyone managed with what they were given. We worked very hard, but we also had a lot of fun. Sometimes after we'd get off work, we would go out for breakfast or go bowling as everything stayed open 24 hours a day. A girl friend and I rented an apartment to help on expenses and we worked the same shift, so we would sleep till noon or a little later and then go back to work. I think we worked five days a week, then have two days off. But if we were not on schedule, we would work overtime—of course that was overtime pay, and remember our pay was sixty-five cents an hour. But that was a good wage for everyone.

I would write my letters to Hiram at least two or three times a week. We would go home to see our parents on weekends when we didn't work. Holidays were the same as any other day, but if it happened to fall on your day off, one could have a day with your family. Otherwise, plan it another time.

I remember one Christmas my friend and I worked our regular shift and got off work at 3 a.m. We wanted to go home and be with our families, so we packed our suitcases and got out on the highway about 4 a.m. and hitched a ride as far as Newton. We stood in front of a church having early Christmas service, waiting for another ride, and luckily, a family picked us up. We got to Lindsborg about the time church service was over and my friend's parents were in church, so we just waited for them in their car and were home for Christmas.

Today one would not do something that stupid, but we wanted to be home for Christmas. It was a different time and everyone trusted one another. Many servicemen stationed in camps would hitchhike a ride to a town if they had a weekend pass. I remember a lady we would ride home with sometimes, and it was a small car, but she would pick up the servicemen and take them to wherever they wanted to go. We would be so crowded in that little coupe, but she was so good hearted and wanted to help the men. They appreciated it and we always had fun. We would sit in each others' laps. Today that would not happen, because we don't trust anyone, but then we did, as our country was at war which was very important to everyone.

Sometimes I wonder what our country would be today if we would have lost the war. All we did was work at Boeing Aircraft our work shift and go home to sleep a few hours. Sometimes we would go downtown Wichita and shop and get a bite to eat and get back to catch our ride to go back to work. We would listen to the radio for news about the war and wonder where all the servicemen would be. I would hear from Hiram but there wasn't much he could write about other than telling me that he was ok. One could send telegrams to the men. They could also send one back. Usually it was a short note saying they missed and loved you.

The work the troops did in the Aleutians, I'm not sure, but I have some pictures that I will put in so you can see what it was like to be living there. It looks like some of the huts they lived in, and one can see all the snow and how bitter cold it must have been.

We would get two weeks vacation time once a year so I usually would take my time in the summer and go home and help my dad harvest the wheat crop. Here are a few pictures—one with my dad on the combine and one of me on the tractor.

I would take the grain to the elevator. We didn't have a truck but a small trailer hitched to the car and I would drive into the elevator and then come back

Wilma's father on the combine.

Wilma, helping with her father's farming.

to the field to get some more wheat. It would keep me busy all day to keep up with the combine and I'd also help take care of the tractor and combine. That was to put gas in both tractor and combine and then there were places that had to have grease to make everything work. That was my job and it was a dirty job. One would get grease all over you if you weren't careful.

I always had a good time with my dad because he always made it fun with the work. My mother was also a big help as she always had a good meal at noon and then around 4 o'clock, she would come to the field where we were working with coffee, sandwiches, cake, or cookies and that was always a good break. She was interested in the harvesting of the wheat because that was their crop to make money to pay their bills. This was a big war effort again as so many things were rationed but the farmers would get their ration books to get extra gas for their farm work. And to get tires for their equipment. It was always fun to help my parents. Sometimes I can't remember everything.

I remember one year my girlfriend and I decided to go to Saratoga, Wyoming, to visit her sister in the middle of winter. We got on the train and did that ever turn out to be an experience! I'm not sure why we picked that time to go as it turned out to be very cold and snowy. We were snowbound in some town in Wyoming for a day, but somehow we made it to her sister's and back to Wichita. We did a lot of crazy things, but we had to do something for entertainment and everything always turned out okay. Time was long for us, but not nearly as long as for the men in the service.

Sometime in the year 1943, some of the servicemen that were stationed in the Aleutians were sent to Japan to another division. Many of Hiram's friend were chosen and he was very sad to see his buddies leave. It was very difficult for all of them. His friends

Alfred Laventz and Ted Welty were among the ones sent to Japan. I'll tell you more about that later. He said goodbye to some of them that he never saw again.

In the summer of 1944, I would get letters from Hiram saying that maybe they would get to come back to the States because they had served twenty-four months overseas. That was exciting news to think maybe we would get to see each other, but he couldn't say much about it because of security. There was quite a long time that I didn't hear from him and then one day, I received a letter saying he was back in the States and when he got stationed somewhere, he would write me. It was exciting to think we would be seeing each other soon.

It was October 8 when I heard he was in Camp Swift, Texas, and he would be getting a furlough in a few days. I was still in Wichita working at Boeing, but I had some vacation time coming, so I asked for time off whenever he would get home. I think he was allowed to call me and I had a call from him around the first, saying he would be in Wichita on the 18th. I stayed with a friend and she was as excited as I. I guess he came in on a train. I can't remember, but I gave him the address where I was staying. When a taxi pulled by the curb, I ran out of the house with my arms ready to hug him, and it was wonderful. Of course, back then, all the neighbors were out on the street to see what was going on and were happy to see a serviceman coming home.

He was given a three-week furlough, so we decided to get married as soon as we could find a minister to marry us. My sister Doris and her husband Everett Pearson came to Wichita to get us and we went to my folks for dinner and started to decide about a wedding. Before I go any further about our wedding plans, Cecil Jacobs, who went into service the same time, came home on furlough the same day. So he rode with us to Lindsborg. I think we went to Marquette after our meal, but I can't remember all of the details. All I know is that is was a very happy time for all.

The day we got to Lindsborg was the 19th, a Thursday. We decided to get married on Saturday, the 21st, but there was a problem because the Freemont Church were I belonged didn't have a minister at that time. Also, the Marquette church didn't have a minister, the reason I don't know. The Messiah Lutheran minister was Pastor James Claypool from Marquette, and Hiram wanted him to marry us. But again, no luck, as he was on vacation. But we didn't give up. We talked to Pastor Smith at Bethany Church, and he agreed to marry us if we would have the ceremony in the afternoon as he had another wedding in the evening. Yes, yes, we agreed, so we were married that afternoon. My sister Doris and husband Everett were our attendants. My sister Violet and Hiram's sister Grace were also with us.

My mother prepared a small reception for us and our family. As usual, everything was rationed and this time sugar, of which no one had a big supply, but between Mom and my cousin Ruby, we managed to have enough sugar so we had an angel food cake made by Ruby, or some kind of cake. I can't remember—with coffee, and I'm not sure what else. But I'm sure Mom made it special for us and we were so happy to be married. Again, the problem of rationing. This time, gasoline, so our little honeymoon was no further than McPherson, about twelve miles from my home in the country. We borrowed

Wedding Day, October 21, 1944.

his parents' car and again the tires were not very good, but we made it there and back. Then we spent most of his furlough with his parents and mine, also a lot of his friends, but most of them were also in the service.

Hiram gave a gift of money to Pastor Smith after the ceremony, but he refused to take it. He said he wouldn't take anything from a serviceman and we thanked him for his kindness and for the wedding. Then we were on our way to a happy marriage, which lasted fifty-five years. We always said our wedding didn't cost very much. I think the marriage license cost $2.00. I know we went back to Wichita to visit with Margaret Laventz and another army buddy of Hiram, Raymond Lampe, who was on leave at the same time. They all would be leaving from Wichita to go back to Camp Swift, Texas. It was sad to see them go again, but we thought maybe I would be going to see him there if he would be stationed there for some time. But as usual, nothing was for certain, and the army sent them some place in California to train and then on to Japan. I can't remember the reason, but that didn't work, so they were sent back to Camp Swift. That was sometime in February 1945, and I took a leave of absence from work and went out be with Hiram for two weeks before the division was sent to Europe as a replacement in the Battle of the Bulge. I think that was sometime in April, so Hiram was there when the war ended.

I went back to work at Boeing and I shared an apartment with a friend, Wanda Ecker, whose husband was also in the army. We worked the same shift and always had a lot of fun together and remained friends for a long time. We sent packages to our husbands with goodies and we always sent them cigarettes. We found out later when they came home they had all the cigarettes they wanted. But we thought it was hard for them to get them.

Whenever we were downtown Wichita shopping and saw a long line, we knew it was something that was not easy to get or a rationed item so we would get in line and buy whatever it was. Sometimes it would be soap, sugar, shoes, or something

that was rationed. It was always fun to see what we'd get. We always had a good time. I remember one time J.C. Penny's advertised that they had sheets for sale and we knew we would have to get there early. So I got on a bus early to be there when the store opened. There were women all over the place. I think a clerk handed out the sheets and if you were close enough to grab one it was yours. I know I got one, but there were two ladies that grabbed the same sheet. They wouldn't let go, and finally the sheet tore in two, so neither one had a sheet. That's how crazy it was for items that were hard to get. I thought how silly that one of them wouldn't give up and try to get another one.

We had a lot of other friends at work and we would go to each other's houses after we'd get off work and play cards, eat breakfast, then go home to get some sleep before we'd go back to work.

The news of the war sounded very bad and fighting was still going strong when we heard that President Roosevelt died. His health was not good when he was re-elected in 1944. Vice president Harry Truman became President April 12, 1945. I remember hearing people say the war would end soon after the death of President Roosevelt which it did, but that was not the reason as the Germans were being pushed back every day. I can still remember hearing the President talking over the radio and saying "I hate war and Eleanor hates war". He had a New England accent that I loved to hear.

The Germans were getting defeated more and more every day and the battles in Japan were very intense. Germany surrendered in June 6, 1945. The news was not good. The United States and England were winning the battles but so many men did not make it through the battles and how sad it was for everyone to hear of all the deaths of the men fighting for their country.

I remember the day we were at work and the news came over the intercom that the U.S. had dropped the atomic bomb on Japan and the Japanese had surrendered. The atomic bomb was dropped on Hiroshima August 6 and on Nagasaki August 9. It was announced that the plant would shut down for the day, so we all shouted and just left our tool boxes and everything right in the place we were working. We went out the door to celebrate. Several of the girls I worked with got together and went downtown Wichita where people were celebrating the news. The streets were crowded. Cars and buses could hardly drive. Everyone was kissing; hugging, crying, laughing. Many soldiers stationed around Wichita were there and saying that now they would be discharged from the army and be back with their families. The surrender ceremony was held on the USS Missouri September 2, 1945.

It was also very sad to think about all the men who gave their lives for our country. I think Boeing shut down for a couple of days. I know my friend Wanda and I went to work, packed up our tool boxes, and quit. Several others did the same thing, but some of them stayed until they started to lay the workers off. That way they could draw unemployment but I guess we didn't care about that. All we were interested in was that our husbands would be coming home soon and we could start our married life.

We each went home to our parents to wait for their return. It didn't happen all at once. I know Hiram was stationed somewhere in Paris, waiting for the orders to come back to the U. S. He said it was the coldest place he spent and he didn't like Paris either. It was very dirty, filthy. I would get letters from him saying they were still waiting for their orders to be sent home, but there was a lot of delay.

One day General Dwight Eisenhower came by and said these troops need to get back the United States now and Hiram said it didn't take long until all the troops were sent back to the States. It was sometime around the 11th of November when I received a call from Hiram saying he was in Leavenworth. He had received his discharge from the army and would be coming to Salina on a train that Sunday evening at a certain time.

Maynard Alhstedt and my sister Violet were going to Salina as they both worked there, so I rode with them and we were at the station right on time. But, no Hiram to be seen. We waited around and went back to see if another train came in, but no

luck. We didn't go to the bus station because we thought the buses were on strike. I was getting very worried that something was wrong and he didn't get on the train or bus. But just as we were driving away, we saw Hiram standing in front of the A. and G. Café where we always went to eat when we were dating. I almost jumped out of the car before Maynard could park. Well he got on an earlier bus and didn't have time to call me. Everything worked out and we were so happy to be together. The first thing we did on Monday morning was go to a men's clothing store and buy clothes. I don't remember how we got back to Lindsborg, whether my Dad came to get us or Hiram's brother.

Now he was a civilian again. It was time to decide what we were going to do to make a home. We both like the country and farming. We rented a farm south of Marquette and started our married life together. Everyone was very happy the war was over, and thankful our country was safe again. Many happy and sad memories of the days of W.W.II.

I want to tell a little about my good friend Margaret Laventz Welty before I end my story. I think I said I'd write more about our days together. We made arrangements to meet in Wichita on a certain day at her brother's home. We were both a little nervous as we knew nothing about each other, only what our husbands had told us. We talked about our families and what we were doing—more or less making conversation—when all of a sudden, her brother came home from work and said, "Where's the beer?" Margaret's eyes got big as saucers because she was trying to be so nice and I was, too. Of course, I said, "That sounds like a good idea," and that's all it took for us to become the very best of friends. We started to laugh and had so much fun the rest of that day and for many years afterwards. We visited with each other many times during the war years. She lived in Nashville, Kansas, so I would take a train out to see her and she would come to Wichita. Alfred, Ted Welty, and Hiram were stationed on the Aleutian Islands until Alfred and Ted were sent to Japan, which made a big difference in their lives because they didn't know if they would see each other again. Ted and Alfred fought together side by side till almost the end of the war. They were attacked by the Japanese every day. I remember Ted telling how each day at a certain time they would be attacked by the Japanese army. They also noticed that at a certain time each day, ladies would come out and hang some clothes on a clothesline. Shortly after that the firing would start. Ted was a very sharp man and he thought maybe this was a signal that the Americans were close by and the attack could start. The next day, the same time, when one lady came out to hang the clothes, Ted took aim and fired and didn't miss, but also the attack stopped.

The men fought for their own lives as well as others. I think it was about two weeks before Japan surrendered that Ted and Alfred were together fighting when a bomb hit both of them and Alfred was killed instantly. Ted was hit very badly with injuries to his stomach and chest. His chances were not good, but he survived. How sad it was for all of us that they made it almost to the end, but that was the case for so many. Alfred told Hiram when he left the Aleutians he would make it through the war and they would see each other again, but that didn't happen. Very, very sad for all of us and that was not ever forgotten.

Ted was in the hospital a very long time, but he made it through and came back to the United States. He was probably in hospital again. I'm not certain about his recovery, but he got in touch with Margaret and wanted to come see her and tell her about Alfred. They kept in touch with each other, and he finally came to Wichita very unsettled with his life not knowing what to do which was understood with everything he had been through. Ted found a job with a contractor building houses. He and Margaret starting dating and later married. They were very happy and raised three very nice boys.

I think how wonderful that they made a happy life for each other with the memory of her husband who was his very best buddy in the army. They went through so much together side by side.

I'm sure I haven't covered all the things during those years of WW II, but I have enjoyed writing the little things I remember. I hope my family will appreciate what I have written. We all love our country and God Bless our U.S.A.

AUTHOR PAGE

Wilma Nelson Larson was born on a farm southwest of Lindsborg October 22, 1919. She lived on that farm except from 1946 to 1956 when she and Hiram farmed south of Marquette. They had three children, Merle, Ann, and Willis. After retiring from farming, Hiram worked at the Lindsborg Golf Course Club House for ten years. He passed away October 7, 1999. Wilma remained on the farm until 2010 when she moved into Lindsborg.

Wilma now.

Her son, Merle and his wife Lisa live in Oakridge, Tennessee. She is director of the Head Start program. He works at the Department of Energy in Oakridge. They have three daughters, Bailey who graduated from the University of Tennessee and plans to attend graduate school; Hannah, a 2011 graduate of the University of Tennessee; and Chloe who attends Bethany College.

Her daughter Ann passed away in 2009 after a struggle with cancer. She left two daughters, Tasha and her husband Tim who have a business building office furniture. They live in Boston. Her daughter Erin will finish her RN training this year.

Willis and his wife Lois live on the family farm near by Lindsborg. Willis works at the Grasshopper Mower Company in Moundridge and Lois works at Cargill in McPherson. They have a son Brooks, and Lois's children Jennifer, who lives in Minnesota completing a post-graduate program and Jeremy is in the U.S.A.F, stationed in Oklahoma. Brooks is married to Erica and works at the McCall Pattern Company in Manhattan, Kansas. Erica works at UMB Bank. Their daughter, Dyhana, is seven years old.

Wilma worked at Bethany Home between 1969 and 1989 as a medication aide. She served in the nutrition center at the Lindsborg Senior Center for seven years after that, and continues serving there as afternoon hostess, beginning in 2007. She just completed a term as president of the board of directors.

Wilma has enjoyed getting to know her new computer better by writing this story. It as a gift from her children who told her if she learned how to use it, they would connect her to the Internet. She asks questions whenever she encounters a computer user, and she has signed up for more lessons at the computer center, Vision_Tek, where meetings were held to make these books. She intends to make good on her children's offer!

DOTS AND DASHES:
NAVY RADIOMAN IN IRELAND AND BEYOND

by Marvin Lundquist

THIS BOOK IS DEDICATED TO:

My parents, Mr. and Mrs. Carl B. Lundquist.

SWEET SPOTS IN TIME

My Uncle Wendell Johnson, world authority on stuttering, sent me a novel when I was a teenager. I guess he considered I was bright enough to "get it." The book was *The Bridge of San Luis Rey* by Thornton Wilder.

The author, like a lot of us, wondered: is fate planned for us or is it just a coincidence or unhampered chance? I'm a Presbyterian and we believe in predestination. The plan of our life is set forth by our good Master, the Lord. The spots of time that I like to recall are certainly timely with positive or gratifying results. Wilder's choice in his story is a Tragic Spot in time. His story is about why the leading characters (or gives the reason) are on that bridge that very instant on that fateful day that the bridge falls a thousand feet to the rocks and rushing water below, and all are killed. If one of them had slept five minutes longer that morning, would they still have fallen? Interesting thought to hang a story on. As is the following…

HOW TO GET TO LONDONDERRY, NORTHERN IRELAND, FOR MY TIME IN WORLD WAR II

I guess I can start way back in high school when my English teacher, Miss Pankratz, got me interested in writing. Even then I helped put out the monthly class bulletin, or was it weekly? I guess my essays ran a little long, because I do remember her remarking that I was a little wordy. Have I improved much in that regard? My dear wife has suggested perhaps not. But writing has been a benefit because it got me through the entrance exam for college and helped me write up hundreds of reports and stories in the past sixty or so years.

The first Sweet Spot might be a bit of a stretch regarding getting to Ireland, but was of note at boot camp in the navy, and the first of many steps getting to Ireland. My cousin, Howard Sandberg, was a whiz on the cornet. His mother, my Aunt Mabel, encouraged me to take lessons from him. I got in the high school band and was good enough for duets, etc. for programs. It does take a lot of practice to get those lips callused enough to hit those clear, clean high notes.

Those of you that know me pretty well agree there aren't many places I go without my camera. I can't remember how old I was when I got my little Agfa 110 camera, but I took my "pitcher takin" seriously. As a matter of fact, I was so captivated with photography that I decided to train to be a professional photographer under the guidance of the Glick Studios in Salina when I graduated from high school. My Aunt Mabel and Uncle Otto had moved to Salina during this time, so I lived with them. Mr. Glick was not dumb. He knew that this kid from the farm and an outdoorsman would probably not last long working in the dark back room retouching negatives of ladies with blemishes on their chins. He was right. How long was it? Maybe six months, or was it four? Apparently, I wasn't needed at home right then, so I decided to move across the street from Glick Studios to Brown-Mackie School of Business. Here was my Sweet Spot because I learned to type. I did try working in an office in a lumber yard, but that didn't work out so well. About this time I got this letter from Uncle Sam that read, "We Need You."

I soon was on my way to Kansas City for the physical and some other tests for the Army. Now I was on standby and went home to pitch wheat bundles onto a rack for the threshing machine. Here is where it gets interesting. As I was saying, it was harvest season and I was needed to make the threshing rounds so I went back home. For some reason – and this really is the Sweet Spot – I happened to be in town on this sunny day, and while crossing the intersection in the middle of Roxbury, Kansas, I met my friend and school mate, Eddie Writer. We exchanged greetings and visited about what we'd been doing since graduating from high school, when out of the thin air came the news that he had just joined the Navy. He smiled big and said, "Why don't you join the Navy and we can both go in together?" I gasped a bit and asked, "Can I do that? I just had my physical for the Army." "Yes you can," he replied.

Thank you Eddie Writer. (Eddie passed away a month or so ago). Maybe not the next day, but very soon, I was at the Navy recruiting office in Salina asking about this matter. August 2, 1942, I was on my way to the Great Lakes Training Station, close by Chicago, in the "Navy." When we recruits arrived at the gates, we were met by a drum and bugle corps to march us to our barracks. Somewhere in checking in, they learned that I played the cornet. I was assigned to the Drum and Bugle Corps. We were there six weeks. I'm not saying I got out of all the KP, drills, and cleaning the barracks, but I missed a lot of inspections and KP because I was out in the Corp barracks practicing or marching new recruits to their new way of life. You had to be there to appreciate why I consider this such a Sweet Spot.

Speaking of Sweet Spots, the next one comes at the end of the Great Lakes Training when they asked what we would like to do as a seaman. I can't remember what I checked on the list of areas we could request. I think one was photography or something related. One must have been radioman because that is what I got. Why? Because I could use a typewriter. Now some more fun begins. We radiomen were out of the Great Lakes Training in time to go to fall semester classes at Wisconsin University in Madison. We were assigned rooms in the men's

Taking in some rays.

dormitory on campus not all that far from the student cafeteria. We appreciated the local people near the campus because they would invite us to their homes for hot spiced cider parties. Their football team wasn't too bad, either, with Crazy Legs Hirsch. The winter was cold. We had all our blues on plus the heavy P-coat, or it is Pee—probably not. I must have known at one time why it was called P. Perhaps parade coat. I know we stood at parade a lot—like marching to the mess hall in the snow and cold.

Now for schooling—guess what we learned for the radioman phase? Dit Dahs! This is what my name looks like in Morse Code—dah-dah dit-dah dit-dah-dit dit-dit-dti-dah dit-dit dah-dit. It took a little bit to learn those dits and dahs, and we could probably make twenty or more words per minute when we finished the semester. Professionals make thirty-five to forty. We had some old Salts (ol' timers) that could sit, smoke, drink coffee, and listen for sentences and type them in. I never did get that good. In additional to dit dahs, we learned how radios worked so we could repair them if we needed to. Thankfully we had technicians that took care of such things at the radio station. Can't recall all the courses, but maybe some English and History?

At the completion of the course at Wisconsin U, the Sweet Spot of all the Sweet Spots came about.

In my "blues."

The class was divided into three groups. One group went to Iceland, one went to Africa, and one went to Northern Ireland—the U.S. Naval Operating Base in Londonderry. We didn't have a choice. We were assigned. I lucked out to go to Londonderry.

From Madison, we shipped out to Long Island, New York. We country boys took advantage of this stop and got leave to go into New York City and Times Square and City Music Hall where all those pretty girls threw up their legs right neat. Wow! We was livin'…But that was a short stay because we were soon assigned a ship to head out. Those of us going to Ireland, or at least I, got on a merchant ship that cruised out into the Atlantic and crossed in fourteen days. It was smooth sailing, seeing seals on icebergs near Greenland, great sunsets with ice, water and clouds, until we were off Iceland and ran into a rough ol' winter northen' bounding us about like a beer bottle at the bottom of a water fall. Well, maybe not that bad, but just about. Only the ol' salts and mates of the merchant ship made it down to mid-ships for breakfast. The bunk beds were attached to the walls. But chairs, tables, or anything not bolted down, including the dishes in the gallery, were racing, sliding, falling from one side to the other as the ship pitched from one wave top to the bottom. I heard forty-foot waves mentioned. I found that I could take it if I stayed in my bunk. They had lights in the bunk walls, so I did a lot of reading on that cruise. Our ship was one of a huge convoy. On the calm days, we sat top side and could see ships far off in all directions. Sitting on the upper decks facing the wind kept me from getting sea sick, and I lucked out pretty well. I didn't see destroyers, but I suspect they were on the outer bounds. If any of the ships were being hit by German torpedoes, we didn't hear about it. We weren't alerted to being in a war zone until we were outside our destination off England when we heard the metallic ping of depth charges somewhere off in that direction. We docked, but my recollections fail me just how we got to Londonderry. My records tell me that we arrived at our base February 24, 1943.

So be it. I guess there is a lot of me in this, but

Base chapel.

Marvin in front of hospital wards.

I realize that there are scores of very kind and helpful people that were involved in getting all the Sweet Spots hooked up: from my generous parents to the radiomen that welcomed me to the Naval Relay Station in Londonderry. Many thanks to all.

A note about my rapid progress of transmission of messages. On arrival at the radio station, we used the key and tapped out Morse Code at thirty-to-thirty-five words per minute. In a little over two years, the operation had shifted from key to inked

I was stationed in Northern Ireland.

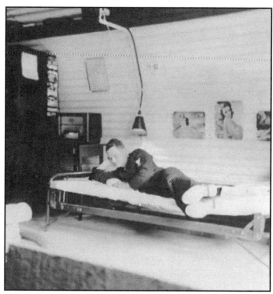

Marvin on rugged duty, July 1944. In my little corner

Marvin (in the middle) ready for Guard duty.

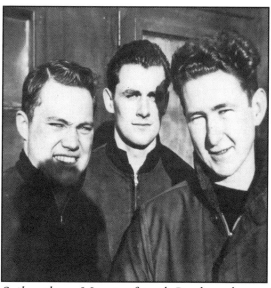

Sailors three: Marvin, friends Brady and Coleman.

paper tape and from transcribing to key on to tele-type at sixty words per minute. On departure, the messages were going out at one-hundred-twenty words per minute by synchronization of two tele-types. By the end of the war, the increased speed was needed because we were flooded with congratulatory messages being exchanged among the allies. Wild! But the news was real cause for celebration.

The sound of crunching leaves under the wheels of the bicycles, the crisp smell of the air, a certain look in the sky, and the mounds of dirt in the field,

protecting the bread of the earth—potatoes—ever hear of Irish potatoes, are lined up and down the center of the fields—along with the oat harvest—all are evident signs of fall in Northland Ireland!"

I found a letter I had written my sister August 1944:

Dear Sis:

After a very rugged day, I feel comparatively good. I think the radio program I just heard, "Suspense," was a bit of tonic for me. At any rate, I feel like writing now and good that I do because I had only an hour here or I'd missed you this week. Being busy or putting off will, I find, often place you in such a precarious position.

I just mentioned a rugged day, and that, it surely was—all except for a couple of very nicely spent hours this eve-

City of Londonderry. Old cities had gates to keep countries south from taking over.

ning. Last night, or I should say this morning, we had the midnight (duty). We couldn't hit the sack this morning as usual because we had a big personal inspection (the first, by the way, for a long time). During inspection, we had to stand at attention most of the time and just coming off a mid, it would have been enough to just stand—period. Man, I'm telling you I was standing there, weaving from side to side, about ready to fall on my face.

The inspection went off okay. I guess I was oaky, at least nothing was said to me. (Some of the boys got restricted because of no hair cuts and unpolished shoes; others just were told to use a brush once in a while). By the time inspection was over, it was 1130, so there was no sleeping in the a.m. However, I immediately hit the sack and immediately fell into a deep sleep which lasted until I awoke gasping for air—cool air. It was a very warm day and the doors of the hut had slammed shut so it was hotter than (you know what) inside this metal hut. I staggered to my feet, opened the door, took a good breath of air, and fell back in the sack. Next thing I knew someone was shaking me for chow. Being in a daze from such a sleep, I didn't know what chow he was talking about. Finally it slowly dawned on me that it was for supper.

Giant Caseway.

To put a nice ending to my story, another guy and I from my hut, Mitchell, went bicycle riding. It was a very pleasant evening. We stopped in one place where Mitchell had some friends and were invited in for a bit of tea. It was darn good and I

One of the off-station activities we enjoyed was bicycling through the Irish country side and visiting neat little villages aong the mostly narrow and hilly road sides.

had some jam and bread and cake along with it. Very nice people, they were, and I hope to see them again. (They got to be like our folks from home.)

I also took down a roll of film that should have some interesting studies in it. I'm anxious to see how my new lenses work.

Oh yes! So you think she'll come into my life some day, eh, well maybe so, but I think, if you don't mind, I'll wait until I get back to the states. The girls shall just have to make good dance partners for

Good-bye, Ireland. It's been swell.

It's harvest now and the farmers are out busy cutting their grain. Oats seems to be the grain that's taking the limelight right now. You should see the way it is cut. Attached to an ordinary farm mower is a rack back of the sickle bar. In the hands of the driver is an affair, which looks much like an overgrown yardstick that is used for a rake. When the rack has the right amount, enough for one bundle, the driver takes the rake and pushes the cut oats off the rack. The mower moves on and the bundler, a man who takes this small pile of oats that has come off the rack, draws a few straws and wraps it around the bundle, and with a twist of the fingers, the bundle is secure with it own straw. Further out in the field, Irish lads are putting up shocks—one by one.

now—(and they did). Maybe I'll get you a picture of a local lassie in it, next roll. (And there was)

What did you think of Jewell going and bringing us a new cousin. Great news!

Good bye for now!

Love, Marvin

German U-Boats collected after war was over.

A Grand Finale—left Londonderry in early summer of 1945. I sailed back on an LDS, a somewhat flat-bottomed boat, that going over waves, tended to buckle a bit. A few, I understand, did break at mid-section. We came across the ocean in fine shape—thankful we didn't meet the storm we had encountered coming over. On arrival in the states, I was given a thirty-day leave. I spent it at home catching up with family and friends.

Again, I went to Kansas City to catch a train, and be the leader for a group of reassigned sailors heading for San Diego. I had no troubles and my charges were delivered to their appointed quarters on arrival, and I was escorted to a naval base outside San Diego.

While in Diego, awaiting shipping orders, we sailors took in USOs and met movie stars. Also somehow, sailors managed to visit interesting Tijuana, Mexico, a sailor-infested community. One night, after a night on the town of Tijuana and feeling no pain, a group of us decided we'd save some money and walk back to our base, but after a mile or two, a group of taxis came along and rescued us. A common occurrence, I understand....I heard it is twenty miles or so back to base. There I was assigned to a converted carrier to head to south seas to bring home Pacific personnel. Upon returning from a shakedown cruise, I was informed that the Navy and Uncle Sam had decided I had acquired enough points to be honorably discharged. It was December by this time. I got on the train and headed for our destination,

of all places, Norman, Oklahoma, and arrived on Christmas Eve, December 24, 1945. The next day, after a very fine Christmas dinner with turkey and the works, we had the Discharge Award Ceremony. I was presented my Honorably Discharged Certificate that is dated December 25, 1945

The folks had held up the Lutfisk, Sil, turkey, and other Swedish goodies for a day or two....Just by chance or otherwise, it was good to be home.

ANOTHER SWEET SPOT

After being discharged from the Navy, I took advantage of our country's program to help fund an education for veterans. I earned a Master's Degree in Agronomy and became an agent for Kansas State University. I helped farmers control wind erosion and save crops on exposed sandy soils of the great bend of the Smoky River in Stafford and Barton counties of Kansas as well as other areas of the state subject to wind erosion.

Continuing is a paper I wrote twenty-six years later after retiring. I still follow the work that was just beginning back in my early days with the Kansas State Agronomy Department. This is another

Marvin at KSU during his agronomy career.

tool that farmers can use in their search for ways to make their farms more profitable. Hopefully this can be considered at least a small part of my taking advantage of a very positive benefit as well as a satisfying result of the government's GI Bill of Rights after my war years in the Navy.

I'VE BEEN THERE BEFORE…(A)

Fifty years of work stared me in the face and it was overwhelming!

It's August 10, 2007. Back in August 1957, we were planning our tillage study at the Sandyland Experiment Field that included our first work with No-Till. Fifty years later I am walking through fields of outstanding remarkable No-Till sunflowers, No-Till forage sorghum, No-Till corn, and a No-Till wheat field going to No-Till wheat again. One field has been No-Tilled for eight years. Some have been longer than this because when I retired twenty years ago, I came to live in McPherson and the County Soil Conservation Service hired me to take on a three-year study to determine how many farmers were involved or interested in No-Till and monitor their work with this recent program.

Fifty years later, I'm still around to look upon the fruits of our labor. Our, meaning the K-State Agronomy Department, the Specialists, Experiment Field Personnel, including me. I was part of this team. Wow!

I am visiting farmers cooperating with the Central Kansas Residue Alliance on the Summer No-Till Tour. Others involved included K-State Research and Extension—McPherson and Rice Counties and NRCS and Soil Conservation Districts—Rice and McPherson Counties. The farms are located in the Smoky Valley river bottom lowlands between Lindsborg and Marquette, Kansas. The summer has provided much above average rainfall. The crops proved that fifty years of research has well prepared the field and farmers to take advantage of this extraordinary summer.

It took me back to not just the late fifties and sixties work, but also reminded me of my remarkable

mentors way back when, like Harold Myers, Ray Olson, and "Throck" was still around at the time. Elmer Heyne and Kling Anderson were included in my adversary committee and were especially good to me. I remember that there was discussion about whether I should go the next mile and apparently they saw something in me that gave them the "go ahead." I do remember Dr. Heyne remarking that it might take me a little longer. And it did. As we continued to tour, I felt I was standing among these administrators, teachers, researchers, all my mentors, many gone now but leaving their imprint mightily among the works I look upon with wonder this day.

We're not at a dry land No-Till field of grain sorghum with beautiful, handsome heads, clean of weeds, no off-types, great stand planted at 45,000 plants/a. Looks like an irrigation seeding rate by twenty-inch rainfall wipes out that kind of dry land mistake this year. I think of Richard Vanderlip—not only concerned about Kansas production ways but also in Africa and other foreign lands where grain sorghum is grown for human food. Milo was the name of the crop and I recall teachers explaining how milo became the Grain Trade name instead of grain sorghum. Ted Walter is standing by, ready to work up the data and would be impressed with yields of this dimension. Seeing the 80 bushel/acre yield, very likely, reminds me of Axelton when he was at the Minneola Field and yields were in the fifteen-to-twenty bushel/acre range during those dry years of the fifties. I think I see him wiping his Swedish forehead and saying, "Ye Viz! That's vot I said." I think Elmer Heyne was saying something else as we rode by a wheat field showing the ravishes caused by fifteen degree temperatures when the tender head was well up the culm. Proof how weather can change it all. A great tour and you can tell that it brought back the past for me very much and though many of the names I mentioned and worked with are no longer with us, their work is still evident and together with all the present workers on the job, the tour and the results were outstanding! Thanks, fellows.

I'VE BEEN THERE BEFORE...(B)

The outstanding Central Kansas Residue Alliance Sumer No-Till Tour of August 10, 2007 took me back too, to the Stubble Mulch Field Days we had back in the fifties and sixties that continued for some ten years. The third Thursday of February, a large group of visionary farmers gathered to hear the work of the Sandyland Experiment Field and Stubble Mulching. We generally had a tour of the field in the morning, lunch in the City Meeting Hall, and then had the program in the St. John High School auditorium. Not sure I earned the moniker of Ol' Stubble Mulch Lundquist, but I still hear that occasionally when I meet a friend of that era.

The Sandyland Experiment Field was established in 1942 with Frank Lowry, as Superintendent, to study ways of controlling wind erosion on the sandy soils of the Great Bend area of the Smoky Hill River. Walt Moore, Superintendent of the Hutchinson Experiment Field, helped in getting the field established. The field was some twenty-five miles south of Great Bend. Severe wind storms were whipping up fields about this time. Superintendent Lowry left the field in 1956, and I was honored to come on board to take his place. They had begun work with V-blades to make use of the crop residue left on the soil surface which was effective. This approach to controlling eroding soils was being studied in Nebraska under the leadership of Charlie Fenster. Also adding in this work was the Noble V-Blade outfit from Hooker, Oklahoma. During this period of the stubble mulch, work was included comparing this new tool to the tillage equipment that was being used. Listers would seem to be a sure bet, but I've seen soil blow off the bottom of the furrow. This was a severe case but gave evidence that this tool wasn't the answer. When the idea of residue being a means of controlling wind erosion on this soils, the Soil Conservation Service began having their specialists estimate visionally how much residue be left for best control and how the different crop residues compared in effectiveness. Since running drills through large amounts of residue, there was a limit to how much would work through between the drill spouts.

This important information came into use when stubble mulching was accepted as an answer to wind erosion control. I believe it was the Nobel folks that came up with a spoked wheel instead of solid blade disks that would pack in some of the residue as well as digging up volunteer and grassy weeds and at the same time preparing the seedbed. Now dealing with surface crop and weed residue, there was the matter of learning what is happening to the fertilizer applied. Did it take more?

It was natural that studies were set up to compare amounts of residue that worked best for satisfactory yields and also studied comparing different tillage tools including the V-blade, disk, one-way, and lister. I don't recall using the mold board plow in these tests. Kinds of fertilizer and methods of application and rates had to be determined. It came to be that in 1957 (I'll stay with this date until proven otherwise) the idea that including No-Till was being battered about "Can we do it with just 2,4-D for broad leaf weeds and Delapon for grasses?" "Why not include no-Till in the above tillage and seedbed preparation studies?" Their Field Advisor agreed to do this. Thus the study of No-Till.

Now all fifty years of it...

Agriculture folks I've worked with in McPherson County: Earl Bondy, State Agronomist, Soil Conservation Service, USDA, Salina St. Office.; Algin Button, County Ag Agent, K-State Research and extension.; John Casebeer, McPherson County Comm.; Dale Ladd, County Ag Agent, K-State Research and Extension, present.; Clinton Lundquist, Farmer and Soil Conservation Service Council; Arnold Serviss, Farm Service Agency, USDA; Baron Shively, Soil Conservation Service, USDA, present; Kenton Springer, County Ag Agent, K-State Research and Extension.; Michael Westerman, Farm Service Agency, USDA, present; Robert Whelpley, Soil Conservation Service, USDA and many farmers and industry reps.

And sweet spots continue...

During my couple years of earning my Masters Degree—two years because I didn't make it in one—I was attending classes as well, saw the Experiment Station meetings on campus and on experiment station and fields out in the state with the Agronomy Staff, learning the profession of the study of crops and soils. Walt Moore, Superintendent of the Hutchinson Experiment Field, kind of took me in hand to help me learnt the "ropes." I had my eye on getting on an experiment Field when I got my degree. But there was no Field available. I decided to go back home to the farm and wait for developments. My folks now lived on a short quarter three miles east of McPherson. We decided it wasn't big enough to make it a joint operation for them and me, but I'd stay on until I got located. I got acquainted with Algin Button, McPherson County Agent, and he ended up giving me some chores and apparently liked my work because it wasn't long before he told me that they needed an Assistant County Agent in Barton County and suggested I apply Four weeks later, I moved to Great Bend or was it less?

An important three years LATER, WITH THE HELP OF WONDERFUL FARMERS and Extension personnel and gaining great experience and training, I get the call!

The land of the Sandyland Experiment Field and surrounding country was suffering severe wind erosion. Not only for the field but the superintendent and his wife. They agreed that they could no longer live here. Upon his resignation, I got the call!

I packed and moved to the Field where I spent more than twenty years of my life work of learning best methods of controlling wind erosion of soils in the Midwest, and this came about because of sand storms making an opening for me!

BY CHANCE...

The Chief Petty Officer is checking the Radio Station personnel at 3 a.m. in the morning. We radio operator are on Dog Watch duty starting at midnight and lasting until 6 a.m. This is a watch we radiomen didn't especially look forward to with great gusto, but it is our duty to show up on time and in top condition. Errors in that page of long coded messages are frowned upon. We sit intent listening for our call letters these dits and dahs coming at us twenty or more words a minute. Our call letters are NST, dah dit- dit dit dit-dah. When hearing this we acknowledge and proceed to type the message and then relay this message to its destination. We are a relay statin between Washington D.C. and London. We're at the U.S. Navy Base at Londonderry, N. Ireland.

We live in barracks, galvanized round top. We're responsible for keeping it neat. The sheets on the bed are taut enough to bounce a coin. Floors are swept and no dirty dishes. Inspections on Saturday mornings were no flybys. Strangers at the beginning but almost like brothers after two or three years. One can't get too far out of line to keep a happy family.

During these almost four years, I am learning about ranks of personnel and their layers of responsibility. There is the commander and all those on down and by achievement. How bad do you want advancement? There is always a place for you but it takes learning, work and desire a bunch. The tour of duty in the Navy gave me Maturity it took to go to college and have a great career in Agriculture.

Since retirement, I've judged crops and gardens in many County Fairs and judged a State 4-H Wheat Show in my eighties. And also been on the McPherson Tree Board for a number of years. Retirement is just an opening for related happy opportunities.

P.S. Spent many years rock hounding since retirement!

AUTHOR'S PAGE

Marvin Lundquist was born on a farm near Roxbury, Kansas, September 16, 1921. He attended school there. After a few months of photography training and schooling at Brown-Mackie in Salina, he was drafted into the Army. Thanks to a friend, he got himself in the Navy instead. He was discharged Christmas Day, 1945, after which he attended McPherson College while helping on the family farm.

Using the GI bill, Marvin completed a degree in agronomy at Kansas State University and went on to earn his Master's Degree. He remembers his total expense for those years was paying to have his master's thesis printed. By then, he was a graduate assistant, receiving a monthly stipend.

Following a long and enjoyable agronomy career, since retirement, Marvin has judged crops and gardens in many county fairs and judged a State 4-H Wheat Show when he was in his eighties. To him, retirement is an opening to many happy opportunities, including marriage to Violet March 4, 1995, who came with a ready-made family of two sons and two daughters. She belongs to a Gem and Mineral Club where she took her grandson and Marvin provided transportation. She is his latest and greatest Sweet Spot. They moved from their home in McPherson to The Cedars in August 2010.

Marvin now.

The Memoirs of
Aubrey McNally

by Aubrey McNally

THIS BOOK IS DEDICATED TO:

Jessica McNally who edited and reprinted Aubrey's story Christmas, 2009.

Hold My Hand

The following is the history of my life as I remember it, or as it was told to me by my parents. Who were my parents? Orval Marvin McNally was my dad and Opal Viola Ham McNally was my mother. I was the first born of my generation and my birth date was February 8th. Orval and Opal were married on January 30th. My birth date and their marriage date were only 9 days apart! Well, plus the 365 days for the year between 1923, when they were married, and 1924, when I was born.

The dates are mentioned to point out that there was nothing going on between Dad and Mom before marriage. They were of the squeaky clean generation, and back then being married meant "from now on." I do recall my dad mentioning how nice "that Ham girl" looked when she was playing basketball and wearing bloomers. For those who are not sure, bloomers were worn to cover the legs to just below the knees. The balance of the figure was left to the viewer's imagination. At that time, the rules restricted each player to only playing in one half of the court, which meant that half of the time could be used to just stand around and look good. Orval noticed.

Our family doctor was Dr. Clapper and he was the attending physician for my birth and charged the huge sum of $50.00 for his services. No credit cards in those days, so I was paid for on the installment plan. The McNally's were short of ready cash. No one had told me of the different methods of birth. My breech birth (feet first) made it rather hard on my mother. Ouch.

Grandfather McNally was very interested in his first grandson and put his pinky finger in my little hand and I grabbed the finger and hung on. Grandfather announced, "He'll make it." Mother heard the comment and she related to me later, "I did not know there was any doubt." After three more sons were born and died within a few hours, she understood that she could have lost me, also. My sister Garnett and younger brother Stanley completed our family. My enthusiasm for a brother was overshadowed by the mail that day-a price sheet showing the value of skunk and opossum pelts. Wild animal trapping was not my thing, so I never helped the family finances by adding pelt sales.

What is there in a name? Every generation of the McNally clan had a David, James, John, and William. Orval became the first to have been given a new name to remember. Orval and Opal agreed that enough was enough and decided on a new name. I always figured that Opal put her foot down for a new name for their first born. No one knew why "Aubrey" except it was in the paper and sounded good, so I was named Aubrey Darrell. The Darrell was mispronounced for years. The name Aubrey has never been a problem, until the mail became saturated with advertising for "female cures." I used to laugh at the mail that was sent to Ms. Aubrey. As long as my wife and family knew that I am a man, the rest can be uninformed. (The problem was the closeness of the names Aubrey and Audrey.)

My memories of my younger years are naturally hit and miss, but a few things come to mind that seem important. My folks were members of the Church of Christ. The local church was located approximately seven miles east and two south of Waynoka, Oklahoma. Our farm house was about three miles from the church house. The family never missed a service unless sickness prevented our going. Since we had no car, we traveled by a buggy or wagon pulled by horses. By today's standards, three miles wouldn't seem very far, but by horse and buggy the trip was long. Orval cared more for the comfort of his team than he did his wife and son. I tried to help by asking him to "make them trot Daddy, make them trot." It didn't work, but I don't recall ever being late to church.

School rules were that you had to reach your sixth birthday before the school term started in order to participate. With a birthday of February 8th, I was supposed to wait a whole year after my cousin Katherine had started. After some negotiation with the teacher, I was permitted to start the day after my birthday. I was supposed to walk across the pasture and save about ½ a mile. I can recall very vividly following a cow path as I walked to school.

That is, until a huge Bull Snake was lying in the path one day. The word "huge" would describe a six year old boy's view of a snake that was probably just 18 inches long in reality. I ran home to tell mother. No sympathy from her. "Just go around the spot, and hurry or you'll be late for school." I went around that spot for another two weeks.

Let me add something about Katherine and me being in the same grade. I caught up with her in school the first year. Katherine was and is a very intelligent person, but she seemed to be slow in school. The teacher had her desk on a raised "stage" area of the one room school house, and the students of each grade would go up on the stage to do our work or recite our lesson. Katherine would almost always stumble or stub her foot on the higher level of the floor. Katherine needed an eye examination, and when she got her glasses, she vastly improved her learning skills.

Back to the problem of walking to school: it was sometimes very cold and when walking against the wind, the cold weather became even more severe. Temporarily walking backwards would help for a few minutes, but was not a satisfactory cure for the problem. During those years, flying became important and pilots wore a skull cap that was lined with sheep wool or other insulation. Manufacturers quickly made caps available to the general public. It took very little persuasion to talk my parents into the idea that it would help protect their son from blizzard conditions. Mother bought my argument and got me a cap that was insulated and had a chin strap that was adjustable. I was thrilled with the new cap and wore it everywhere. I changed my mind when I would get home with red cheeks that were hard and sore to touch. The instructions said nothing about if the chin straps were tightened to keep out the wind, then the straps would cut off the blood circulation in the cheeks. Two hours in the wind to freeze my cheeks and two weeks to thaw them out!

I don't recall what age I was when I milked my first cow, but I do recall that as soon as I could carry a bucket, I began feeding the calves. In the good "old days," the cows were milked and the milk was

run through a separator to separate the cream from the skim milk. The only thing that was of monetary value was the cream. You couldn't waste the saleable cream, so the calves were treated to skim milk. My dad worked in the field until it was dark, then came in for supper and then the chores. Milking and separating was the last to be completed. That meant that feeding the calves usually took place at eleven and sometimes even midnight. Mother came to my rescue and told my dad, "You either milk earlier so that the calves can be fed before 10 p.m. or you feed them yourself." I was finally able to get some sleep.

While on the subject of cows and calves, let me mention the fact that it was always a difficulty to predetermine the date of birth for a calf and to determine the date of a winter blizzard. When a cow had been bred to drop her calf in March, it seemed a winter storm would change its date of arrival to the last week of February. Calves dropped during a blizzard usually meant them being born after midnight, and the weather meant frozen ears and tails and death if the calf was not warmed up quickly. The newborn calves would be brought in the house and laid on blankets behind the warm kitchen stove. We could save their life, but not their ears or tails. A frozen ear meant the hearing would be unharmed, but the ear would remain twisted and funny-shaped for the cow's entire life. Frozen tails would thaw out, but would lose the long hair on the end of the tail. The thawed out calf would start making noise and try to walk around, usually before Mother had breakfast ready. Then they were taken out to the barn and introduced to their mother.

One of the natural, instinctive uses of the tail is to switch at flies, and with a little imagination, you know what happens when a cow is being milked that had her tail frozen as a baby calf. The long hair would never re-grow and make nature's natural flyswatter. Now imagine sitting down on a milk-stool with your head in the flank of a cow and the cow feeling that there are flies on her back. She flings her tail and hits the milker in the head. Talk about headaches.

One time my dad was milking out in the corral, and to make the cow stand still while being milked, he had put a halter and rope on her and tied her to a fence post. Now he could milk her. When the switching of flies started, and without considering all of the possibilities, he grabbed the end of the tail and tied its long hair to the fence. Problem: the rope had been tied too long and the cow moved. The hair of the tail stayed. That's right; now the cow had a club for a tail instead of a flyswatter.

Twelve was a Good Age

By having a good banker, the cow herd all became registered Jersey cows, and a new barn and milking machine were purchased. The principal reason for the milking machine was the ability to milk over forty cows twice in a twenty-four hour day. The milkers were quite an improvement over the hand method, even when the milkers didn't always work like they were supposed to. The milkers were attached to a vacuum line that created a suction that literally sucked the milk from the udder and deposited it into a container- that is, except when the teat was not of sufficient size to allow the suction to hold the milker cup on to the teat. That is when Aubrey became big enough to milk. Almost without exception, the heifers were under-developed in size. The teats were not large enough to hold the teat cups on. Aubrey was given the job of milking, by hand, two gallons of milk from each heifer twice a day.

There was also the problem of the heifers not wanting to be milked and kicking the person that was trying to do the job. Kickers would have to be applied to the legs to prevent the kicking problem. Also, the expression "milk by hand" would be more accurately described as "milk by thumb and index finger."

Besides the cream for sale, we had all the baby bull calves to supplement the farm income. The heifer calves were grown and fed until they were old enough to drop a calf of their own. The bull calves were sold to anyone willing to feed them until they got to be butchering size. A Jersey cow was not really a quality beef breed and we finally dropped the asking price to $5.00 each. There was not much profit in raising bull calves, but no one figured out how to change the 50/50 male-female ratio of calves being born. The only planning that could be done was that the cow could be bred approximately 9 months before you wanted her to drop her calf. The sex of the calf could not be pre-planned or determined. We kept the bull penned up so that we had a choice of breeding date.

Another thing that was important on the farm was realizing that Jersey bulls were mean and therefore dangerous. Our bull pen was designed to keep the bull in a section of the pen away from the person who was feeding him. The wooden pen door would swing across the pen and make a restraining wall. All you had to do was to chase the bull into the far portion of the pen and swing the gate across and then feed him in the feed trough. There was a latch on the gate that could prevent the bull coming in for his food. One time Daddy didn't latch it properly and was putting the feed in the trough when the bull pushed the gate back. The bull hooked him with his horns and knocked Daddy down. Fortunately, no physical damage was done-the bull only wanted his feed. Otherwise Daddy could have been killed by not latching the gate.

Before we built the new barn, the bull was kept in a fenced pen made with woven wire. We soon learned that the fence would not hold the bull, so an electric fence was installed. The bull was very much afraid of the new barrier. Daddy also had great respect for the fence's electric shock and would turn off the electricity whenever he needed to go into the pen. The bull would check the fence and when anyone forgot to turn it back on, he would be gone. And when he was gone, he would be found in the pasture with the cows and had no intention of being driven back into the pen. He was not afraid of any man on foot. The only thing he respected was the Allis Chalmers "WC" tractor. So it was my job to drive him back home. He would run a few yards and then turn and face the tractor, lower his horned head, and paw the dirt with his front feet. "Make me!" was the message. As long as I was on the tractor I felt safe, but I was still very cautious. It would take a long time to convince him to go home. When the bull wanted to look over the neighbor's herd we would get a phone call from the neighbor's wife: "Come and get your male ox cow." "Bull" was not part of her vocabulary.

Since I was a farm boy and had passed the diaper stage, my size made me a favorite when teams were chosen for a ball game. The only problem was that I had to learn to bat left-handed because I made too many home runs batting right-handed. The youngest Seachris boy was about my size, so every noon recess we would try out our wrestling skills on each other. Made a lot of washing for my mother. Marbles were also important to our education. My milking experience made my marble thumb strong and I still have my dad's agate marble.

For my twelfth birthday, my folks thought it was time to present me with a .22 rifle. Any new rifle needs the sights to be adjusted to obtain any accuracy in shooting. Before any adjustments were made, the preacher stopped by for a visit. Daddy was proudly showing off the new rifle and a hawk was circling by as it floated in the wind. Daddy fired once and the hawk dropped like a rock.

I was real proud of the rifle and decided to take it with me as I walked to bring the cows in for milking. As I walked toward the cattle, a pretty little blue bird was sitting on the fence approximately 50 feet away from me. The sights had still not been adjusted and since I never had fired a rifle, what could I shoot? My conclusion was: nothing. Since I didn't think I could hit anything, my logic was that all I could do was scare the pretty blue bird if I shot at it. Wrong! The poor thing dropped dead. I got the cows, but I cried all the way home and was still crying when I told my mother. I didn't want to kill the bird.

Another time I was trying to kill sparrows with the rifle and was in the barn aiming through a split in the wall boards. I aimed at a sparrow sitting on a post in the corral. I fired the .22 and the next thing I saw was one of the Jersey cows shaking her head. She had walked in front of the post just as I fired and the bullet went so close to her head that the noise that the bullet made as it passed by her head scared her. I had told my mother about the blue bird, but I never told anyone about the near miss of the Jersey cow.

High School Days

High school was a little different back in my day (1938). I was a farm boy and there were no school buses. My mother's mother and dad lived in Waynoka and I stayed with them. My granddad was not in very good health. My job was to help him get out of his chair and help him walk to wherever he had to go. At least I got to go to high school.

Back to the topic of school: freshmen male students were supposed to prove their ability to take whatever the upper classmen wanted to dish out. For the first week, it was a "belt line" before classes started in the morning and before the bell rang after the lunch period. That added up to ten times the first week.

What was a belt line? A belt line meant our bottoms were sore for the first week. All the upper classmen would make two lines opposite each other. They would take off their belts and whack you as you ran down the narrow lane between the two lines. The belts were supposed to be doubled and the two ends were held so that the doubled end would really hurt. The seniors got their revenge for the punishment they had to take when they were freshmen. If someone in the line really didn't like you, he might just happen to not hold onto the belt with a strong grip and one end would come loose and it was usually the buckle that struck your bottom. Ouch. Make that double ouch.

There was one big farm boy that defied the upper classmen. He just backed up to the schoolhouse wall and said "Come and get me!" He never had to run the belt line. Nope, it wasn't me. The last couple of days, James Buckner and I had had more than we wanted so we waited in the old shed across the street until the bell rang and then we ran to get to class. It was a lot better than sitting on the welts made by the belts.

Living in town had its advantages. I tried all the sports that were offered. It was the first year for football, so we had no experience. We won no games that first year. I did make a touchdown though. Peewee Curtis broke through the line and blocked a punt. I was playing right end and the blocked ball hit me in the stomach. As I caught it, Peewee hollered "Run!" It was only ten yards to the goal line. I was slow, but not that slow!

Baseball season was a little better. I remember one game when we played the Alva "Goldbugs." One of my cousins played left field for them. My turn at bat. Their pitcher was pretty good. Strike one. Strike two. Then the pitcher got real fancy and threw me a drop ball. I had missed the first two by swinging below the ball. This time he threw right into my bat. He threw hard, and I swung hard. The ball went over my cousin's head in left field and into the canyon behind him. I ran the bases and was standing at home plate when he finally came up out of the canyon.

My best sport was basketball and my best game was against Dacoma High School. Another cousin was their best player. He had been averaging 20 points each game. Our coach gave me instructions to "stay on him like a dirty shirt." He was able to make only six points that game and I made twelve, which was my best point total for the entire season.

My greatest pleasure was the agricultural class and the Future Farmers of America club. Our instructor was Harold Dedrich. He was instrumental in any success I have had in school or in my teaching days. He was not what you would call a regular teacher. One example: two of the sophomore boys were always picking on or fussing at each other. Mr. Dedrich tried to stop the verbal display, but to no avail. So finally he had the class move all the chairs and tables to the outside of the room, leaving an open center. He got out two pairs of 16 ounce boxing gloves and had each boy put on a pair. To better picture the opponents: one was large, fat and slow. The other was small, skinny and fast. The rules were three minutes of boxing and one minute of rest for the entire class period. After the second round, the fighting had become a physical hardship on both of the boys. Would you believe that they got along very well after their battle? All was well until the superintendent called Mr. Dedrich to his office. "Don't ever pull that again…unless I'm invited to attend the show."

For three years in a row, I was elected to one of the offices of the FFA club and during all that time

I tried out for all the contests and honors that were available. One state-wide contest was about the use of levels in laying out terraces, etc. At the state contest, we were to start from two predetermined points and measure that angle and distances between three trees and then plot a map showing them on paper. Those in charge gave all the teams blank paper to work with. It quickly became obvious that the paper furnished was not big enough to properly plot the information. We had some larger sheets that we had brought along with us. We could see all the other teams struggling with their report. Our best analysis was that the only reason we came in first place was because we used bigger paper.

During the four years of vocational agriculture class work, we were required to keep accurate records of the projects that we took care of at home. As seniors, we could turn in those records and enter the Junior Master Farmers contest. My project as a senior was to feed and care for a bull (steer) calf. Our records were sent to the state office and an inspector was sent to the school to make a final inspection. We were not informed of when the inspector would be there to inspect our project. When the inspector arrived, Mr. Dedrich told me and I immediately called Mother and told her to expect him within a couple of hours. Mother did the thing that I should have been doing every day. She went out to the pen where the steer was kept and cleaned up the pen and calf. I got the Junior Master Award of the state FFA, but mother should have gotten the honor, not me. The Lt. Governor also wrote me a letter of congratulations and suggested that he would be pleased to help me with anything I might need. Later that summer, we had the privilege of asking for help. The Lt. Governor was a banker that lived in Stillwater, OK.

Another big item in my senior year was the planning and construction of the new barn on the farm. The general plans were made by my father Orval, the ideas by my mother Opal and me. The barn served as a dairy barn for over 15 years. The foundation was the main reason for the longevity. The barn remains standing real proud today after 60 years. The hay loft was in the center, the south wing was the milking area, and the north wing had five individual grain bins. Each grain bin was on a concrete floor and to prevent moisture from entering the grain from below, the concrete was covered in tar. During the pouring of tar, dinner was ready, so pouring stopped. A kitchen pan was being used to pour the tar into the low parts of the concrete. When dinner was over and we went back to work, I picked up the pan and the tar had stuck it to the concrete where it had been sitting. I got a handful of soft, hot tar. Since the laborers were watching, I did not cry-until I told mother. Mother was able to clean off the tar without leaving any burns.

Another plan for the barn was to hire a professional installer of the corrugated iron on the roof. My dad was a perfectionist and expected the installation to be perfect. After only one half day of work, it could easily be seen that the sheets were running crooked. The professional installer was relieved of his job and paid nothing. My cousin and I put on the roof and after 60 years it still looks good.

College at Oklahoma A&M in Stillwater, Oklahoma

The decision was made to enroll at Oklahoma A&M. Daddy and I drove to Stillwater to investigate the possibility of college. We asked for information about finding me a job and room. Everyone we talked to was sympathetic but could not help us. After seeing everyone we were referred to, Daddy asked if I had brought the letter that the Lt. Governor had sent me. I had it with me and we went to the bank that he owned in Stillwater. He read the letter and asked what he could do for us. "A place to stay and a job to pay for my room and board." Without hesitation he phoned someone at the college and gave us a name to go see. Within the hour, I was enrolled, had a room at Cordell Hall, and a job in the dining hall of the same dormitory. We concluded that it is not *what* you know but *who* you know that really counts.

My first purchase was a notebook to keep a record of my out-of-pocket expenses. My first semes-

ter expenses totaled $395, and my second $405. I had noticed the girls on campus-and in those days girls dressed, walked, and talked like girls.

My grades were not very good the first semester. My folks received a report from the college and I received a letter from my dad. His letter was short and to the point: raise that D or come home and milk cows. I was able to raise my grades to a high C or low B. Grades were harder in college. My study habits were not very good, but my ping pong was getting better. My room was on the first floor and just below my window was the basement where the ping pong room was. No more ping pong until I raised my grades.

The local preacher was Wilburn Hill and I took several Bible classes under his teaching. I had been baptized (immersed) when I was 14, and have never regretted that decision. And thank God for all the blessings that have been mine over the years.

College and the "Jap Trap"

Second year was more eventful than the first and things worked out better. My grades held up to a B average. My job was serving dinners to two tables and working in the kitchen doing dirty dishes. We worked as waiters and served a three course meal-main plate, drink of choice, and then dessert. On one of my best days, I recall serving over 60 within the same lunch hour. Of course, another waiter served 90 during the same hour and his tables were farther from the kitchen than my tables were. I think he was better organized.

The real excitement was the Sunday radio announcement that the Japanese had bombed Pearl Harbor. Everyone that had a radio had it on and had several people around listening to every word that was broadcast. Everyone was affected personally- or would be soon. Many of the older, more mature-thinking students knew that they would soon be a part of the war and when Mr. Roosevelt declared war on the Japanese, Germans, and Italians, many men decided to enlist in their choice branch of the service. The rest of us waited until the army recruiter told us if we would sign up with the enlisted reserve corp., we would be allowed to finish the school year. He wasn't too far off-we finished the semester and ½ of the second semester. But we did get credit for all of the second semester on our records at school.

All college men that signed up were inducted and sent to Fort Sill, Oklahoma, for our shots and further instructions. Speaking of shots, the one with the "square needle" got the most attention. A "square needle" was one that was not accurate, perhaps even dull (but still round). We went in line between two medics, one for the right arm and one for the left. A big football player must have thought the square needle rumor was for real-when he was hit from both sides, he passed out cold. They revived him and the line continued. No, I was not the man.

You may have heard that the army was slow. Not so-we were sent to Camp Maxey, Texas, for our basic training. The basic training was to learn to say "Yes, sir" and "No, sir" and to toughen up those muscles that we thought were already ready-to-go. In thirteen weeks, there were a lot of boys that became men. Our training camp was what we called the "Jap Trap," because it was built for the purpose of holding Japanese prisoners. The army soon learned that the Japanese didn't give up. Their understanding was that to die for the Emperor was a sure ticket into their heaven.

The "Jap Trap" was all new, even to the double barb wire fence that enclosed the camp. There were some real men in camp and some that were "Dodo Birds." Even "Dodo Birds" couldn't describe some of them. One man at the other end of the barracks (named Briscoe, I think) smoked big square Havana cigars and the smell would get to our end of the barracks. The smell was great. I had never smoked but that smell almost made me want to.

Then there was a man who had lost most of his good marbles. To tell the story, you need to understand that we were issued all of our clothing and with the shoes we were to wear: leggins. Leggins were to protect our ankles and were worn as an extension of our shoes. They were held in position by a small strap that went in front of the heel of the shoe and wrapped around your leg. They were made with canvas and were tied on with shoe strings and hooks.

Now, the Dodo Bird was smart enough to put his leggin's on with the hooks on the inside, since if they were on the outside, they were difficult and slow to put on. Orders came down for us to pack out 75 pounds of gear plus our rifle and to get ready to start a 30 mile hike (15 miles out and 15 miles back), with a campout at the end of the march on the first day. Each man had been assigned to a spot in the company and was to be ready for inspection at 9 a.m., ready to march.

All went well until we were marching along in front of the commander's headquarters. Then the Dodo Bird's leggin's, which were hooked on the inside, decided to hook together-which meant that both of his legs were suddenly tied to each other. Down went Dodo Bird, flat on his face, pack, rifle and all. We helped him up and went on our way to the 15 mile stopping spot. As far as I remember, the Dodo Bird never put his leggin's on wrong again. He still had a few marbles left and they took such a shaking up that his memory improved.

At the end of the first day's hike, one soldier decided to tell his officer what he thought of the whole situation and apparently used some language that offended the officer. "Dig a six by six hole and make it six feet deep and to complete the job, move the hole over six feet!" The zipper for his mouth was installed good, and the experience installed many zippers in other people.

Another man had been playing basketball in college and had a trick knee. He could throw the knee joint in or out of place anytime he wanted to. So, after the 15 mile hike was over, he yelled "Medic!" and threw his knee out of place. The medics had not been trained in knee problems so they called for an ambulance. Off to the camp hospital and we didn't see him again. He went back to college and played basketball. Another man was about 45 years old and tried hard, but just couldn't take the physical abuse. He went to the hospital and received his discharge. No more army for him.

163

The army comes up with some peculiar ideas. Since they had a bunch of college men, they decided to send several to Eastern Kentucky State Teacher's College to take training in engineering. I never did know what they wanted with engineers, but it was a school and that's what was ordered, so away we went. Only thing I could rationalize about it was that engineers could be used to build bridges. We were there for six months.

During that time, J.D. Coble and I went to church in Louisville. An older couple invited us to dinner every Sunday and took us to see some of the horse farms in the area. On one trip, we visited the farm where Man o' War was stabled. He was nick-named Big Red and had won the derby and now was only being rented as a stud. His breeding fee was too high to even imagine. I don't remember it exactly except that it was in the thousands of dollars. But to a rich horse filly owner, what was money? If he could get a colt that could win some races, the investment would pay good dividends. One amusing event that occurred was a newly-married couple was touring the stable and the man was trying to explain what the breeding harness was used for to the girl. She sure wasn't a farm girl.

Those in charge of the school decided that, in order to keep everyone from copying each other, all tests would be given in the gymnasium. There was one man that made almost every test with a perfect score. Another man was flunking almost every test. So the man who was flunking made an arrangement with the good student to sit in a chair where the lines on the floor crossed and each quarter of the area could be designated as A, B, C, or D (all the questions were multiple-choice). The smart one would move his foot to the area that matched the right answer. Well, our dummy got behind on the answers and had to guess on some of the questions. The result was that the dummy beat the smart guy!

College and then to Camp Swift, Texas

Our favored college status was about to stop and did when the six months were up. Back to Camp Swift, Texas for more training in being an infantryman. We all knew that our time was getting closer to actual combat. So I wrote home asking if my mother could get a bus ticket and come to see me some weekend soon. She could and did. It was a good weekend 'cause I had always enjoyed mother's kisses and hugs. We both knew time was running short. We went to church Sunday morning and it was the first time I saw my mother go to sleep in church. The bus ride and the emotional time just about wore her out.

Someone must have decided that the troops needed to see their families because furloughs were passed out and I was home with my family on June 6th, D-Day, when General "Ike" invaded France. I was extremely happy to have been home then. And another reason for being happy to have been home was that the troops that were still training went on a practice run of marching against the enemy and having the mortar team shell the area ahead of the troops. One of the shells fell short of the target area and a staff sergeant was killed. It could have been me if I had not been home.

Since Europe had been invaded, the need for infantrymen became urgent. We loaded on a train and headed for the east coast and our training was over. I spent many hours watching the Gulf and countryside go by while standing at the end of the train car. It was a long but interesting ride along the southern coast and up the east coast to a camp close to the ocean.

Our first orders were to clean up the barracks area. The camp was filthy, but we did not blame the troops that just left. They left knowing that they were going into combat and had very little interest in the way they left the condition of the barracks. I have no recollection of making the camp squeaky clean when we left.

We spent our time sitting through lectures: 50 minutes of listening and then ten minutes of a break. The break period gave me a chance to remember Brisco and his Havana cigar. For small change I purchased and tried my first —and only- cigar. The only thing that I learned was that lighting and smoking for ten minutes and then putting out the cigar for

50 minutes was not the ideal way to enjoy a first smoking experience. The cigar became extremely strong during the time of stop and start. Once was enough; never tried it again.

New Jersey and the Port of Departure

On weekends, we were loaded up in a truck that would take us to Trenton, N.J. The United Service Organization (USO) had a place in town that you could sit and talk and play cards or ping pong or visit with the local girls that were there. One blond, feminine type I tried to get a date with said, "No, you drink too much,"- to a man who had never taken a drink in his life! I was at a loss for how I got that reaction. One weekend, I was visiting with a little dark-haired Italian girl and asked if I could escort her home. I found her to be very smart because when the bus reached her getting-off place she said, "See those boys on the corner? They would pick a fight with anyone I was with." So she got off and I stayed on the bus. I don't consider myself a coward, but rather a good judge of a bad situation.

Then came the day for preparing us for our boat ride. The chances were slim for our boat being sunk by the Germans, but since they did have several subs in the Atlantic, and there were orders to sink all American ships, the army decided that we needed special training for "what if?" The idea was to teach us how to make a life preserver out of our pants. Tie a knot in each trouser leg and then soak the trousers in the water. By flipping the trousers in the air a certain way, air could be trapped in the trouser legs and then you had a life preserver. Sounded like a bad deal to me. In the first place, I had not learned to swim and to take off my trousers and prepare them for being a life preserver seemed to me to be a lost cause. I found a shade tree and caught some sleep.

When orders came down to clean up the area, we all knew that our ship had come and we were on schedule to "be on our way." New York City was our departure city. The sight of the "Sea Wolf" looked massive to a farm boy. Actually, it was one of the smaller ships. It was built by the Kaiser ship build-ers, the same company that was later to build the Kaiser car. The Kaiser car was never accepted with much favor by the general public. I always figured that anyone that had made a trip in a flat-bottomed Kaiser ship would never catch himself owning a Kaiser car.

We assembled on the dock with all our possessions and had an army band to play for us before we left. I wonder why we got the feeling that maybe we should have volunteered to be a part of the army band. I did not even know how to toot my own horn, so I suppose I was not qualified.

Up the gangplank, single file and then down a long internal ladder to the bottom of hold number one. Along the sides of the ship were our sleeping accommodations. They were canvas bunk beds stacked five high with about two feet of space between each bunk. We were to live in that space for several weeks. The troops scattered and put some identification on the lower bunks quickly. I chose the top bunk for head room. It was a little problem to climb to the top, but when that was all you had to do for days it was the easy way to spend time sleeping or whatever.

Everyone had heard of sea-sickness and by the first morning at sea, most men knew from experience just how sick you could get. The gentle rolling of the ship caused by the waves of the ocean meant almost everyone gathered around the trash can that was located in the center of our area. Our area was hold number one and was separated from number two by a steel wall with only a door to pass through between areas.

The first morning I didn't feel sick, only a little woozy. So I looked over the side of my top bunk and there was our trash can surrounded by sick men heaving up their breakfast, and since we had not had any breakfast that day, it must have been yesterday's breakfast, or lunch, or supper, or last week's meal, depending on how sick you were. I did the wise thing and didn't try to get up. I stayed in bed all day and got used to the rolling of the ship so I never did get sea sick on that trip.

Our second day at sea was better; almost all men had been able to get their "sea legs" under themselves. We were all awakened by the top sergeant yelling "Everybody up. Hot cakes, hot cakes!" This happened every morning, noon, and evening. Our hot cakes looked and tasted like a boiled egg and a boiled potato. I wonder why there was no one asking for seconds.

The ship's bulletin board had a notice attached asking for someone to volunteer for a job of bookkeeping. Most everyone had learned that in the army you never volunteered for anything. It might sound like a good job, but most of the good jobs became KP duty. "KP" meant "kitchen police", which usually meant peeling potatoes or washing dishes. My good friend, Rowland Maas, read between the lines and decided to volunteer. He applied and got the job. It was to help in the office of the ship's crew. A little bookkeeping or recordkeeping all day, which entitled him to eat with the ship's personnel. A real restaurant-type meal, even pie for dessert sometimes. Roland was smart enough to not come back down to his bunk and brag about his meal. I'm glad he got the job. He was later killed by a German artillery shell during our first battle at Flosdorf, Germany.

Our ocean travel was kind of like having a loose steering wheel: we were always changing direction. Actually the entire convoy of ships, troop ships, and the navy escort vessels changed directions several times each day in order to avoid the possibility of being torpedoed by the German "U-boats"- submarines. We were never attacked.

France and Camping Out

Unlike all the previous convoys that stopped in England, we went straight to France. Remember that D-day was June 6th, 1944. We landed at Cherbourg in the early part of September 1944. Of course there were no docks to tie up to so we had to unload into small boats and were brought to land that way.

Since by September, the Germans had been chased out of that part of France, we were not destined to spend time in a hotel or any special vacation resort. We walked to a preplanned farming area where we could put up our own personal pup tent and dig our own latrine. We were not coed so we did not have to put up "His" and "Her" signs. The pup tents were put up by the buddy system. Each man had only ½ of the tent. My buddy was Sergeant Doyle. I personalized my half of the area by digging a shallow hole to put my hips or butt in so I wouldn't have a sore back from the bad mattress.

There were cattle everywhere and no fences. Hedge rows were the only limiting line for each farm. The cattle wore ankle bracelets on a front foot and the bracelet was tied to a peg in the ground that the farmer would move when the grass was eaten down short.

Our Chaplain's assistant was a member of the Church of Christ and he knew several that would like to meet for worship services on Sunday morning. He passed the word around and made available the bread and grape juice for the emblems, and men walked five miles from three different directions to come. And as I recall, there were as many as 12 or 15 soldiers that attended the service. It was my most memorable service, held under a large cottonwood tree. The only uninvited guest was a rusty field cultivator that had been left there during the occupation of the German troops.

Our time spent in France was short, only long enough to make arrangements for a French train for transportation through north France. The train was an old one that got its name from World War One. The cars were known as "Forty and Eight." Each individual car could hold forty men or eight horses. I have no experience of the eight horses, but I can agree with the forty men. It was really crowded. Forty men could not all lay down to sleep at the same time. If you could find two men that were lying on their right side at the same time, you might be able to squeeze between them. A few men arranged for a little comfort and went to the finance car that was behind the engine. It was amazing how much extra room suddenly appeared when six men went to that empty car.

The other problem was that there was no restroom available and no stopping of the train for a chance for a person to relieve his pain. After traveling through most of northern France, we had to stop for fuel for the engine and another man and I decided to take that time to relieve our stored up used-food supply. Just off the tracks was a loading dock that was empty. With no one around, we both backed up to the edge and dropped our pants and squatted down. When we had bared all, here came two French girls who were obviously headed straight for both of us. Since neither of us knew the language, we assumed that they wanted to thank the Americans for running off the Germans. Thanking verbally was not enough; they insisted we shake their hands. We were still in our squatted position so it did not take us long to finish our "project." I'm not sure we even thought about the usual wiping required. We were too embarrassed and red-faced to care. We were back on the train just in time to pull out for Belgium, German front.

We were sure that we would soon be, should we say, "too close for comfort." Actually our only problems had been very minor compared to what we would soon experience. We were moved to what we found to be an unoccupied area. There had been Germans there, but they had moved farther back into their own country. Our job was to take up a defensive position, to prevent the Germans from changing their plans and to try to retake the area. I was given a very comfortable job- almost a continued vacation. The German troops had left a farm house and a listening post that was located in a low place in the backyard. They even had built a place to house or hide a soldier with a straw bed and a roof for protection from the weather. The German troops had abandoned the area we moved in.

When I say "we" I refer to the man that was assigned to be a lookout with me. The only problems we had was the barking of a dog that was in the house. Everything would be quiet, when all of a sudden, the barking would start. As we manned our outpost, our concern was who made the dog start barking. Was it a German who had come back to see what was going on? We finally sent word for someone and we felt better about our situation. In

fact, when the company headquarters sent to question whether I wanted to change my job, I could not see how I could improve, so I declined the offer. A roof over my head and a straw mattress for a bed-it seemed to me that any change would be worse.

And our change came soon-our first battle/engagement with the enemy, whatever you want to call it. Our camping out privileges were canceled and we assembled at about 4:30 a.m. on a beet field (about a 50 acre field of beets that was a good stand and provided a hiding place if you wanted to crawl on your belly.) No one preferred that approach to the little town of Flosdorf. The town looked to be about three blocks long, and at that time of the day, the number of German troops was not known to us.

The First Battle: Flosdorf, Germany

Our company assembled in the canyon that was across the beet field. It was dark, so we really did not know about the beet field or what our objective was. The plans called for going across the field and into Flosdorf at daybreak. Daylight came and we delayed our advance. Why? We were waiting for a group of 12 tanks to arrive and go with us. Finally, at 10 a.m., we started our advance across the field. You can be sure that the Germans were surprised, what with the noise of 12 tanks rumbling around getting in position to go with the infantry if needed. We didn't advance 100 yards when the artillery started coming in from the right side. So they sent in the tanks to help us. The tanks were no match for the artillery. The Germans had "88" artillery that was actually an overgrown rifle that was fired directly at tanks, men, or anything they wanted to hit.

And hit they did. The tanks were ordered to pull out or back up and leave us. Six of them were already hit and couldn't retreat. The artillery fired on our position for the rest of the day and you could set your watch by the timing of the shelling. From the right side of the field, the shelling started on the house and shelled the entire field. The next hour they started all over again. Remember, our only protection was the beet leaves and the six inch tracks left in the soft ground by the tanks. Early in the shelling was when my good friend Rowland Maas was hit. The medics carried him off. He later died from the wound.

I was hit twice by the fragments from the exploding shells. The first was a hit on the top of my helmet resulting in a dent that cut the camouflage netting. The second wound actually was caused by the shrapnel going through my coat, the clip of rifle ammunition, and through my trousers and underwear, finally hitting the flesh in the area of the right kidney. It proved to be a minor flesh wound. The bleeding stopped due to the hot metal, I think. No trip to the hospital or official record of my wound. Only evidence was a scar that disappeared after a few years. The tank tracks were apparently not deep enough. I was in them as far as I could get.

The shelling continued all day and started up against the next day. About 10 a.m. two air force P-42 fighter planes started to fly around over the area. We had had no German planes so we wondered what the U.S. planes were doing there. Both planes were carrying 500 pound bombs under their wings and the pilots were watching for the artillery muzzle flash to locate the guns. When a gun muzzle blast was observed, the P-42s would dive down and drop their bombs on the target. The shelling ceased and our troops proceeded into Flosdorf.

As we went, we passed one of our tanks. We could not observe any evidence of it being hit by the enemy. It appeared that after the order to retreat, it had backed into a German foxhole and got stuck. The German foxholes were a slit trench and the tank track had dropped into the trench. This would compare to getting a car stuck in the mud with the wheels hopelessly spinning. One tank track, having fallen into the split trench, would spin because of no traction. The tank driver had tried to move it forward and backward to no avail. The tank was abandoned where it was stuck. Personally, my concern was that there was not one of our troops in the foxhole when the tank tried to move.

My squad picked out a house that had a basement to get a night of rest. No electricity, so a basement without lights was real dark. I had the crazy idea of going back to the disabled tank and using the battery to hook up the light system. A large 24 volt battery would be heavy and one of the men volunteered to help. Here is the crazy part of the idea: all European countries used 240 volt electricity systems. The lights only had a faint glow. No real light.

The real sad part of Flosdorf was that 50 percent of our company was lost by either death or injury. Losing a member of your squad is like losing a member of your family. When you spend months of togetherness with someone, he becomes a part of your army family. Then come the questions: Why Roland? Why not me? I was hit by shrapnel from two shells and lived to tell it. Why? God must have had other plans for me. There were other situations that made me wonder. I thank God for the guidance and protection and pray that I have been what he wanted me to be.

Forty Miles Northwest of Aachen

The 102nd Infantry Division was to be a part of the Ninth Army. The Ninth was composed of an English division, the 84th Infantry Division and the 102nd Infantry Division. The Ninth was to maintain or hold our position along a river northwest of Aachen, Germany. We were not going anywhere; our object was only to hold our position.

Aachen, Germany is best known for The Battle of the Bulge. The Battle of the Bulge was where, just before Christmas and during a winter blizzard, Hitler had gathered his best troops and tanks for a surprise attack to push back the American troops. The surprise part worked, but what he did not know was the true temperament of the U.S. soldier. When the Germans had surrounded one outfit and their general, the Germans ordered the general to give up. His answer was, "Nuts!" I would rather think that his answer was longer than the one word, but that was all that it was reported that he said. Anyway, the weather cleared for three days enabling the air force to fly in and help stop the German assault.

Our 102nd Division was about forty miles northwest of the Bulge, and our position and plan was to hold back any advance that the Germans might try, like they did at Aachen. When the Germans attacked Aachen, the 84th Division was sent to help clean up and retake the lost ground in the Aachen area.

The 102nd was scattered out to take over the 84th's portion of the line. I can't recall the town's name, but it was along a small river with the Americans in possession of the town and the Germans in possession of the area northeast of the town. They had earlier planned for the line to be a defensive line for they had fortified the area with concrete bunkers/ pill boxes. My foxhole at that time was to the extreme left of our company area and I can recall listening at all the noise that the enemy made. One distinct identifiable noise was at about 10 p.m. every night; the soldiers would receive their evening meal. It was delivered to the German soldiers by a horse-drawn cart. That is, we assumed it was a horse-drawn two-wheeled cart because we were able to hear the horse walking on the hard surface of the road. Klippety-klop, every evening at the same time.

Orders came down to try to locate the sound by compass readings from several positions along our line, and from that information, fire or lob mortar shells. It worked…well, kind of worked. Shells were fired and all was silent for about five or ten minutes, then klippety-klop. For three nights in a row, we tried to hit the horse. Never did stop the klippety-klop.

The Ruhr River crossing was our next major move and complication was the next order of business. The date had been scheduled, but someone told the Germans of our plans. "Berlin Sally" was an English-speaking radio announcer from Germany and she advised us of the plans. Even the date and hour of our plans were known. I never knew how she could be so accurate, but she had been right before and was again. I wanted to get a letter from home before the crossing and I did. By "V-mail" in five days from Oklahoma. I kept that letter folded in my helmet along with my toilet paper (to keep it dry).

We were advised that plans included our staying in this area for some time. If we were to stay for awhile and two of us were to occupy the foxhole, why not make it first class? Snow had covered the ground about four or six inches and I was sent across town to a position about 200 yards out in an open field and on the slope towards the German line. Now it was not best to dig a foxhole out in the open facing the enemy in broad daylight. Two of us made the change, moved back some snow and started digging. The snow moving was no problem, but the ground was about ten inches frozen solid. Sent for and got six one pound TNT explosive charges that helped our problem. We'd chip a small hole with our bayonet and then explode it with our TNT. The ground was loosened up enough to be able to dig with our shovels.

Remember that this was in the afternoon and in a place that Germans could watch our every move. They had been watching us and, different than the horse and cart we tried to hit after dark, with binoculars the enemy could see everything clearly. They decided to discourage us and fired an artillery shell. Their right and left sights were set just exactly right. The shell landed 50 yards below our hole. We had had time to dig enough of a hole that we could get a little protection from the frozen ground. There was a black spot in the snow where the shell landed. The second shell came in about 25 yards below our hole and left another black spot in the snow. Missed a second time. We were anticipating a third effort on their part and they did not surprise us. They adjusted the elevation and fired again. This time you could hear the whine of the shell as it came over us and landed 50 ft above our position. It was target practice and apparently three shells were all they could spare for practice shots. We went back to digging and made a hole deep enough to sit up in.

We borrowed a barn door for a roof, a small stove and some coal. We were comfortable for several days. Then came the early snow thaw and we soon found out that we had put our foxhole in a dead-furrow. We came out and ditched around the hole to divert the unwanted water. We had the conveniences of home, but we preferred not to include running water. A German plane flew over but paid no attention to our position.

We were trucked to another area of the front lines. Trucked sounded good to us men of the infantry. The trip turned into an R&R period. We were scheduled for hot showers and church service and a practice working with tanks. The hot showers were in a coal mine in Holland. That was a memorable occasion. I'll always remember when we passed through this Dutch Holland town. It had rained the night before and the streets had mudholes that were hit by the tires on the truck. When the sidewalks got wet, there was a little old lady with a broom sweeping off the water and mud that was splashed her way. She impressed me as being one who had been raised to be clean.

Our church service was conducted after the shower session. The part of the service that I remember was the communion part. I knew the reason why, but the Thursday time was a problem for me. Thursday was not the first day of the week, and Paul had stayed longer than necessary so he could be there on the first day of the week. I quickly decided that while Thursday was not the day, it had been so long since we had met under the cottonwood tree and there was no promise of life later on so I partook.

After our shower we lined up to practice walking with the tanks. The objective was to determine what gear or speed was compatible with our marching. The tank driver asked me if I wanted a ride, so I quickly gave my rifle to another man to hold and crawled in the tank. It didn't take long for me to decide that the cramped position and the can't-hide problem were not for me. And, considering our past experience with tanks at Flosdorf, I was back-walking as quickly as I could.

Back to our front line positions, with a little change in plans. We were instructed to form a patrol of 30 men to go to the enemy lines and bring back a prisoner. The whole idea seemed to not be logical to me. 1. No one spoke or understood German. 2. What were the chances of taking a prisoner without losing some of our patrol? 3. If we were lucky

and captured a prisoner, what would he know that he would tell us? The rules of war were "Give your name and serial number only." We were told to get one man from our squad and I asked for a volunteer. A man from Tennessee with a wife and four sons at home, who was a replacement for our injured, said "I'll go as far as you do, but not one step farther." The patrol assembled and went close to the German lines but the patrol leader set off a mine and was killed. His name was Greenblat.

We were issued snow white coveralls/ pull-over suits to get ready for a push against the Germans and their pill boxes. At about 4 a.m., we were instructed to move across No Man's Land, make no noise, and have no conversations. I was the squad leader, and there was about four inches of snow on the ground. In the middle of the street was a small hump in the snow. I thought it might be a shoe mine. Being scared of mines, I went through a gap in the garden hedge and was walking through the garden when I heard a loud explosion behind me. Then I heard a yell for a medic from my friend in Tennessee. He needed help. It was a shoe mine and he had stepped on it.

I hurried back and found my friend from Tennessee down with one foot missing. The shoe mine had blown off his shoe, sock, and all of his foot. All that was left were his toes, hanging on by a little skin that was a part of the arch of his foot. The medic and I gently folded his toes up against the ankle bone and poured sulfa powder over the area. Sulfa powder was the antibacterial that was available back then.

My friend looked at me and asked, "How bad is it?" Neither a lie nor a truth could be profitable at this time. I did not lie, nor did I tell all of the truth. "You will be gone for three or four days." I can't recall his name. All I know is that he was from Tennessee, had four sons and was an amputee. I have written letters to all I could and even put my senator on the "Find him, please!" list. Nothing.

Everyone had been issued a white coverall that would hide our movement early in the morning. White suits for moving in the snow was a good move and it worked out. Concrete bunkers are built to face one direction, so it is impossible to turn around and fire in the opposite direction. By being extra quiet, we walked on the back side before the Germans knew we were even there. The Reserve Company that followed made too much noise and woke up the Germans and was fired on. We were already three hundred yards behind the German line. The firefight didn't last long. The Germans realized it was a no-win situation and they decided being a prisoner would be better than what they were now.

Crossing the Ruhr River

We packed all our belongings in our bed rolls. I forgot to include a 12-inch bowie knife I had asked my folks to send me. I made the mistake of putting it under the belt that the roll was tied by. Right, it was a mistake. Someone stole it from me. Just as well, I had no use for it anyway.

Now to the river crossing. Orders were to be ready by 5 a.m. But by 5 a.m., the Germans had decided to open the gates of the dam upstream and the river that was usually 30 yards wide was out of its banks and now flooded the river plain to about half mile wide. Orders were to delay our crossing until the water had receded. After a five day delay we gave it a try. Water was still moving at an eight-mile-per hour speed. The ground was not dry yet but could be walked on through the trees toward the cliff where a huge pill box was facing our advance. We loaded into small row boats (the stackable kind that were designed to hold 12 passengers). That meant ten from our squad and two engineers. They were in charge of the crossing. One in front and one in the rear of the boat.

When you are paddling in water that is moving eight-miles-per hour you go down stream at a fast clip. We moved across the main river pretty good–that is until we floated into the plum thicket on the opposite bank. There we were held by the branches from going anywhere and the engineers had not been trained to know how to go through the brush. They told everyone to paddle hard upstream. Pad-

dling upstream was getting us nowhere. So I told them to part the bushes and go through the tangle and then paddle to shore. They approved and we made it ok. All except one of my squad, who was hit in the stomach. I asked him how bad it was and he said, "Go on, I'll be alright." I never saw him again.

Since we did not know where the enemy was we just plodded on through the mud until I saw a small tank in the trees up ahead. Our bazooka man was with me and I asked him for the weapon. I aimed and fired. I was in a hurry and had no training in firing a bazooka. The round fell about 25 feet short of the target. Since no one was firing from the tank, I decided it was abandoned in the mud and we went on out of the river basin and up the slope toward the huge pill box.

Now the Germans had a rather simple way of directing the enemy into a narrow space that was in front of the machine gun port hole. The method was simple. Put a mine field on the right and one on the left of the path they wanted us to follow. They even put up a single wire fence and hung signs that said "minen." Since I had developed a sincere respect for mines, I walked into the machine gun path between the fences with the "minen" signs. We treaded quietly past the huge concrete bunker/ pill box in front of us. It never fired a shot.

We later found that there was a good reason for no one firing at us. The bunker had been shelled by our own "Big Bertha" artillery gun, the biggest of our artillery weapons. It was a 240 millimeter gun and the spotter that aimed the gun from a distance was responsible for one direct hit. It turned out that there were two German soldiers in the bunker but they were shell-shocked from the exploding shell and were back in the corner of the bunker all shook up.

We proceeded on to the top of the ridge and dug in for the night. We planned to go on the next morning into the little town that lay in a valley. We could see German soldiers retreating and trying to salvage one of their wheel-mounted 88 guns. I fired at them as they fled, but saw no signs of coming close. At the quarter mile distance they might have been scared a little.

As our company settled in for the night, I was designated the job of contacting everyone on the left side and Sergeant Wise everyone on the right. I found one older man that was shaking like a leaf and I told him to report to the medics the next morning. In his condition he was of no value to anyone. When I got back to the command post, Sergeant Wise had not shown up and never did that night. Found him later in front of the line and hiding in a German foxhole. He said that he got lost and some Germans started firing at him. Remember that it was dark. He jumped into the first foxhole he came to- fortunately it was empty. He stayed there the rest of the night.

We marched to the town and for the first time used "marching fire" as we went toward the Germans. Sergeant Wise was near the German lines and said that marching fire was the most effective way of traveling. He said he wouldn't stick a hand out of the foxhole. Marching fire was simply shooting from the hip as we walked toward our objective without using our sights for accuracy.

Attacking the town was mostly uneventful but there was a personal happening that nearly cost my life. We had entered the town and I had stopped in a corral and was standing under a shed roof. A U.S. tank came across a field and started firing a machine gun. Every 5th bullet the machine gun shot was red. This tracer-bullet was designed to show what you were hitting. I have no reason to think that they were shooting at me, all I know was that the red tracer bullet appeared to be coming straight at me when it hit a fence post and veered off in a different direction. Saved again.

Crawford and Marching Fire

Crawford was one of those men you couldn't forget. If he had done just half of the things he told you, you could not forget Crawford. I recall him receiving a letter from home and his parents were reporting that the food situation was bad due to shortages in certain food items. They concluded that they would make it through the winter ok since they

were able to accumulate 20 pork hams that were hanging on the back porch. Crawford remarked that "that must have been a big hog to have had 20 hams!" At least he understood where hams came from. He obviously was not a farm boy.

Now back to Germany and our advancing on a bigger town than usual. Three of us were walking across a wheat field, and a jack rabbit jumped up and ran in front of us. A good opportunity for practicing our marching fire. Using our sights was not necessary- the puffs of dust would tell us where we were hitting. First a broken leg and then a few more shots and it was all over for Jack. From all that we could see the town was empty. We found out later that perhaps over a thousand soldiers and citizens of the town had gone to an underground shelter for protection.

Since we had reached our objective we figured a two-story house would be satisfactory for catching up on our sleep. Beds were all made and enough for our use. As a soldier you slept in your uniforms so you'd be ready for anything to happen. And it happened. Orders were to assemble in the street and be ready to march in one hour, going to march toward our next objective at daylight. Roll-call was made and everyone was there except, you might have guessed, Crawford.

We looked everywhere and no Crawford. Finally, upstairs in a bedroom we could hear some heavy breathing. Crawford was behind the bed and out like a light. He and a friend of his (I use the word "friend" with reservation) had found a bottle of Schnapps (German whiskey) and the friend had talked Crawford into drinking all of the bottle. We were not able to sober him up in the time we had left to be ready to march.

By giving his equipment to others to carry and by putting Crawford between two of us, we were able to march/ drag him along until he finally sobered up and could handle himself. The rules stated that you would always be ready for any order all the time. Crawford didn't qualify and by the rules could have been arrested and court-marshaled. And the results could have been the firing squad. At least we avoided that penalty.

We marched the rest of the night and on the morrow we reached our objective, a highway along a big grove of trees. Our platoon reached a small bunch of trees at the edge of the field and the men from another platoon had reached another bunch of trees across the field, about a quarter of a mile away. Our officer in charge wanted to let them know and wanted information from them and without radio contact, the only communication we could make was by walking across the field. I volunteered and took another man with me. We got there without incident but on the way back things began to happen.

The field was muddy and difficult walking through, so on the return we agreed to walk on the blacktop road that was there waiting for our use. As we were moving down the road we were interrupted by two Germans that had their foxhole dug in the road ditch. All of a sudden two rifles were seen with a leaflet each. The leaflets were dropped by the air force and promised safe passage if they would surrender. Remember, we had crossed the field about 75 yards in front of them and it would have been easy for them to have killed both of us. We motioned them to get out of their hole and to march down the road with us.

We had just started when German machine gun fire started shooting at the four of us. And, almost as if by a signal, machine gun fire from the American side also started shooting at the four of us. We jumped back into the foxhole. It had been dug along a gas pipeline and we could use the pipe for a seat. We couldn't see anyone while sitting. So I stood up and about the same time our artillery began shelling the trees across the road behind us. Having been under artillery shelling from our side many times, I was sure the trees were the target and we were in no danger. However, the German soldier was very scared and pulled on my trouser leg and motioned me to sit down on the pipe. He held up three fingers and tried to tell me that for three days they had been shelled. When the shelling ended we got back on the road and went to our platoon without further incident.

I had been having some dizzy spells and reported to the medics and they sent me to the hospital for a physical checkup. As I look back on my condition, I have concluded that I had reached my limit of mental torment- battle fatigue would maybe describe my problem.

At the hospital, I was put to bed and was given all kinds of tests, mostly "mental conversations" with a doctor. Some things happened that I hope will be of interest. First and possibly the most interesting was the man who carried his helmet everywhere he went- to meals and even to the latrine. Why the helmet? It was a souvenir that he planned to take home with him and it would be of value for anyone to keep. On the right side were two holes made by a German machine gun. When you were hit by a German machine gun, you could count on being hit twice and that is what happened. The two bullets had entered from the right rear and made a complete trip around the helmet and exited just above the left ear side and had left two grooves made as the bullets circled the inside of the helmet. Seeing was believing. He was not about to let anyone steal his miracle.

I never expected mail while in the hospital but it did catch up with me. A bundle of 96 letters and only two that had a similar name but was not mine to receive. I was glad to get the old letters, no matter how long it took to get to me. The couple of the letters that I knew were not for me had a return address of some manufacturing company and was a news letter.

Tidbits to Remember

There is always something else that comes to mind that should be remembered and told.

There were not many farm houses. It seemed that most of the farmers lived in town and went out in the country to do their farming. All except this one home that was "self-contained" in the country. It had a house and barns for cattle and work horses and was enclosed on all sides, making it a small community by itself. We went in the house and were looking for soldiers or anyone we might find. It appeared to have been a German place for soldiers to stay.

As I was surveying the house, I found nothing upstairs and headed for the basement area. One U.S. soldier was already in the basement and had found a lady of about 25 years. All three of us had come to the same conclusion that we knew what the American wanted and the German had already determined that she was not going to be a willing participant. Since I outranked him, I told him to leave her alone and take her as a prisoner to the captain. I'm sure I did the right thing by her, but it didn't work out like I had planned. The soldier got permission to take her back to the back area where the prisoners were kept. I am sure the lady was in the house to entertain the German soldiers but that did not give the American soldier the same privileges.

At another town that we took they had a barn full of milk cows that were still in the stanchions waiting to be milked when the farmer ran off. One of our men caught and killed a hen and cooked her for our evening meal. Along with the milk that was ready for the taking, we had a feast. We invited the captain and he approved of our conduct. The cows were let loose from the stanchions.

After another taking of a hill in front of a little town, we were told to dig our foxholes and wait until tomorrow to attack the town. About 4 p.m. we received orders to back the line of foxholes about fifty yards. The orders were not accepted with pleasure but orders were orders. So we moved back and dug new holes. At 10 p.m. "Bedcheck Charley" flew over and dropped a bunch of personnel bombs along the line of the original foxholes. Bedcheck Charley was always on time at 10 p.m. This was the first time for us with a bombing run.

A couple of things that should be added: One was the U.S. air force and another was the buzz bombs that the Germans fired at London. The B-17 bombers flew too high for infantry troops to be able to see them. In contrast, the B-24 bombers flew much lower and we would watch them as they flew over the front lines and into Germany, making their bombing runs.

The B-24 bombers had two primary problems from anti-aircraft guns positioned on the ground and from the German fighter aircraft that was very active as soon as our bombers crossed into German territory. Since the problem of fighter planes was serious and the only protection was from the machine guns mounted in the bombers, the B-24's flew in tight formation so that they could help protect each other. The machine guns were mounted in the wings to fire ahead and the top turret could fire to either side and above. Then the poor tail gunner was to protect the rear.

I never saw any planes being attacked by German aircraft, but anti-aircraft guns was a different situation when the planes flew over, both on their way to cities in Germany and then on their return trip on their way back to England. As I recall, they must have been flying in groups of 15 or 18 bombers and on the crossing of the front line both ways you could see the bursts of the exploding shells. And since the bombers were clustered close together for protection from fighter planes, every trip we would see two or three bombers hit and come down and crash. The sad part was that sometimes you did not see even one parachute bringing down a bomber crewman floating to safety. When the bomber came down and no parachute could be seen, you knew that all the crew was lost.

Now to the problem of buzz-bombs. The Germans had developed the ability of firing a huge payload of destruction without the loss of planes or men and could strike London by firing from inside Germany. The ground troops could hear the bombs being fired and could follow their flight as they were on their way to London. The engines that propelled the bomb were noisy and the nervous part for the infantry was the fact that the bombs crossed our lines at a very low altitude and when the engines would cut out we would wonder how far this one would go. The engine would start roaring again and we would know it was on its way to London. Every buzz bomb that was fired would stop and start its engine. Never did see one fail to complete its journey.

This part is written to relate another story of a good soldier that will go unnamed. Why unnamed?

Because I can't remember his name after 55 years! Let's call him George. He was a 5 foot 9 inches a 190 pound man like I was in those days. He was not in my platoon but we did meet every once in a while at the same dinner table. And as usual when the meal was finished we would push back our plates and, without a verbal challenge, our elbows would be on the table and a quick game of arm wrestling would ensue. We would lock our hands together in a tight squeeze and then the game would start. George won the first time or two and then I would catch on to the timing and won my share of the bouts. It became a never-ending game for both of us.

George lost the last game, and that is what I want to relate to you. The medicine of Imodium was unknown in those days, but there was need of such medicine whenever a soldier got a bad case of dysentery. Time was of the greatest importance. We soldiers called it a bad case of the GI's. The "GI's" was a quick way of saying Government Issued. And when the GI's hit, you don't waste any time or you'll regret it.

Now to the situation with George. When you are on the front you never knew who was moving in the darkness, so guards were told to protect the rest of the troops from any enemy that might try to infiltrate the area. The proper password would identify anyone that was told to stop or halt. George had a bad case of the GI's and was hurrying to the latrine. "Halt, who goes there?" the guard asked. George said, "You know me," and kept going towards his destination. Now the sad part: one rifle shot and one dead George. Was the guard right or wrong? He did as he had been trained to do. George had been trained to stop and give the password. Since he was not in my company, the information was told to me.

The next day we made our move to take the little town in front of us and here came the company of tanks to help in case we needed help. You'll recall my past experiences with tanks, so you can understand I was not impressed. This bunch was different. They came roaring through our lines shooting up the town in front of them. The tank commander was directing traffic from his position on the tank. The turret door was open and the tank commander

was giving orders since he was above the tank turret from his waist up. He showed no fear. He was a black man and my impression of black men soon changed. We had no problems taking our town. We had the kind of help we needed.

Now back to my being in the hospital. I received orders to report to one of the cigarette camps. What was a cigarette camp? The cigarette companies furnished a pack of cigarettes to everyone, and for thanks, the camps were named after the company. Camp Home Run, Camp Lucky Strike, etc. Even if you didn't smoke you took the free cartons and sold them to the French for spending money or whatever favors you desired.

I remember one camp I was sent to was a camp for receiving our own men who had been prisoners of the Germans. At that camp were also folks from the United Service Organization (USO) and they specialized in furnishing coffee and doughnuts. I remember one man that had been starved at his prisoner of war camp and went through the doughnut line several times. He did not realize that his stomach had shrunk and that the combination of hot coffee and doughnuts would swell and his stomach burst and he died. The USO put a limit on trips through the line after that.

Also at that same camp was a short landing strip and I saw my first P-51 fighter plane there. It was standing on the concrete runway, warming up the engine. When the pilot was ready to take off he revved up the motor and held the brakes. When the tires began to slide he released the brakes and he was airborne almost immediately. I was much impressed.

Another thing that happened at the camp was one of my friends and his friend were visiting in the tent when the barrel stove went out and we got cold. My friend had some kerosene and poured it into the stove. He looked for live coals but didn't see any and then next thing we knew flames shot out of the opening on the top of the stove and my friend was on fire. He ran out of the tent and his buddy was faster than he was and tackled him and put out the fire. I was shipped to camp in Le Harve, France, soon after so I never saw him again.

Le Harve, France, was home to Camp Home Run and was designed for small units to either come in or go out of the area. The small units could be either single persons or small groups. The USO used our camp as a come in and go out area. For example, the USO brought entertainment from the states.

One man I recall was an amateur ping pong player that was rated in the top ten of amateurs in the United States. He was good and proved it while in camp. We held a tournament each weekend for three weeks. Remember that my college days were almost shortened due to ping pong. Over there it didn't bother my grades if I played in each tournament. Each week I ended up in the finals with the USO man. He let me get that far. And I'm not joking- he told me of his time while playing in the United States:

A sergeant wanted to play ping pong and our USO man was willing. They played three or four games and our USO man let the sergeant win enough points that the USO man would only win by two or three points. After three games of almost winning the sergeant pulled out a five dollar bill and said, "Let's make this interesting." The USO man didn't want to wager but the sergeant insisted. So the USO man decided to teach the sergeant a lesson. He matched his five-spot and proceeded to "skunk" the sergeant. Didn't let him make even one point. He picked up both fives and left with the sergeant just standing there.

So my conclusion was that he let me make a good game out of the finals. The USO man was so good that he put so much top spin on the ball that it appeared to come off the table parallel to the table top. No bounce. By playing defensively and being young and active, it looked good to the crowd that was watching and cheering me on.

On the shipment home schedule there was a black man that came to the office to complete his paperwork and was struggling with his duffle bag. It was heavy and when we asked him what he had in the bag he replied, "A chunk of concrete from a German bunker. There's a lot of men that will give good money for a small chunk of that." I couldn't see any profit in carrying it all the way to New York and then breaking it up in small pieces and hoping to sell it for a big profit. Made me wonder how much he had paid for it in the first place.

And there was the officer that came in wanting to fill his fountain pen. There was ink at the far end of the counter. He went down and proceeded to fill his pen and after he was gone, I looked at the ink bottle and found that the label on the bottle said "correction fluid." I was sure happy to have never seen that officer again.

I found an announcement that read, "Select a college course at Shrivenham University in Shrivenham, England- American professors." I signed up and was selected to go at government expense. Shrivenham was about 60 miles north of London. Signed up for a dairy class. Thought it would be easy for a student from a dairy farm. It should have been a push-over except for the weekends spent in London. Our income was very thin. My roommate and I purchased an electric iron and I used my study time to iron shirts and trousers for those that could afford it. My transcript from OSU has a D on my record for the class from Shrivenham. I possibly learned more from my trips to London on the weekends than from Shrivenham University.

I found a church to attend in north London and went there each Sunday. While I was in London, a family invited me home to eat with them and that was an experience to remember. Nice meal if you like everything made from vegetables. Right in the middle of the meal the lights went out. The husband asked for coins and when he had found what he needed, he went out to the meter and the lights came back on.

There were cheap rooms to rent that had several bunk beds in one big room. The maid came with the rent money. She did a good job of making the beds and cleaning up the room. But I'm sure she got very little in wages. Her primary purpose of working there was to find herself a husband that would take her to the United States. Not my type so I didn't fall for her game. In the park there was always a bunch of girls that had the same plan in mind. I did meet one very pretty British girl that I found out that had married a US soldier and when D-day came, her husband was among those that went. She never heard from him again. He was probably among those that were killed on the beaches of Normandy.

I applied for and got a furlough and spent a week in Belfast, Ireland. North Ireland was open for visitors but they were not allowed in the south. My relatives came from the Belfast area anyway and that is why I wanted to go there- to find out about the McNallys. I found one McNally that was friendly. He said that the McNally clan came over from Scotland and were in the cattle business. I was afraid to ask what kind of cattle business- cattle thieves was a category I did not want to hear about. The man was nice and took me out to a farmer that spelled the name the right way. It was a cold day in the winter and the man did not even invite us into the house to visit. So I told my friend that I had seen enough of the McNallys.

I did ask him why all the different ways to spell McNally existed. He explained that it was real easy- if a young McNally from North Ireland met and wanted to marry a pretty lass from the south, he could not be successful with his name and had to change it to one of several different ways so that she could accept his proposal of marriage. So now we know why there's McAnallys, McNeelys and other different spellings.

I did see the original Ferguson Tractor factory. I met and stayed with a family that were of the Church of Christ in Belfast. One of the daughters was a pretty and loving girl- I didn't ask her to marry me but all indication was that she would have said yes. A little young for me- she was about five as I recall.

Furlough was over and back to France and by then the point system was good for me to be on the go-home list. Came over in a Kaiser tub and found the same ship was anchored for boarding for the trip home. There were two major reasons for not being real pleased with the Sea Wolf. It was a flat-bottomed boat and the radio was good for only 50 miles so we had to stay with and follow another Kaiser tub. The weather was wicked the first day out and the sea was rough. Since the Kaiser tubs were flat-bottomed, as the waves got bigger the ship would roll up and the

bow would come out of the water and then the flat bottom would hit and the ship would shake and quiver from stem to stern. Everything came up from my stomach and I discovered what bile looked and tasted like. It isn't good.

The captain of the other Kaiser tub wanted to take a shorter route to New York by taking what was known as the Northern Route. Our ship had to follow because of the radio problem. On Sunday morning the ocean was calm and we went to church services. Out at 12 p.m. and we were in for a surprise- little patches of snow floating on the surface of the water. It did not snow while we were in church. The sky was clear. What we saw were chunks of ice that had been snow last winter floating on the surface of the water.

By 1 p.m. the scattered chunks of floating ice had become a field of snow. Just like a snow storm in the wheat fields of Oklahoma or Kansas. The normal ice flows that break loose from the Arctic area had started their journey south about one month earlier than normal. We were now plowing through ice that was averaging six to eight feet thick and the chunks were so packed together that you would have been able to walk anywhere if you had been crazy enough to want to.

Our ship kept plowing on through the ice flow because if we had stopped the ice would have closed in on our propellers and that would have meant being stuck out in the middle of the ocean. So we and our sister ship kept on moving. The other ship did have a scare when the bow of the ship received a rip in the bow and in the front number one hold was filled with water. A lot of take-home items were soaked and lost their value. Our ship withstood the plowing without any problem and escaped being damaged.

Some of the men tried to get me to go below deck and play pinochle. I refused. There was too much to see and besides the noise sounded like a rock crusher below deck. In addition, the icebergs were all around us and I wanted to see what we hit. Finally as evening approached the ice flow had been passed through and our journey was uneventful for the rest of the ocean voyage.

Home again.

I should mention that all the stairs were impassable since all the high finance men were placing their money on the roll of dice. Anyone that wanted in on the dice game had to sell their watches or other valuables. The men that were running the dice tables had all the money and watches hung from their wrists to above their elbow. I'm glad I never got the gambling fever.

The sighting of the big girl with the torch in her hand was a welcome sight as we pulled into the harbor in New York City. The first troops to arrive in the good old USA had bands and parades to show the troops that the home folks did care and to thank them for the victory. Well that was for the troops that arrived home the first summer after the war had been won, not the one-year later troops. All we got was a small tug boat squirting a stream of water as we sailed past and the band on the dock did not show much enthusiasm either. They had a job to do and they played a couple of tunes for us. We were not really surprised. We were in New York but still were not home yet. I knew the welcome that my folks would give me is what I needed.

Final Remarks

I had looked all over the USA, France, Germany, England, and Ireland but found no one that

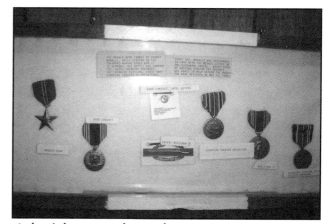

Aubrey's honors and awards.

Awards and memories.

Veteran shares his experience in memoirs; wants future generations to know life-impacting realities of war

By DAWN QUANE

Sentinel Staff Writer

Aubrey McNally, a World War II veteran and McPherson resident since 1952, has written his memoirs for posterity. He wants not only his children and grandchildren to know the life-impacting realities of war, but to share his harrowing experience with others as well.

McNally wants to encourage education regarding WWII as early as possible for our youth. His hope is that kids won't have to go through what he and many others did. McNally's message is, "Avoid war at any cost."

After the bombing of Pearl Harbor, McNally knew it wouldn't be long before many from the United States would be called to war. McNally was a college student in Oklahoma at the time. He eventually volunteered in the Enlisted Reserve Corp; it was 1942.

The college guys were told they would be allowed to finish out the school year -- they almost made it. McNally said

WORLD WAR II

Aubrey McNally receives news while still stationed in France -- the war is over. McNally said there was much excitement at the news.

found some protection in the six-inch tank tracks. He was hit by shrapnel twice during that incident. The first hit was to the head -- it dented his helmet, the second went through his coat, trousers, ammo belt, underwear and broke the skin just above his right kidney, McNally said the hot shrapnel prevented a lot of bleeding. His friend Maas was not so lucky.

McNally said not many knew what they were there for -- being shot at every day -- but Hitler had killed a lot of people and somebody had to stop him; it had to be done.

The troops were sent to go in and break down Hitler's power structure, to remove the atrocity.

The next stop for McNally and the 102nd was Aachen, Germany, the locale where the Battle of the Bulge was fought. McNally's most poignant memory of this assignment was lying in his foxhole, looking at the pill boxes and considering the very real possibility of facing the machine gun fire.

During a short reprieve from Aachen, McNally recalls the

other "adventures" in his memoirs -- memories from 55 years ago that he recalls vividly, as if they had happened yesterday -- the life-long impact of war.

The ride home in the spring of 1945 was apropos -- the troop spent the trip dodging icebergs. McNally was happy to see Lady Liberty and anxious to get back to his folks.

McNally said war is an experience you never forget -- war is hell, and he hopes today's youth won't ever have to go through what he did.

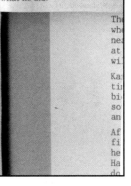

The
whe
nea
at
wi

Ka
ti
bi
so
an

Af
fi
he
Ha
do

they were half-way through their second semester when they were called to go for basic training. He was sent to Camp Maxey in Texas.

Just before D-Day, June 6, 1944, McNally found out his division, the 102nd, would be sent to France. Fortunately, McNally was given a furlough and ended up being home on D-Day. Shortly after, he was sent to France.

McNally's division traveled on The Sea Wolf. The quarters were extremely tight and the ship was not able to travel in a straight path due to the possibility of being torpedoed by German U-boats. Many of the men suffered terrible seasickness, but thankfully he didn't, said McNally.

Upon arrival in France, the men had to be sent to Germany by train. McNally explained the trip would be best described as the ride in the "sardine can" -- sleeping could only be done on one's side and there were no restrooms.

The first area McNally was sent to was an area that had been deserted by the Germans. His squad's job was to take a defensive position and make sure the Germans didn't come back into that area. It wasn't long before they were sent on to attack the little town of Flosdorf, Germany.

A soldier didn't often make friends, said McNally, because the friend might not be there the next day or even the next hour -- this lesson was sadly learned at Flosdorf.

McNally had made friends

with a man by the name of Rowland Maas. They had been together since basic training -- he died at Flosdorf. The orders had been given to cross a beet field and take the town. McNally said the Germans allowed the U.S. troops to get 100 yards onto the field and then started shooting. The tanks were taken out immediately and the infantrymen were stranded in the middle of the field with only beet plants for cover.

Every hour on the hour, the Germans would sweep the field with artillery. McNally said he

opportunity to attend church services.

He remembers considering skipping the partaking of communion because it wasn't the appropriate day of the week but, as McNally put it, "I was not given a promise that I would live to see another chance to partake."

McNally included many

Dorothy's ration book.

suited me or could meet the high standards that I had set. Couldn't find a Momma Dorothy anywhere-that is, until I got back to college and attended the first church get-together for college students. There she was, a Christian, a farm girl, and pretty too. And when you are a man who has looked all over half the universe for a girl and find her right at home, you don't look any farther. And her white sweater was out of this world too!

Tomorrow, August 30, 1999, we will celebrate our 52nd anniversary. Along with three daughters, one son, and their spouses, we have seven grandsons and three granddaughters and three great-grand-daughters (two adopted from Russia) and one great-grandson.

I want to thank God for his protection and the blessings that have been mine to enjoy.

Praise to his name.

My Life as a
World War II Nurse

by Alice Nelson

THIS BOOK IS DEDICATED TO:

My brother Paul and all of

his companions in war..

My brothers John and Paul got me involved in being interested in the war and joining the army. Paul graduated from high school and was enjoying himself. He and his friends were looking around for what they were going to do next when Paul was drafted in the spring of 1943. He left our home in Minnesota on June 20 for Camp Robert, California, where he received his basic training, and two weeks before Christmas, he was on the way for the European theatre.

On arrival in England, he was assigned to the headquarters company and whatever his particular duties were, we do not know. But he wrote that he considered himself the luckiest boy in the army. But this joy didn't last. Just as he was assigned to a course in engineering with the Specialized Training Program after the end of his basic training, that program was discontinued.

It seems that after leaving England, his mail never caught up with him for more than two months at a time. His typical characteristic expression was always, "It isn't too bad." Even then, in rain and cold, eating "K" rations and going for weeks without as much as a change of stockings or a chance to wash, he tried to be cheerful when he did have a chance to clean up and write a letter, although it is with

My brother Paul Carlstedt.

noticeable difficulty that he did so.

He soon became sick with scarlet fever. When he was about ready to be dismissed from the hospital after about six weeks, he had to undergo a severe operation for mastoids. He was finally dismissed on June 7, after more than three months in the hospital.

The invasion of Normandy 1944 had taken place the day before he was dismissed, so he was left behind and after a month's recuperation, was assigned to an infantry company and shipped across the Channel. His first letter from "somewhere in France" was written July 7. The next letter was from "somewhere in Belgium," probably written in August, and then in September, he was "somewhere in Germany" which, as we have seen, turned out to be in the neighborhood of Aachen.

On October 2 from "somewhere in Germany" he had just been granted a rest period behind the lines after six weeks on the front. He had shortly before finally received mail, twenty-two letters at once. He says, "After reading letters from home, it leaves the body and soul separated. It is a tortuous state to be in, but please keep writing anyway." He had just received his pay, too, for three months, and sent some of it home to take care of the arrears on church dues and missions.

There are some quotations from his letters to indicate the thoughts and longings of some of the soldier boys away from home, and in situations of danger and privations that we little understand.

"It isn't too bad, others have it worse."

"Pray for the boys. They need your prayers."

"We went to church, but the sermon was over before we found the place. I came in time for communion anyways."

"Pray that the war will be over soon so that we may all come home."

"God definitely means more to me than He did before as well as to most of the fellows over here."

"No matter how tough things get, I can always find plenty of things to be thankful for."

"When I see you next, I may not be much older, but I will be wiser. I know more than before about the stuff humans are made of."

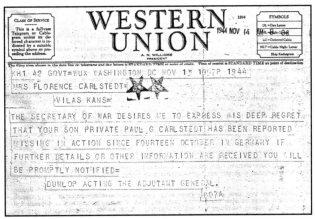

The telegram declaring Paul missing in action.

According to expectations, he would be changed off ever so often, as a battalion runner. Three days out and then three days rest. Accordingly he had a chance to rest also on October 14th, but some special urgency of war seems to have upset the schedule and forced him to be out on the front then.

Paul was declared "missing in action" on October 14, 1944, but it was years later that his body was found.

It was August 30, 1948, that his remains were found and November 30 before he was buried in Ardennes Cemetery. The government presumed he was dead on October 15, 1944, but it was a year later before our family received news from the government, making about four years in which we wondered whether he was dead or alive.

Paul's burial site in Ardennes Cementery.

The family was very happy to receive some definite word about him. A close boyfriend at the time couldn't understand how one could be so happy over news of the death of a brother, but knowing someone is dead is so much better news than wondering what his circumstances might be.

Two letters from close friends of Paul's were found with his remains. Our family knew the two young people very well and so were satisfied that it was indeed Paul who was buried at Ardennes.

The next news that would us even happier would be to know what he was doing in England at the Headquarters Company, when he claimed to have "the best job in the Army." I wrote to Army Headquarters early on, but was told that their records had been destroyed in a fire and they could tell me nothing.

It is easy to picture him seeking cover, possibly wounded in a bomb crater, as some other bombs exploded nearby. Perhaps he was killed and buried at once with a bomb attack. Anyway, God knew the best time to take him. In the end he is not dead to us. He is still speaking to those who knew him and corresponded with him. He remains as young as he was, 21 years, 9 months, and 14 days. He knows something we do not, and will say some of those things when he sees us next. Perhaps he is waiting more to see us than we, to see Christ and him.

After graduating from high school, I spent one year at the Lutheran Bible Institute and two years at Augsburg College before registering for nurses training at Bethesda Hospital School of Nursing in St. Paul, Minnesota. By the time I graduated from the nursing program September 14, 1944, I had accepted a post-graduate course at Highland Hospital in Asheville, North Carolina.

Paul's story was very important to me and to my choice to join the Army Nurse Corps in 1945. I joined the Cadet Corps, a program of the United States to prepare nurses for service. The women in this program had to promise to stay active as nurses for at least six months, for which they received a small salary. There was an urgent need for nurses because of WW II.

St. Paul Pioneer

ST. PAUL, MINN., FRIDAY, JANUARY 19, 1945

Enlist In Nurse Corps

The urgent call for more nurses for both Army and Navy has resulted in 97 recruits since Jan. 8, Mrs. William A. Nyman, secretary of the St. Paul Red Cross Nurse Recruitment committee, said Thursday. Five nurses who arrived at the recruiting desk at the same time, are pictured above. From left to right are Catherine Haas, 1875 Laurel ave., Navy; Alice Carlstedt of Vilas, Kan., nursing staff member at Bethesda hospital, Army; Mary Esenik of Eveleth, Army; Peggy Re-

Alice in uniform.

I remember hearing the news of the bombing of Pearl Harbor. After one brother was missing in action, I felt the need to do something for my country. I went down to the local recruitment office to enlist in the Army Nurse Corps. I called a number of my classmates, suggesting that they should enroll too. We went to the St. Paul Red Cross Nurse Recruitment center and enrolled together.

By January 1945, I was given a release to make application for military service. In the meantime, my brother David had joined the Army and was serving in France. He was wounded in February 1945, and if that had happened before I enlisted I would have hesitated, thinking that was enough military risk for one family.

I was first appointed to go to Camp Carson in Colorado. Most of the patients there had foot problems, following the Battle of the Bulge. It was a very deadly fight during the winter that created a lot of foot and leg problems. Camp Carson was a difficult assignment. Most of the young men had or needed amputation of arms or legs.

On Easter Sunday our company (about 15-20 women) drove to The Garden of the Gods for Eas-

ter Sunday Services. There was singing and musical instruments that played. We were captivated by the scenery, the music and just being together in that beautiful setting on Easter Sunday.

Following basic training at Camp Carson, April 1945, I was sent to Fort Leonard Wood, Missouri, for a short stay. A fairly new Army training location at the time, eventually more than 300,000 soldiers passed through Fort Leonard Wood on their way to service in every World War II theater of operation. There was a serious shortage of nurses, and we worked twelve-hour shifts. Not long after the end of the war in 1945, training declined at Fort Leonard Wood and ceased completely by the spring of 1946.

The war with Germany was over, Hitler had committed suicide, and I was sent to Fort Lewis, Washington to train for duty in the South Pacific. We were to replace nurses who had served there.

Fort Leonard Wood, Missouri.

Bivouac at Fort Lewis, Washington.

General Somervell.

Part of our training was a two-week bivouac where we lived in tents, ate out of mess kits, and washed in our helmets, preparing for the South Pacific.

By the time our training was over at Fort Lewis, the focus of the war was on Japan, and we were not sent to the South Pacific. Instead, I was assigned to Ashford General Hospital in White Sulphur Springs, West Virginia. Formerly the luxurious Greenbrier Hotel, this was Sam Snead's hometown and his famous golf course was near the greenbrier. The Army had turned the resort into a temporary Army hospital. This is where I learned to play golf, a game I played most of my adult life.

While stationed there I had the privilege of caring for General Somervell, while my good friend took care of President Dwight D. Eisenhower. We each received autographed pictures of our "patients" soon after. The pictures were kept on the mantel above the fireplace as long as we were at White Sulphur Springs.

General Somervell was responsible for the U.S. Army's logistics during World War II, head of the Construction Division of the Quartermaster Corps. His most well known project was the Pentagon in Washington, D.C.

It was while I was at Ashford, our family received news that my brother Paul was missing in action. My brother David had returned from the service and was attending Augustana College, where my brother John had attended earlier.

I was soon assigned to Pratt General Hospital, formerly the Miami Biltmore Hotel in Coral Gables, Florida. My last two assignments were in stark contrast to the earlier ones, especially our training at Fort Lewis, Washington.

The decision about what to next after separating from the service twenty months later was harder than my previous decisions. I chose to attend Augustana College on the GI Bill where I enrolled March 1, 1947, and graduated with a Bachelor's Degree in Nursing one year later. I went to work at Wadsworth Veterans Hospital in Los Angeles.

When one of my classmates took a job as a Speech Correctionist at the Crippled Children's School in Jamestown, N.D. and they needed an R.N. to serve as head nurse, she recommended me. Ironically, the only specialty I didn't consider was pediatric nursing. But, I received a telegram asking me to fill that need and I accepted, believing it would help me to know whether or not public health nursing was what I wanted to do.

At the Crippled Children's School I was privileged to learn to know Dr. Ann Carlson. Dr. Carlson was a remarkable woman who forged ahead despite having lost both arms and legs. She made a deep impression on everyone who knew her.

While I was working at the Children's Hospital, Jamestown experienced a terrible flood. The

Dr. Ann Carlson.

Alice Nelson now.

children were all evacuated and there was no way to get around except to wade through the floodwater. We did find a boat that was then used to float through the rooms picking up whatever we could find to salvage.

At one time during the two years I spent in Jamestown, the head of the Children's Bureau visited and suggested that I ought to go to the University of Chicago and study nursing of children because that particular course emphasized child development, something that would be right for my job. That didn't appeal to me; after all, I didn't intend to spend my life giving childcare. I had been closely involved in raising my seven younger siblings and had done au pair work as a college student. That was enough, I thought. I saw myself working with adults

if I stayed in public health. But when my boss was asked to start a School for Handicapped Children at Iowa State University, he asked me to join him as Head Nurse when he had it going, that sounded like an interesting change and I accepted, September 1950.

I did enroll at the University of Chicago on the GI Bill and received my Master's Degree in Nursing of Children, June 1954. While I was in Chicago, I met Armour Nelson. We were later married. Armour was from the Salemsborg, Kansas, area. When Armour retired with heart trouble we moved to Lindsborg to make our home in Armour's home area.

I Suppose You Thought I Was Never Going To Write Again:
George Osborne, Jr's War Letters

by Emily Jones

THIS BOOK IS DEDICATED TO:

The memory of George Osborn, Jr.
and those that left this world
before sharing their stories.

George Osborne, Jr. was your typical Kansas boy when World War II erupted. Leaving his "mom and pop" in McPherson, for training in August 1944, he wrote home as often and dutifully as time allowed to his mother, relatives, and friends. His concern for them is apparent as he frequently inquired about their health, the weather, and if there was news of anyone else he knew who was involved in the war. George Osborne's letters to his parents are insightful and poignant from his training days in various camps to his involvement in the occupation of Japan after the War. His letters invite us in to share his thoughts, fears, concerns, complaints, and the hopes of his youth and future.

His wartime experiences began in the fall of 1944, when Jr., as he signed his letters, enlisted in the United States Army as a senior at McPherson High School. He settled into training mode at Camp Hood, Texas. From the outset of his wartime correspondence, he initiates a pattern of apologizing for being unable to write regularly to reply to his loved ones. In early November he writes,

"Dear Mom,

I suppose you think I wasn't going to answer your letters but I just haven't had time to think between cleaning my rifle every night & all the other things. I don't have much time to write letters it seems like I have a lot of letters to answer."

If it is a soldier's right to complain, then Jr. was surely going to take advantage of that notion, and rightly so. The weather would be a constant source of aggravation for the next few years. The heat, cold, and rain never quite suited him. Descriptions of the weather wherever he was stationed had a consistent presence in his letters. Jr. was also always very curious as to how the weather would be treating the folks back home. On November 28, he made such an inquiry to his mother.

"Dear Mom:

How is every thing going at home ok I

hope, I suppose it is pretty cold there now it is pretty nice weather down here now except for it being cloudy all day long."

Jr. shared with his mother what camp life was like. When one wasn't overwhelmed with routine and training, boredom had a tendency to set in. He described to her range practice and the subsequent cleaning of his rifle. At times, routine was shaken up by the business and less glamorous side of the service, in which he had to receive injections, sign up for insurance, and get food and pay stamps in order. October 21 was of paperwork.

"Dear Mom,

How is every thing at home geting along Fine I hope we just got back from taking our shots one in each arm now we are laying in our barrack waiting to move to Co. B we haven't done anything except wait we go to chow at 5:30 in the morning & at 12:00 noon. We got our payroll book this morning. We also signed up for insurance & Bonds I am sending a couple…of papers home about the Insurance & Bonds."

Jr. also explained to his mother in this particular letter that he has recently learned the tenure of his tour of duty.

"The talk around here we are in the occupational for the Duration & two years. The duration might be all right but the two years after ain't going to be no picnick."

Between explaining the goings on of camp, Jr. makes small requests of his mother. His tone is apologetic that he should be such a bother when asking for funds so that he could purchase a few creature comforts from the PX.

"Dear Mom:

Say if it isn't to much to ask I would like to have a shoe stamp & also some gas stamps of the boys I have been running around with brother living in Houston & they let us use there car every once in a while as long as we can get the gas which the coupons are perty hard to get"

In the same letter, one can detect a hint of homesickness and regret that he can't get around to answering all the letters that he has received.

"I should go to bed now so I can get up in the morning & we will be out in the field late tomorrow night so write when you can maybe I can get time to write you more letter If you see any of the Boys tell them hello for me & I will right when I find time which is very limited"

When the new year rolled around, Jr. began to ponder the possibilities on where he would be sent next.

"When we get through with our training here this I suppose most of the boys will go to Ft. Ord, Calif, & the Rest will go to FT. Meade. As far as I know now I will go to Camp Benning, Ga. for 4 or 6 weeks more training 1 week of physical training if you fall out during that week you get a 5 day furlough & then get shiped across as an infantry man which I am right now so you see you don't lose anything if you do wash out & if you don't you get 10 days at home & $50 more a month so I don't think it will be such a bad deal."

Indeed, he did spend a few weeks in Georgia, as he had believed he would, before being sent to Ft. Ord, California. In the first few days of March, he described the weather to his mother, only to conclude that "this country is sure funny." Despite his mild complaints about the shifting cloud cover, he appeared to have truly taken to sunny California.

"I would like to live out here because it is nice & warm all the time you folks should live out here I think because you never feel the winter here."

In this letter, dated March 4, 1945, Jr. acknowledged some earlier news from home that he must have received in a letter from his mother. His brother, Marion, who also was in the service, was due for an upcoming furlough to visit their parents in McPherson.

"I suppose Marion is home now or will be in a short time at least I hope he can get home before he has to go across."

Next, he explains that he will be making his way overseas very soon.

"Speaking of going across we are about to ship now we are getting our ... inspection now we get our hair all cut off yesterday or at least most of it there isn't much left of it think it don't look funny & also feel funny I went"

"Well it looks like we are going out in a very short notice maybe tonight we are all packed up now & ready to move out but that doesn't mean any thing I have a box of stuff of mine & Eugene's stuff we are sending home"

Shortly thereafter, Jr. left the United States behind, sailing for the Pacific Theater. Due to restrictions on censorship, he is never clear on what he will be doing when he reaches his destination, wherever that may be. Yet, he wrote home on April 29 that he was somewhere in the Philippines, which he didn't find too impressive.

*"Dear Mom & Dad
Well here we are on a beautiful island, if you think so I don't, there isn't anything here on this Island they do have little water-*

melons about the size of our mushmelons there at home & also some coconuts that the natives want 3 or 4 packs of cigarettes but I don't have enough for my own…"

Though he found little to admire on the strange foreign island, Jr. was kicking himself for forgetting his camera. He asked his parents to please send it to him, along with some film with his usual "Say will you…" Even more distressing for Jr., he encountered a new kind enemy, besides uncooperative weather, on the island.

"The ants are about to eat me up sitting here on the ground. I never saw them as bad as there are here you can't do any thing with out them getting all over you."

"We have been quarantined here on account of the mumps & it seems every day some one breaks out with them. Dale had them on the boat & I haven't seen him since we got off the boat, he was pretty sick with them on account they …on him. I don't think he knew he had them for 3 or 4 days and then it was too late to do much about them, I think he is getting along ok now."

In a postscript, Jr. makes note of the recent victory in Europe and his hopes that now he is one step closer to returning home.

"It looks like the Germans have given up at least. I think it is a good thing if they wanted any thing left well the sooner the better we get this thing over with the sooner we all get home so we just hope for the best."

Unfortunately for Jr. and all those still involved, it would not be until August that the entire war would come to its devastating end.

By late May, Jr. and his outfit had moved on from Manila. Though he thought it was a "nice town" it couldn't compare to those at home. They continued moving, in what we can assume, in an eastward direction towards Japan. Along the way, Jr. found less and less time to write; yet he can never keep busy enough to avoid feelings of homesickness.

"Dear Mom:

I am going to try & scribble a few lines this afternoon to let you know I am ok, we haven't done a hole lot since we left Manila, but what little we do keeps us so we don't think of home so much of that doesn't keep me from dreaming at night when I am off guard but laying all jokes aside, so far it hasn't been any worse than living at Hood, only we are farther away from home."

He goes on to tell his mother that he has heard from Marion, who was finally shipped to Europe and is now part of the occupation forces in Germany. He then makes an unlucky guess as to what will happen in his case when the war will finally conclude in his part of the world.

"I suppose you have heard from Marion I wrote him a letter a couple of weeks ago so I suppose I will get word from him soon, he probly got in the 15 Army over there in German, occupational army, I hope we don't have that over here but I don't think we will."

Aside from his excitement of crossing the equator, he expresses disappointment that something is preventing the mail from coming through regularly.

"I should be getting some mail one of these days. I haven't gotten any now for letters in a month I don't know what is hold it up, I suppose when I do get some, it will be a whole arm full"

In the first few weeks of June, his mail finally begins to catch up with him, as well as a case of tonsillitis. Bored with the same old movies that play over and over again, he told his mother that there is more training for them coming up, an idea he doesn't relish. With his loathing of heat, thankfully it is only in the morning.

> "Dear Mom:
> Well I guess we have to start training this morning again how I hate to. We have a little…to start the week off good, we only have to train during the morning then we are off till retreat so I guess we can take it, it is about the same as we took in the States. After we had been on the line for two weeks they say we are too young to fight so here we are but I believe we have a pretty good deal, I think we can take it though. It is just Camp Hood all over again."

Later that month, he seems to have had a few happy moments. A game of catch and a couple of beers is the closest he has felt to home since his departure. The gloomy realization of time sets in.

> "I have only been in it for 9 months with 4 months of that overseas not bad but it will probly be close to 24 months overseas before we see the U.S. again but I hope it isn't that long."

Occasionally, Jr. replied to his parents' inquests about his combat experience. But his answers are brief and vague, a simple yes or no, accompanied by the length of time spent on the front line. Whether he is not allowed to say anything in regards to battle details, or chooses not, he seems to think that they will find his trips to villages of more interest. For the most part, he is not allowed to be near the front because he is so young. In several letters, he mentioned a "boystown," where men 19 and under are sent during the fighting. These vignettes are simultaneously tinged with shame and relief. Understandable emotions for a young man who no doubt wanted to be in the thick of it with his peers, but also aware of his own mortality.

At any rate, his camera, once he received it, was

usually left behind or was out of film. Lack of film and shoe polish would plague Jr. throughout his stint in the Pacific. The highlight of July was a package containing a compass from the Boys Scouts, which also included addresses of boys he went to school with. If only he had the time to write them all.

On August 9, Jr. writes home from the island of Luzon, an island that saw more than its fair share of blood during the island hopping to Japan between January and August of 1945. Jr.'s weariness of battle is evident, but what he has seen, heard, smelled, and felt he kept to himself. All that he shared was that the experience was enough for a lifetime, however, he was aware that it could happen again.

> "Dear Mom & Dad:
> I received your letter of July 26 & was really glad to get it as to your questions yes, we were up near San FABain when we joined the co. it wasn't to bad but I have had too much to suit me, I just hope there isn't another campain that I have to go through but that is probably asking to much but it sounds pretty good since Russia has declaired war on Japan. Maybe some day this will all be over with & we can all get home once again."

Included with this letter were birthday wishes for his beloved mom and dad, as well as a poem dedicated to his mother.

The unknown of the future began to weigh on Jr. Never certain on what is the next step while he was in the Army, his future after the war also loomed before him. The fact that he will be home was his only assurance. A few weeks later he wrote,

> "I don't know just what we are in for now but I hope it won't be too long before we will able to come home and start all over again I haven't desided just what I will do as yet but I think start back where I left off work for Ed Honner."

Jr.'s next letter, dated August 29, expresses much the same. He takes some pride in the fact that his outfit has had the longest time on the front line, at 129 days, but he has grown tired of it. All he wants is a break, since it is impossible to return home. He has yet to learn what their next move will be, but wherever he goes next, Jr. desired a break from the island heat.

"I hope where we go next is a lot cooler than here because a guy really bakes here on this place even sitting in my tent writting this letter I am really sweating, I thought

Kansas was hot during the summer but that weather is cool to what it is here I hope we move from here to the States but that would be asking too much, there is a rumor around her that Walter Winchell said on one of his broadcasts that the 25 Divisions would make a parade in Washington D.C. the 26 of Nov. but I don't believe it have you heard any thing about it"

In October, a letter to his mother explains that they have remained on their boat in a Japanese harbor for 29 days with no idea as to when they will be able to disembark. They were allowed to tour the harbor town for a short while, but had to remain in large groups so no one would get lost. On October 8, they are still on board. Jr. was teased into thinking that they would be going ashore, but he found it no laughing matter when the equipment was reloaded onto the ships.

```
THOUGHTS FOR YOU ON

YOUR BIRTHDAY


On this your birthday my thoughts
   are with you.

It would be wonderful if I could
   greet you in person on
   this day;

Since I cannot, then I will
   say I wish you many,
   many happy returns of this
   occasion.

May you be blessed and kept
   in all happiness by the
   One who is able and
   willing to be our Keeper.

It is my desire that all your
   future days will be filled
   with a goodly portion of
   sunshine, good health and
   much laughter which comes
   from a heart filled with
   joy.

Though we are separated today
   by time and distance; I am
   with you in thoughts, and in
   the spirit.

May this spirit which binds us
   today,

Be one of true friendship which
   will ripen, and bloom in
   full, through the years.

   "HAPPY BIRTHDAY TO YOU."
```

```
A SOLDIER'S TRIBUTE TO MOTHER


Mother, I will not forsake thy law
   of love.

It shall be bound continually upon my
   heart, and tied about my neck.

When I go, it shall lead me; and when
   I sleep, it shall keep me; and when
   I awake, it shall talk with me.

For thy love is a lamp, and thy faith
   in me is a light, and thy reproofs of
   instruction have shown me the good
   way of life.

My heart doth safely trust in thee, so
   that I have no need of spoil.

You have done me good all the days of
   your life.

Your children shall rise up, and call
   you blessed.

Many of your children have done virtuously,
   but thou excellest them all.

Strength and honor are your uniform; and
   you shall rejoice in time to come.

I shall honor thee, that my days shall
   be long upon the land which my God
   giveth me.
```

"We have been on this boat & that has been a long time, we left Tarlac three weeks ago today & come down to Linguen Gulf where we loaded the boats, we stayed there about a week on the beach then got on this ship & didn't move out for about a week or more, we are now sitting at one of the little Islands of Japan, I don't know just what one they started to unload yesterday & then they quit & put the LSTs back on the ship & we are just sitting here, I don't know what we are waiting on we all thought we were going to unload yesterday because they gave us 80 rounds of ammunition & enough rations for 3 days"

His next letter is dated November 17, and land-lover and boredom-hater that he was, Jr. was probably very ecstatic to be off the boat. He does not reveal much as to his new duties, but he casually mentioned being on guard at different shifts throughout the day. And later, his duties on base included a truck that he was issued to drive for assumably a variety of purposes. Perhaps, what is most striking in this letter is a life-changing decision that he had been mulling over.

"Say don't go too high now because I have something I am going to say so hold your seat. I have been thinking about it for a long time now & I have about desided to reinlist for 18 months I will get a 60 day forlough & we are supposed to be home by xmas but I haven't really decided yet & besides it doesn't look like the boys are going to get home in time for xmas"

The rumor mill was going full tilt in December. Jr. has heard that he may get to go home the following March since he has been overseas since March 2. He didn't put much faith in that rumor, nor any other that he heard, yet his skepticism never prevented him from asking his parents if they heard rumors concerning his homecoming.

The reality of finally being able to return home is still illusive.

Strangely, there are no letters dated from the month of January. But February's batch included a typewritten one from Nagoya, Japan. No word yet on his return. Another letter from February gave a small indication as to Jr.'s location. Thirteen miles from Osaka, he described it as a "hell hole."

Letters are touch and go for the next few months. From Osaka on May 22, 1946, he wrote with obvious frustration,

"Dear Mom & Pop:

How is things going now, I suppose things are getting ready for harvest. & it is proably pretty hot but I would sure like to be back there any old place in the states would be better than this hellhole & I mean every bit of it"

He also shared with them the latest rumors circulating, but as always, there is nothing concrete in what he has heard.

"I sure hope they start sending them home pretty soon. I have 19 mo. in now & I sure hope I don't have to sweat out 24 month like a lot of guy that have gone home already."

Jr.'s final letter home to his parents is from June 12. Poor behavior and lack of points resulted in the truck he had been issued taken away from him. He has become apathetic and bitter towards life in the Army. He refused to get up in time for formation and reverie. He admitted to his parents that his fellows have begun to complain about him, but as he says repeatedly, he just doesn't care anymore. His tone is one of desperation.

"I have been pretty busy up until this week when they took my truck away from me. but I don't really care anymore because things are getting so it doesn't pay to do any-

thing, since they took my truck I haven't done anything but lay in Bed until 7:30 in the morning & get up & make my bed then lay back down on it again it is really getting to be a life here in the army, all the guys are hollering about me laying in Bed every morning while they …to get up & stand reverie but I can't see getting up & going out side for any formation at 6 in the morning. they can count me absent first I don't care. this life is really killing me when I get home I won't be worth a darn They say army life builds you up but I sure can't see where it has done anything for me but make me lazyer than what I was before I came in."

Epilogue: A word from author, Emily Jones, Bethany College History Major

Happily, George Osborne, Jr.'s story does not end here. Although what remains of his letters is a mystery, and there are most likely several missing. Jr. would lead a prosperous and fulfilling life. What we do not learn from his letters is that he was the youngest of five siblings, Marion being the third oldest. His older brother and sisters are mentioned repeatedly throughout the span of the letters, as well as several other relatives. Despite his final claims of being lazy, Jr. managed to find some time for courage. His list of medals include the Meritorious Unit Award GO 19 25th Inf. Div.; the Philippines Lib-

eration Ribbon with Bronze Star; the Asiatic Pacific Campaign Medal; W.W. II Victory Medal; Army of Occupation Medal; and Good Conduct Medal. He also managed to find a way to get "his truck" back. For many years after the war, he was an independent truck driver.

Whether his dampened spirits ever came around again, I do not know. I would like to think that they did. From his story, though, we can learn a valuable lesson. War changes people, its effects creep up on you and suddenly you may no longer want to rise from your bed. In the year and half's worth of letters, I detected a change in Jr. from his waiting days as a wheaty in Montana to his awe at the California sun to a weary fighter who felt his youth slipping away in time and violence. I believe that even he noticed his transformation, as slight or as great as it might have been.

Towards the end of this project, which I have so proudly been a part of, a bittersweet discovery was made about George Osborne, Jr.'s letters. Donated to the project, we had believed that they were unwanted, without a home, and no loved one who would take them in to cherish as a remnant of departed Jr. And then, suddenly, the error was noticed. Jr.'s wife of 32 years resided nearby and we learned of his many rewards, during the war and after. A reunion is planned. His family's lack of involvement, through no fault of their own, is my only regret in taking on this task.

An Infantryman's Letters and Recollections

Experiences with a rife platoon of the U.S. Army's 99th Infantry Division in Western Europe during World War II

by Joel Weide

THIS BOOK IS DEDICATED TO:

David J. Nutt, a Lindsborg boy who went to serve his country in World War II.

David J. Nutt was born and raised in Lindsborg, the youngest child of David G. and Fannie Nutt. Graduating from high school in 1943 he received his military induction notice about six weeks later. "Prior to my military service, I'd never traveled beyond the borders of Kansas."[1] David would later write that while on active duty in Europe, February 11, 1945, it was his birthday, "I had turned 20 years old and was no longer a teenager.[2]" David trained in Texas and in the fall of 1944 departed the United States for service in Europe and stayed there until the German surrender in 1945.

During his time in the European theatre he wrote letters home to his parents who saved the letters. The letters described scant descriptions of combat conditions because David knew that his parents were desperately worried about his safety and did not want to increase their concern by describing the terrible conditions that existed in the war, also the letters were subjected to military censorship. In 2003 David would publish a book about his experiences in World War II. This work would include his letters home as well as his recollections about his combat experiences. A brief summary of some of his experiences are described in the following pages.

"Letter writing was a chore. Occasionally we were allowed to write a letter and were given a sheet of v-mail paper. The v-mail letter was then taken to a rear area, photographed and the film sent to the US where a copy was made and delivered to the addressee. V-mail was slower than airmail so my parents often enclosed a stamped airmail envelope in their letters so I could reply by airmail. I used one of

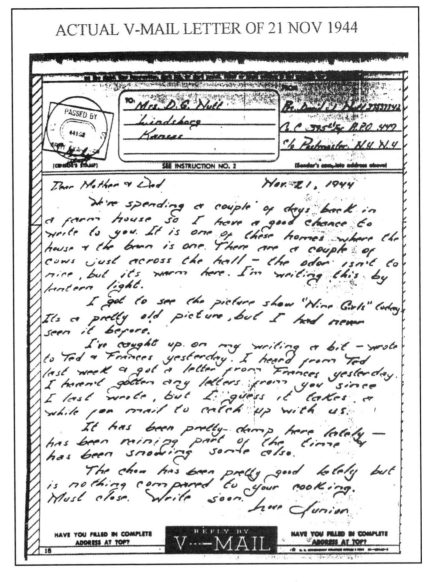

ACTUAL V-MAIL LETTER OF 21 NOV 1944

those airmail envelopes (because) I didn't have any writing paper in my foxhole, I write it on a couple of sheets of toilet tissue taken from a K-ration box[3]."

While spending considerable amounts of time in foxholes many letters were written to help pass the time. David recalls that letters were "written in pencil and the words (were) barely visible on the paper. I probably used a cardboard K ration box or maybe my rifle stock as a writing surface and the damp outdoor atmosphere no doubt contributed to the faintness of the writing. The pencil address on the envelope is equally faint but someone thoughtfully used a pen to trace over the words of the address making it legible. The tracing ink matches

1 Page i
2 Page 30

3 Page 9

that of the censor's signature on the envelope so I can only assume it was Lt. Eldon J. Bradley, Executive Officer of Company C and the censor, who did the good deed. It was not his responsibility to make the address legible enough for delivery but suspect (that) the feeling of camaraderie among us and a desire to help one another when possible," contributed to the action.

Spending Christmas of 1944 in combat David writes how a gift of the "Lindsborg News Record" was a much appreciated gift. "Had a fairly nice Christmas considering it was spent on the wrong side of the ocean. We had turkey and some of the fixings for dinner. Also was fortunate in receiving my first package from you,…the Lindsborg paper of Christmas day. Sure enjoyed the package - you couldn't have chosen anything better to send-Thanks a lot.[4]" In a letter dated February 13, 1945, David writes home that he "received 3 Lindsborg New's last week…thanks a lot.[5]

In a letter dated April 30, 1945, David describes meeting liberated American prisoners; "have had a chance," he writes, "to see a few Americans who have been held as prisoners and have been liberated. They are the happiest bunch of men I have ever seen and it sure makes one feel good to do something for them[6]." Coincidentally April 30th was also the day Adolf Hitler committed suicide in his bunker as Russian forces overran Berlin.

After returning home, David writes in more detail about his war experiences. David describes experiencing his first combat related death, Saul Kokotovich of the 2nd Platoon. "We had a number of casualties. . .I especially remember his death because I helped lift and carry his body a short distance to the rear. It was the first time I'd touched a dead person and I was shocked at the rigidity of the corpse, no doubt resulting from the rigor mortis and the cold temperature. Under normal circumstances, his body would then have been transported back to a burial site by support troops; however such activi-

ties were so disrupted by the Battle of the Bulge, the disposition of the body became unknown and Saul Kokotovich was listed as missing in Action (MIA) for more than 50 years. In 2001, searchers found his skeletal remains, with identifying dog tags, in a shallow grave on a wooded hillside near where the battle occurred.[7]"

David also writes about the frustrations of war and testing his mental capacity to the "breaking point.[8]" "We continued occupying our defensive foxhole positions on the ridge and were subjected to sporadic shelling by the Germans. Life became more difficult when I got diarrhea. Getting out of the foxhole, loosing several layers of clothing and squatting in the snow to relieve oneself was complicated by the uncertainty of when the enemy would start shelling us again. My sickness, and the difficult living conditions made me despondent."

I began thinking of what infantrymen refer to as the 'million-dollar wound.' That is, a wound that did not kill but was severe enough to require return to the US for the duration of the war. Once when we were being shelled, I stuck my leg out of my foxhole hoping it would be hit. It wasn't hit and I never did that again but at that moment my mental capacity to continue was near the breaking point." [9]

"There was a feeling of great relief and joy that the fighting had ended. A feeling of wonderment at having made it through all of the death and destruction and a deep sadness for the many who had been so close and had not survived. Attrition in a combat infantry unit is enormously high. The second platoon, of which I was a part, had 41 members when we entered combat. My recollection is that at the end of the war only two of us had been with the unit during the entire period of combat. All others had been killed, wounded, captured, evacuated for disabling conditions or transferred, although many with less serious wounds or disabilities had returned to the unit by war's end.

My relief at having survived the war in Europe

4 Page 19
5 Page 31
6 Page 53

7 Page 16
8 Page 25
9 Page 25

was tempered by the fact that war with Japan continued and I feared I might be shipped to the Pacific Theatre. Occupation duty in Germany was much preferable. The German people were as sick of the war as we were.[10]

David J. Nutt was discharged from the US Army at Fort Leavenworth Kansas on March 14, 1946, and currently resides in Walnut Creek, California.

References

All notations are from David J. Nutt's book *"An Infantryman's Letters and Recollections, Experiences with a Rifle Platoon of the US Army's 99th Infantry Division in Western Europe during World War II,"* 2003 Walnut Creek, California

Joel Weide

My Memories of
World War II
And Military Family Members

by Elaine Ragan

This book is dedicated to:

Disabled American Veterans and the loving memory of my husband, SSG Joseph B. Ragan, Sr.

My name is Elaine E. Ragan. I was born July 4, 1930, and I am eighty years old. My hometown is located in the southeast corner of the state at Parsons, Labette County, Kansas. I lived there the first nineteen years of my life.

Parsons was the hub for the Missouri, Kansas, and Texas or Katy Railroad. If you wanted to go north, you took the train to Kansas City, Missouri, or to St. Louis, Missouri. If you wanted to go south, you took the train to Oklahoma City, Oklahoma, or San Antonio, Texas. They also had a spur line to Junction City, Kansas. It took a half day to go there and a half day to return. The railroad also had repair shops and a roundhouse located about eight blocks from my home.

Parsons also had the Kansas home for epileptic and mentally ill. It is now used as a state training school for people with learning disabilities.

They had a place called the Baldwin Shirt Factory. They made dress shirts, fancy dress shirts with monograms on them and gym shorts.

Just before the war, a new industry was built about eight miles east of town. It was called KNOP or Kansas Ordnance Plant. There they built bombs and it was in operation on a smaller scale until 2009 when it was moved to Oklahoma. Before it was in operation, we were allowed to drive through the complex. They had a lot of storage units above ground made of dirt that looked like Quonset huts.

I was eleven years old when the war was declared and the oldest of three siblings. My mother was a homemaker. My father worked for the Railway Express Agency. We lived on the edge of town and had two cows and chickens. We sold milk, cottage cheese, eggs, and sometimes butter. When the new chickens got to be what was called fryer size, we sold some of them and froze a lot. Also we sold some of the older hens.

My father worked from midnight until 9:30 a.m. He loaded and unloaded express and mail from the night trains. He would come home at 6 a.m. and milk the cows, eat breakfast, and deliver the milk on his way back to work. There he would deliver the express that had come in on the trains to the stores. Then he came home and went to bed.

On Sunday, December 7, 1941, we were in church and someone announced the bombing of Pearl Harbor. We came home after church and turned on the radio and we learned the gravity of the news. War was declared on December 8, 1941.

One of the first things I remember was drives for newspapers, magazines, tin cans, metal, and old tires. Tires were rationed and hard to get. So they took the best tires to be recapped. The others were used to melt down to put on the tires chosen to be recapped.

We had gas rationing. Since we had what was called a dairy, and my father's job was essential, he was able to get a little more gasoline than some. Later when my father went to work on the trains, we had to give up our dairy.

There were War Bond drives. We had Saving Stamp Books and could get stamps at school for ten cents each. When our books were full, which was $18.75, we could purchase a $25.00 War Bond.

In 2001, Peter Gwillim Kreitler copywrited a book entitled *United We Stand, Flying the American Flag.* He is an Episcopal priest, environmentalist, preservationist, cultural historian based in Southern California.

This book contains pictures of American Flags, Pledge of Allegiance, Patriotic Songs and Poems.

War stamps.

The idea for the campaign was the idea of Paul Mac-Namara, a publicist for Hearst magazines.

This campaign was to have "United We Stand" on magazines with Old Glory on the cover of July 1942 magazines. Nearly three hundred magazines took part and were backed by the National Publishers Association, the newly formed United States Flag Association, and Henry M. Morgenthau, Jr, Secretary of the Treasury. He also urged them to put "Buy War Bonds and Stamps," on the magazines.

The book contains one hundred and eighteen copies of the magazine covers. They include *Life, Saturday Evening Post, National Geographic, Readers Digest*, sport magazines, industry magazines,

July 1942.

July, 1942.

New Yorker magazine cover July 4, 1942.

Town & Country July, 1942.

patriotic magazines, comic books, movies, farming magazines and so forth.

The Pledge of Allegiance, which was written by Francis Bellamy in 1892, is included in the book. He was the circulation manager of *Youths Companion* magazine. Congress officially adopted the pledge of allegiance as he wrote in 1942. In 1945 the phrase "Under God" was adopted.

Newsstands and over 1,200 department stores had magazine covers and flags flying in their windows in July 1942. It was the greatest symbol of our nation's unity everywhere.

This book *United We Stand* was published in November 2001 in conjunction with the Smithsonian Institution's Museum of American History. It complimented a SITES traveling exhibition in July

2002, which opened in July 2003. It honored the patriotic pride, spirit, and remains a moving tribute to a nation and people standing together. Sixty years after they first appeared, the images still retain their power to move people's spirit.

People planted victory gardens. My parents always planted a large garden every year anyway. They raised potatoes, green beans, onions, tomatoes, corn, and many other vegetables. My mother did a lot of canning. She also canned fruit and made jellies and jams. We ate a lot of chicken also.

We had food rationing of such things as meat, coffee, sugar, butter, and many other items. We saved our sugar for canning. We used melted saccharine tablets, white Karo syrup, and honey for sweeteners.

When we would buy oleomargarine or oleo, it would be in one pound bricks. It was white in color with a yellow capsule containing food coloring. It reminded me of a one pound brick of lard. We would set it out to soften, then work the coloring in until the color was like butter. As we had a butter mold, Mother would put the oleo in it and it came out looking like a pound of butter. Some people did not bother to put in the color and ate it like it was.

I was working on one of my Girl Scout badges and I went to the railroad station with my grandmother on Monday evenings. There were cookies, doughnuts, cake, coffee, and drinks for soldiers in the lounge and on the troop trains. Sometimes it was just a car attached to the regular train.

As the war progressed, my father was promoted to Express Messenger and worked on the train. It was his duty to unload mail and freight. They also carried bombs in the baggage cars. They had to watch that the bombs didn't shift around.

I had a cousin who was killed on a bombing mission over Germany. Two of his brothers were also in the Air Force. One was a navigator and the other a bombardier. I asked one of them if he was on the atomic bomb raid. His answer was that he wasn't allowed to talk about it. The oldest brother was a carpenter and he became a Seabee (Construction Battalions). He was stationed on an island in the South Pacific.

War stamps.aMt. Fuji Island, Japan, where my husband, Joe took basic training.

On D-Day, June 6, 1944, we were awakened by a newspaper boy at 6:30 a.m. shouting, "Extra. Extra." At first I thought it concerned the end of the war. Instead, it told us about the invasion at Normandy by the Allies.

There are many important dates that I remember. I have placed them at the end in chronological order.

As I am the widow of a retired Army veteran, I will include his story in my book. I am also the mother of a retired Navy veteran and have another son who was in the Navy, and a grandmother to an airman in the Air Force on active duty.

My husband, Joseph B. Ragan, was in the occupation of Japan. He started his basic training at Ft. Lewis, Washington, and was transferred to Japan to finish his basic training. He completed it on Mt. Fujiyama and then was stationed at the 28th station hospital in Osaka, Japan and went to Medical Technician School.

The last of December 1950, he was sent to Ft. Carson, Colorado, to reopen the Army Hospital there. It had been closed except for one building. It was opened to house the wounded soldiers from Korea.

In 1958, he was stationed in Germany at a McPheeters Barracks outside of Bad Hersfeld, Ger-

A modern area of Osaka, 1948.

Hospital where my husband went to school

McPheeters Barracks, where we lived in Bad Hersfeld, Germany.

Our quarters at McPheeters Barracks.

German road signs.

many, in the Fulda Gap. The children and I were there also. We lived five miles from the Marianborn checkpoint, which would take you into Russian territory. We were there during the building of the Berlin wall. We were able to get a border pass and go up to what was to be the wall. It was wire strung along where the wall would be built.

It was nothing to see Russians sitting on the autobahn looking down at the Kaserne with binoculars. Also they would be at the PX gas station on the autobahn to Frankfurt, Germany.

During this time our husbands would be pulling border duty. Mine was there driving a field ambulance, which was a jeep with litters in the back. They would be out five days and home long enough to wash and dry their field clothes and go back.

1960 International Day in Bad Hersfeld, Germany.

Treating civilians in Vietnam's rainforest.

For the last one and one-half years, he was stationed in Frankfurt, Germany, at the 97th General Hospital. We lived at the Drake Edwards Kaserne close to the town of Tanus and the Tanus Mountains.

My husband went to Viet Nam for the last ten months of his twenty years in the Army Medical Corp. He was stationed at Puch Phen near the Cambodian border. There he worked in an aid station and went into the rainforest to give the civilians immunizations.

Joe also had the duty of inspecting the mess halls. Some of them were in the tunnels the Viet Cong had used. He spent the last month at Bien Hoa waiting for his discharge and retirement papers. Joe returned home in May 1967. He passed away May 4, 1984 at Brook Army Medical Center in San Antonio, Texas. He is buried in the old Army Cemetery at Ft. Riley, Kansas.

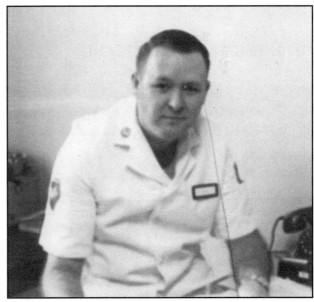

My husband, Joe, just before he retired in 1957. He re-upped with the Army in Germany, came home, and went to Fort Belvoir, Virginia, before going to Vietnam.

In Vietnam with field ambulance.

Our oldest son went into the Navy in September 1969. He had his training at Great Lakes Naval Training Center and became a medic. His first assignment was on a cable tender in the Atlantic. When he came back, he was stationed at a medic clinic in Portsmouth, Virginia, and then over to Navy Hospital at Norfolk, Virginia. He then put in for school at Bethesda Naval Hospital in Bethesda, Maryland. There he became a Cath (cardiac) Lab Technician. He went overseas during the second

Lebanon conflict and was stationed on a hospital ship off the coast of Lebanon. They went into the mainland and gave immunizations to the civilians. He returned to Bethesda and spent the last of his twenty-one years in the Navy teaching and editing textbooks. One of the textbooks has his name on it. He retired June 30, 1990. He has been a cardiac technician since that time at a large hospital in Charlotte, North Carolina.

Our daughter was a Navy wife for four years. Her ex-husband was on the aircraft carrier USS Forestall.

Our youngest son went into the Navy in May 1972. He took his first six weeks of training at Orlando, Florida. He then went to Great Lakes Naval Training to train to become a Boiler Technician on Destroyer Escort (D.E.) stationed at Norfolk Naval Base. It was renamed a Fast Frigate (F.F.) He served in the Mediterranean Ocean and made several trips to Guantanamo Bay, Cuba for training.

Two years after leaving the Navy, he became a policeman in McPherson, Kansas. Two years later, he became a member of the Kansas Highway Patrol (KHP).

During Desert Storm, he was called up with the Navy Reserve Evacuation Hospital from Hutchinson, Kansas. He was stationed on the island of Bahrain in the Persian Gulf. It is reached by a bridge from Saudi Arabia or by ship. He was no longer a Boiler Technician, but now was with Navy Security Police. He was able to see the fires and smoke from the fields in Kuwait. The smoke hung over Bahrain all the time.

In 2004, he retired from the KHP. He now holds a same rank he retired at as Director of Traffic at Ft. Riley, Kansas.

My grandson is in the Air Force and has been stationed at Whiteman Air force Base in Missouri for seven years. During that time, he spent six months in Kyrgyzstan at an American Air Base refueling airplanes. Kyrgyzstan used to belong to Russia. The Kyrds seceded from Russia when Stalin was the ruler of Russia. The air base is across the fence from the Russian Air Base.

This concludes my story. I have lived a life with many family members involved in the military, beginning with my own memories of World War II, living in Germany with my husband, my sons, and now I'm following my grandson's military career.

Following are important dates of World War II that I lived through and remember clearly:

- December 7, 1941: Japanese attack on Pearl Harbor
- December 7, 1941: Japanese declare war on USA
- December 8, 1941: Allies (except Soviets) declare war on Japan
- December 11, 1941: Germany declares war on USA
- May 4, 1942: Surrender of all US Forces on Philippines
- June 4, 1942: Battle of Midway—four Japanese carriers sunk
- November 8, 1942: Operation Torch begins—Allies invade Northwest Africa
- January 14, 1943: Casablanca Conference begins—US President Roosevelt demands "unconditional surrender"
- May 12, 1943: Surrender of Axis in North Africa
- September 3, 1943: Italy signs armistice
- October 13, 1943: Official Italian Government declares war on Germany
- June 6, 1944: Operation Neptune/Overlord—Allied invasion of Normandy
- December 15, 1944: Battle of the Bulge begins—Germans attack through Ardennes
- January 16, 1945: German Ardennes "Bulge" eliminated
- February 4, 1945: Manila falls to Allies
- February 19, 1945: US landing on Iwo Jima
- April 1, 1945: US invades Okinawa
- April 12, 1945: US President Franklin Delano Roosevelt dies; Harry S. Truman becomes president
- May 2, 1945: German forces in Italy surrender
- May 5, 1945: Ceasefire on the Western Front
- May 7, 1945: German unconditional surrender
- May 8, 1945: VE Day declared
- June 22, 1945: US forces capture Okinawa

- August 6, 1945: Atomic bomb dropped on Hiroshima
- August 9, 1945: Atomic bomb dropped on Nagasaki
- August 14, 1945: Japanese surrender
- August 15, 1945: VJ Day declared

AUTHOR PAGE

Elaine Ragan was born on Independence Day, 1930, and gets teased about everybody in the U.S. and other countries joining her to celebrate her birthday. After graduating from Parsons High school, she completed one year at Parsons Junior College before starting nursing school at Bethany Hospital in Kansas City.

Joe Ragan, stationed at Fort Riley, traveled to Kansas City one weekend while Elaine was in nursing school. She agreed to a blind date with Joe, accompanied by a friend and her date. They attended a swim show with performers in and out of two or three tanks, almost like a circus. Elaine had not seen anything like it before or since. She and Joe were married September 8, 1950, which meant she quit nursing school. Students could not be married.

Elaine began work at Fort Riley as a nursing assistant, the first of many positions with hospitals, clinics, and pharmacies wherever Joe was stationed. Their oldest child, Joe Jr, was born at Fort Carson, Colorado; Eva, at Fort Riley, Kansas; and Steve at

Elaine Ragan, now.

Fort Sam Houston, Texas. At one time, both she and Joe worked EMT.

She worked at the Fort Riley Hospital between 1983 and 2000 as a nursing assistant. After troops returned from Desert Storm, she worked in troop medical clinics and spent six years working in a prison section. She then went to Irwin Army Hospital to work in the OB/GYN clinic until her retirement.

Joe died May 4, 1984, seventeen years after finishing his military service. Elaine considered moving to McPherson, but with a lovely mobile home comfortably situated in the Fort Riley countryside, she chose to stay in Junction City. She moved to Bethany Home from Junction City.

WORLD WAR II:
WAR IN KANSAS

by Jack Turner

This book is dedicated to:

3rd Staff Squadron, U.S. Army Air Corps.

My name is John Turner. I'm known as Jack. I served forty-four months in the Air Force. I was drafted out of Chicago, Illinois, and went to Camp Grand, Illinois for indoctrination. I was sent to Jefferson Barracks, Missouri. I was inducted March 28, 1942. After I got to Jefferson Barracks, it was March. We had eight men to a tent. There was coal rationing, and we were allowed three pieces of coal in a bucket. If it got cold in the night, someone had to get out of the tent, go to the coal pile, come back, and get a fire started again.

After several weeks of basic training, they mustered all of the school squadron into a large tent. There were an even six hundred of us in the squadron. Five hundred-ninety-nine of them were sent to Hawaii. I was sent to Sherman Field Kansas, which is at Fort Leavenworth. Sherman Field was built in 1917 and has been there ever since.

The Third Staff Squadron was our outfit and we were there in support of the Command in General Staff School, which instructed Field Grade Officers in the strategies of war. Basically our mission was to see that the pilots going to school would have aircraft available to them, so they could stay current with their flying skills and status, also so they could receive their flight pay.

I was sent to Fort Leavenworth as an aircraft mechanic. After pushing a broom for several weeks, I realized since I had not been to an army school for aviation mechanics they were not going to let me work on airplanes. So I transferred to photography and ask to go to photo school. They assigned me TDY to Lowry Field, Colorado photo school, where after three months, I graduated as a laboratory technician and a photographer.

At Sherman Field, our work consisted of personnel, engineering, and just general photography.

Kansas World War II Army Airfields

From Wikipedia, the free encyclopedia

During World War II, Kansas was a major United States Army Air Force (USAAF) training center for pilots and aircrews of USAAF fighters and bombers. Kansas was a favored because it has excellent, year-round flying conditions. The sparsely populated land made ideal locations for gunnery, bombing, and training ranges.

Contents

- 1 World War II
- 2 Postwar use
- 3 See also
- 4 References
- 5 External links

World War II

The USAAF established fifteen airfields (AAF), under the command of Second Air Force, headquartered in Colorado Springs, Colorado between 1942 and 1945. These were:

- Coffeyville Army Airfield (Now Coffeyville Municipal Airport) (CFV)
- Dodge City Army Airfield (Closed)
- Fairfax Army Airfield (Closed)
- Garden City Army Airfield (Now Garden City Regional Airport) (GCK)
- Great Bend Army Airfield (Now Great Bend Municipal Airport) (GBD)
- Herington Army Airfield (Now Herington Regional Airport) (HRU)
- Independence Army Airfield (Now Independence Municipal Airport) (IDP)
- Liberal Army Airfield (Now Liberal Municipal Airport) (LBL)
- Marshall Army Airfield (Military) (FRI)
- Pratt Army Airfield (Now Pratt Industrial Airport) (PTT)
- Sherman Army Airfield (Military/Civil Joint Use) (FLV)
- Smoky Hill Army Airfield (Now Salina Municipal Airport) (SLN)
- Strother Army Airfield (Now Strother Field) (WLD)
- Topeka Army Airfield (Now Forbes Field) (FOE)
- Walker Army Airfield (Closed)

Kansas World War II Army Airfields

Part of World War II

Locations of World War II USAAF Airfields in Kansas

Type	Army Airfields
Built	1940-1944
In use	1940-present
Controlled by	United States Army Air Forces
Garrison	Army Air Force Training Command

The training that was given to the airmen stationed at these airfields gave them the skills and knowledge that enabled them to enter combat in all theaters of warfare, and enabled the Allies to defeat Nazi Germany and Imperial Japan.

The majority of these airfields were located in rural farmland, near small farming towns. The effect of stationing thousands of airmen brought the reality of war to rural and small town Kansas. In addition to providing training for servicemen, the air bases provided jobs for many civilians. Civilians were employed in maintenance, repair, and secretarial work.

We also did crash pictures. We had only two fatalities, one of which was an enlisted man who drowned trying to save a pilot in the Missouri River. The pilot survived. The second incident was a student pilot trying to impress a girl at Saint Mary's College. He never recovered from an inverted spin.

In June of 1942 we had seventeen B-17s fly into our field. They had been on their way to Europe and were turned around over the Atlantic and flown cross-country. Our field was one of the smallest ones, and they used it to keep people from finding out about us as a way to go west. We did not know it at the time, but these B-17s were on their way to Alaska to fight the invasion by the Japanese. (This is called the forgotten war). Dutch Harbor Attu were part of this campaign. These aircraft stayed overnight at our field, refueled, and had to take off with a full load of gas on a very short runway over a railroad bridge. These were big, big airplanes on a little tiny field. (VERY SCARY).

The students at the Command in General Scout School were pilots and had to fly to keep up their flying status. Flying pay was fifty percent of base pay. That's one of the reasons we were there.

So that the students at the school could fly, we had all types of aircraft from PT-19s, BT-13s, AT-6s, B-25s, A- 20s, to an old B-10 martin bomber. We got to do a lot of flying with these students, especially if they were flying twin engine aircraft because anybody could fly as a co-pilot. Fortunately I got to fly a lot. While I was there, they brought in a bunch of Dutch cadets from the Dutch West Indies, and they were going on primary training on PT-19s. These were Javanese and also Dutch West Indies guys and while they were there, they lost one cadet to a crash. We had another crash into the Missouri River and we lost one of our non-comps, but they did rescue two people from the aircraft.

Sherman Field is built on a peninsula in the Missouri River and every year in late May and early June, we would have floods and we would build dikes.

While I was at Fort Leavenworth, I noticed they had squads of soldiers with shoes that were painted red and green. They reminded me of a story about the song of WWI, Hay Foot, Straw Foot. The reason for hayfoot, straw foot terms is because these soldiers couldn't tell the difference between right and left, and that's exactly what happened in WWII. They used red and green shoes to know which foot for which shoe. If I hadn't seen this, I never would have believed it.

There's other thing about being on the home front. We were outside of Kansas City. I had a cousin who lived in Kansas City. His wife told me that I was welcome any time, but do not ask for coffee and do not ask for bacon. These were in short

supply. After I made First through Third Grade Staff Sergeant, I was allowed to buy bacon at the commissary. I brought a slab of bacon, about eighteen pounds, and took it to Ruth along with about two pounds of coffee. I never saw anybody so happy in my life.

Couple more things I remember. I married a Lindsborg girl who was working in Kansas City at a hospital. She was an RN and we would travel on the streetcars in Kansas City.

I was what they called a paper bag soldier. Because they were paying rations in housing meant I wouldn't eat at the Mess Hall, so we carried our lunches. One of the other non-comps had a car and we all shared the expense of the car and the gas rationing. Thank goodness we had enough to get back and forth from the base.

Isla Rose, my wife, and I were on a streetcar one time. Before we got on the streetcar, it had been pouring rain and she'd just brought a new dress. And the dress, you couldn't believe, how fast it shrunk. It

Jack and Isla Rose Hagstrand, 1943.

Wedding Day, March 21, 1944.

was clear up to the top of her stockings by the time we got home. Of course, she was very embarrassed. Another time, Isla had bought a brand new pair of shoes, and the first thing the clerk told her, "Do not wear them in the rain because they will dissolve." At least this time, she was warned.

We had to clear trees at the end of our runways because the runways were so short. At Fort Leavenworth, they had a huge military prison. It's not a guardhouse; it's a prison called the Disciplinary Barracks, and these are for hard core criminals. Because we had to have the trees cleared out, guardian service said we could have the prisoners do the work if we supplied the sentries and guards. So we did. Several months of that, on-and-off, as everybody took a turn. We would take these men down to the runways. The first thing they would do, if it was cold, was build fires—one for the guard and one for themselves and then they proceeded to clear

out the trees. Command had told us that if we lost a prisoner, that we would have to serve his term instead, which scared us very badly. But it was not true, which we found out later.

I was discharged from Scotfield on December 3, 1945. I have included here a history that was written by Tim Lindshield after he interviewed me.

Jack Turner by Tim Lindshield

Jack Turner was born on June 26, 1918, and spent the first twenty-two years of his life in Chicago, Illinois. He currently resides in Lindsborg, Kansas. He has two younger siblings, a sister eighteen months younger, and a late brother who was five years younger. Jack married Isla Rose Hagstrand on March 21, 1944 – now deceased. Jack was very active in photography and fishing. Jack and Isla had four children: a daughter Susan and three sons named Jim, Hal and Keith who have given them several grandchildren. Jack is an active member of Bethany Lutheran Church.

During his high school years he worked at a railway express agency in Chicago, until the news about the attack on Pearl Harbor struck the nation. He had worked all night on December 6th and was sleeping when the attacks occurred. He only found out after asking a girl out on a date and watched her puzzled reaction to his request on such a horrible day. Like many thousands of Americans, Jack went to enlist two days after the attack—on December 9, 1941. He attempted to enlist in the Navy, but was turned down when he could not obtain a waiver because of his eyesight. He then tried the Coast Guard, which was controlled by the Navy during wartime, and was also turned down for the same reason. He didn't want to be a "foot soldier" in the Army and decided to wait until he was drafted to enter the military. The wait was short and he was drafted into the Army in March 1942. After his induction in Chicago, he was sent to Camp Grant, Illinois to receive his uniforms and also to take a "test." He then was sent to Jefferson Barracks, Missouri, near St. Louis for Army Air Crops basic training. This twelve-week training cycle consisted of military law, articles of war, close order drill, customs and courtesies and the usual military discipline of being a soldier. He said they trained him how to make his rack and how to salute officers, but not how to be a combat soldier. He received no weapons training and the training equipment was very limited. For example, old cars and trucks were painted with the word "Tank" instead of having actual tanks for the training. He still remembers his assigned serial number of 36397707. The three digits at the beginning meant that he was a draftee and the last four were his own individual number.

His basic training squadron consisted of six hundred men and upon graduation, five hundred ninety-nine of them were sent as Army Corps Engineers to Hawaii. Jack was sent to Sherman Field, Kansas that is located where Fort Leavenworth is today. The Army did not tell him why he was the only one to be sent to Kansas, but he had received some specialized training in aircraft maintenance. Since he had never officially been trained at an Army mechanic school, he was not allowed to work on aircraft. After growing tired of the "grunt work," he transferred to Lowery Field in Colorado for photography school, where he was trained on how to use a camera, do aerial photography, and process the photographs. This school was very sought after for intelligence purposes and it trained soldiers twenty-four hours a day, six days a week. After graduation, he returned to Sherman Field, Kansas and married Isla Rose in 1944.

Jack assumed that it would be only a matter of time before he was sent to Europe as many men were beginning to disappear from his unit, some without any warning. He recalls several times when his company was lined up in formation and every other man, regardless of rank or specialty, was selected and sent to Army infantry. Jack was always odd man out. Because of the dwindling numbers, Jack did most of the flying for the aerial photography even though he did not have flight status because of his eyesight. He was sent on missions in the states, to photograph rivers, airfields and factories where B-25s were being built for the Russians through Lend Lease. The Army Corps of Engineers used some of the photo-

graphs for future dam locations while he received no explanation about others by the officers seeking them. He would receive the orders, fly the mission, develop the pictures, and send them off to whoever ordered them. This led to a funny story about how he received his flight status in 1944.

"I was a "Buck Sergeant" and I was doing all of the flying because our chief aerial photographer had just returned from Burma and he refused to fly. A major called one day with a mission and I said I would not fly for two reasons: I don't have flying status and I am not getting paid. The major asked, "Why not?" I can't get a flying status because I wear glasses and I am only a Buck Sergeant. He said, "You report to the medics, now:" I went over to the medic's office and there was a Corporal waiting for me. He said, "Take off your glasses. What's that chart say over on the wall?" I said, "E", you know the big "EE, and he said, "OK, you passed." I reported back to the Major and he said, "Staff Sergeant Turner, are you going to fly this mission?"

Jack received a promotion and flying status just so he could fly this particular mission over the Missouri River. Although he enjoyed the extra money, he never trusted the Army after this incident, because he didn't like how the officers could make up their own rules.

On September 2, 1945, the war ended on the deck of the *U.S.S. Missouri* with the surrender of the Japanese. Even though Jack was drafted in 1942, he was never sent outside of Kansas. After the war, soldiers were being discharged at an enormous rate based on a point system. Jack was offered Master Sergeant to stay in, but he turned it down and was discharged in December 1945. He was married, ready to try another occupation, and most of all he just didn't trust the Army. He joined the inactive reserves and was later called up during the Korean War, but was sent home three days later with hay fever. Since then, Jack worked as a painter, carpenter, photographer, mail carrier and for anybody else who would hire him for a dollar per hour. He also received money from the G.I. Bill as part of this paycheck with these jobs.

Jack has a great dislike for Franklin D. Roosevelt and feels that the President was not honest with the American people. He believes that Roosevelt was "lying through his teeth" when he said American boys would not fight on foreign soil during his presidential campaign in 1940. He said Roosevelt forced Japan into the war with the oil embargo but this was justified because, "Japan was raising hell in China." He also believes that Roosevelt knew about the attack on Pearl Harbor, but didn't expect the damage to be so great. He used the conspiracy theories of the missing aircraft carriers and the intercepted Japanese messages as justification for this argument. He believes that the government underestimated the destructive power of aircrafts and didn't realize that they could destroy a battleship. He cursed Roosevelt for not alerting the American troops and using them as pawns for entering the war.

With regard to the German troops, he said Americans believed them to be the best in the world. The newspapers reported that the German soldiers were trained from the age of eight and Jack had a lot of respect for these men. He noted, however, that the American sentiment following Pearl Harbor was that our GIs were going to "whoop their asses" and there were never any dissenting views toward an American victory in Europe. He did not hear about the Nazi death camps until late 1944 and the extent of the casualties was not made public until years later. He strongly believes that it was the right decision to strike Germany first before Japan because of the strong European relationship with America. He said, "When you look at Europe, you have people like us, but China and Japan are completely alien to us."

The attitude towards Japan was completely different than the German sentiments. The propaganda from the radio and the newspapers portrayed the Japanese as weak, and America was going to completely wipe them off of the map. He believed that the Japanese were "bandy legged little guys who couldn't keep up with the American soldiers." The Army also led him to believe that the Japanese couldn't fly a plane and that the battle was going to be a joke. There was a lot of hatred directed towards the Japanese because of the widely publicized Rape of Nanking during the Sino-Japanese War and also the Greater East Asian Co-Prosperity Sphere. He said it wasn't long after the fighting began that, "we knew we had a hell of a fight on our hands." He lost only one friend in the Pacific and considers himself lucky with the amount of American casualties that were suffered during the Island-hopping campaign. He firmly believes that the use of the atomic bombs over Hiroshima and Nagasaki in 1945 was the right decision and it saved America lives. When I asked about the number of civilians that died he said, "What about Nanking and Pearl Harbor? How many civilians did we lose there?" Speculating that America had invaded Japan, the amount of casualties on both sides has been estimated at one million. Jack strongly feels that this decision saved lives in the big picture.

Since Jack never left Kansas during the war, what about the effects of rationing impacting Americans at home? "It affected our lives," he said laughing. "We had to get a coupon if we wanted a pair of shoes." He had an advantage of being stationed at a military base because meat and other valuable items were usually available at the commissary. "I could get ham, or sugar, or a big slab of bacon which was not available in the civilian world." The shortages resulted in a lot of frustration over the lack of common items that we take for granted today.

He also noted that he didn't experience the struggle to find the necessary supplies like civilians and his wife had. He complained about the lack of meat at the dinner table only once, and then he found out that his wife had spent the day going from shop to shop in search of meat. "I almost lost her that day; she almost divorced me," he said.

The rationing of gasoline didn't affect him greatly because he did not own a car and usually carpooled to the base. People began walking more and taking the street car as an alternative to driving. Even though people were bitter about the rationing, he said they generally accepted it. A common response to any complaint about rationing was, "Don't you know there is a war on?" In response to

C-54 photographed by Jack Turner, Staff Sgt., June 1945.

all of the negative feelings toward rationing he said, "People had enough to eat. We didn't lose weight like the English. You didn't get to eat what you wanted sometimes, but you could go to a restaurant and order a meal." This quote says a lot about the actual hardships of rationing compared to the perceived hardships felt on the home front.

His general feelings at the end of the war were that we now had to stop the Russians. This new threat of communism scared him worse than the Germans or the Japanese ever did and there was a real fear about Communism taking over the world. This coordinates with the growing suspicions between the two super powers during the Teheran conference in 1943 and the Potsdam Conference in 1945. Perhaps the media helped establish these fears.

Jack's experience in the military was unique. The fact that he was drafted and remained home throughout the war is absolutely extraordinary. This was a wonderful source of history because he experienced the war both as a service member and also as an American on the home front. He flew aerial photography missions, supported his family, sacrificed along with the rest of Americans in the home front, and lived under constant threat of being sent away at a moment's notice. His conduct during his service warrants credit as well. As thousands of service members were being discharged after the war, he was offered a promotion to stay in. He was more than willing to

serve overseas in both the European campaign and in Korea, but fate had different plans for him.

AUTHOR PAGE

Jack Turner was born in Chicago June 26, 1918. He was drafted from there into the Air Force in 1942. Meanwhile, Isla Rose Hagstrand was in nursing school in Kansas City, where they met at a U.S.O. When he had completed his service, they moved to Lindsborg, where he was employed by the Postal Service. They had three sons—Jim, Hal, and Keith, and one daughter, Susan. Isla Rose worked for Doctors Fuller and Fredrickson. Jack retired from the Post Office in 1975, sat on his porch until Bethany Home's administrator (who lived next door) told him he was tired of seeing him sitting around, doing nothing. Jack became head of maintenance at Bethany Home for eleven years. (Jack's mother was a resident at the time.)

Wherever Jack has been or whatever his employment, he continued his interest in photography, taking wedding pictures from 1942 to present day, and filling other requests. His work inspired his son, Jim, to follow his footsteps and earn his way as a photographer. Isla Rose died August 14, 2010, and Jack continues a full and active life in Lindsborg. He participated in an Honor Flight to Washington, D.C. November 2010.

Jack Turner, now.

World War II:
A Personal Story

by Warren Webster

THIS BOOK IS DEDICATED TO:

All the thousands of servicemen who lost their lives before they could tell their story.

GOING TO WAR

This is a story about a great war, but also a story about a great nation who, after the First World War entered into isolationism. This nation was so disenchanted with war and the events which led to it and the way it became involved in it, that the United States felt it could stay out of future conflicts by staying out of world politics. We felt that this was a nation unto itself. We could stand alone. We did not need anyone else.

This was our policy for the next twenty years until a Sunday morning, December 7, 1941. Everything changed. All at once we became embroiled in a world conflict again. Our isolationism had come to an end.

The attack on Pearl Harbor should not have been that much of a surprise. With all that was going on in the Pacific, the Japanese had been slowly moving south through the countries and the islands until they had almost complete control of that part of the world. We could not see or we would not believe what we were seeing. We felt secure. After all, what did we have to fear from the tiny nation of Japan? We failed to understand or believe that Japan had become one of the greatest powers in the world and that their mission was to have complete control over the Pacific.

I remember scrap metal drives in the late thirties. Japan was buying up all and every kind of scrap metal we could provide. It was extra money for the depression era US people. Little did we know how that metal would come back at us. We found out that they did not buy up the metal to make plow shares! The Japanese Admiral that commanded the Pearl Harbor attack made a very true statement when he said, "I fear that we have awakened a sleeping giant."

We were in a war for which we were woefully unprepared. Our standing army was small, ill equipped. Some of our weapons were leftovers from the First World War. Our Navy had been badly hurt by the sneak attack on Pearl Harbor. Our war effort nearly had to start from scratch. War with Japan had been declared. War with Germany had been declared. War on two fronts spanned nearly the whole world. Things looked bleak and things were bleak, but we had this special something going for us—the American spirit.

In this period of crisis, the people all pulled together in the war effort. For the first time in history, the effort was almost 100% toward a common goal. Almost overnight the factories turned from producing civilian goods to war materials. Young men, volunteers, and draftees were called into service. From the cities, from the farms, from the hills, they all came. Many had never been more than a few miles from where they were born. Many coming out of the Great Depression had never had dental service and limited medical care. Some were illiterate; some had never slept on sheets. These were the men who were called on to fight a war which was really a war of survival.

As tough as the basic training and boot camp were, these men had seen tougher times. In fact, many had never had it so good with regular meals, clean sheets, a warm place to live. Women were called into the effort, too. They went to work in the factories, the shipyards, and various other jobs that men had held before they joined the service. The three branches of service had put woman units in force. Nurses were called into service. It was really an all-out effort.

MY STORY

My part of the story starts March 20, 1923 when I was born one and one-half miles south of the small town of Roxbury, Kansas. I was in the middle of seven children, four boys and three girls. It was a tough time during the depression, raising seven children, but we did not realize that things were that bad. Most everyone was in the same boat.

We all managed to receive an eighth grade education. I graduated high school in 1941. Since there was not much to do around home, my uncle who was president of the employees' union at the Coleman Company obtained a job for me in Wichita in July. Coleman Company was making some war materials then, as the nation began gearing up for possible military action down the road. December came and Pearl Harbor. By this time, Coleman had gone full-scale into manufacturing war materials.

I, along with many boys, went down to try to enlist. They basically told us that they were not ready to take on more people and told me to go back to my place of work where we were producing materials for war. In early 1943, I received my notice to report (greetings!). I was sent to Fort Riley for induction and while there, they gave us a choice of service. I had always leaned toward the Navy, so I chose that branch. My two older brothers were already in the service by that time. Winston, my oldest brother was in Patton's Army. Wendell, the next son, was to serve in New Guinea. I was sent to Kansas City where I was inducted into the Navy.

My younger brother Ronald, who was a high school senior and was to graduate in the spring of 1944, registered for the draft. He was offered a deferment to stay with my father on the farm. He said, "I don't want to be a draft dodger," and my father who already had three sons in the service said, "If that is what you want, you can do as you wish." Ronald enlisted in the Air Corps in September, was eighteen in November, and was called up in December. His diploma was mailed to him.

This must have been hard on my mother, having four sons serving at the same time, always wondering where they were and if they were safe and alive. She knew what it was like, even if it would not have been her choice. Five of her brothers had

served in World War I, and four returned home safe. One died in the trenches of influenza in France.

I was sent to Farragut, Idaho, for basic training (boot camp). No one could understand why a naval training station was built in Idaho. The favorite story was that when Eleanor Roosevelt was flying over the state and saw a lake below, she thought that would be a good place for a naval training station. I don't know if that was true or not, but the general opinion was that it could be, and no one could come up with a better answer! I do not have fond memories of boot camp, not because it was so tough, but because of the sickness in our company, which put us in quarantine the whole five weeks. After five weeks of training, I received a leave to go home.

While on leave in Roxbury April 1943, I met my wife-to-be as a kind of a pick up date. I had a car and they wanted to go somewhere, so my friend and I were tabbed.

After leave, I reported back to Farragut to be deployed. They told me of a new service that had been started which was the Armed Guard, a group of Navy personnel to man the guns which armed merchant ships. I volunteered for it and was accepted. Merchant ships were privately owned steamships under military orders. I was sent to San Diego to Gunnery School at the Destroyer Base, and after completing the training there, was sent to the Armed Guard Center Pacific at Treasure Island in San Francisco. While there, a crew was formed, about thirty men, and we were shipped to Portland, Oregon to the Kaiser Shipyards where we were assigned to a brand new Liberty Ship, the SS Dunham Wright. We sailed empty from Portland to San Francisco where we took on cargo consisting of 1000 and 2000 pound bombs, aviation gasoline in fifty-gallon drums, and various explosives. The deck was then covered from stem to stern with trucks. The only way to get anywhere on deck was by catwalk which was installed for that purpose. We learned to be very careful.

We didn't know where we were going. Only the captain knew this. This was necessary as any loose talk could jeopardize the voyage. It was almost certain that we were not headed for Europe. The only other destination was the South Pacific. There were slogans all over the ship reminding us of the danger of loose talk. "Loose lips sink ships." Once at sea, we were told of our destination, the New Hebrides Islands, which were in the Coral Sea northeast of Australia. We plotted a zigzag course designed to confuse any enemy vessel which might be following us. We were not in convoy. Throughout the trip, we were told to expect an initiation when crossing the equator, September 23, 1943. This would transform us from a "Pollywog" to a "Shellback." A word about the pain and torture we had to endure. We were told that we had to "cleansed of all the loathsome creatures" before entering the domain of Neptune Rex. We had watched the preparation for this ceremony more of the time since we left port. The old Shellbacks (those who had been initiated) were busy building a dunk tank and making up paddles covered with canvas and filled with sawdust, then soaked in salt water.

On the day of the initiation, the Pollywogs (that included me) were gathered together, commanded to strip of our clothes and get on our hands and knees on the catwalk of the ship. The Shell-

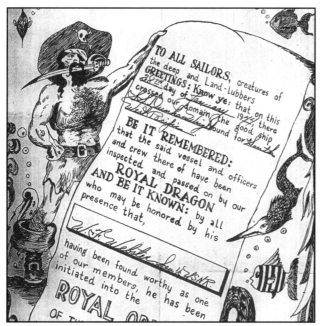

Proof of initiation to cross the equator.

backs (formerly initiated) were on each side of the catwalk, urging us to cross the ship on the catwalk by using the paddles on our bare behinds. When we reached the ceremony area, we were blindfolded and subjected to various other methods of torture, including being covered with red lead primer paint, getting a "Southern Cross" haircut (one swipe with the clippers from forehead to neck and one swipe from ear to ear, exposing the scalp both ways), and a dunk in the tank! Now I was a Shellback!

Another milestone was crossing the International Dateline, which we did in January 1944. No initiation this time. Just a certificate verifying our location.

After twenty-eight days, we arrived in Espiritu Santos of the New Hebrides and anchored out in the bay off the island. The cargo was unloaded onto barges and while this was going on, we had some time on our hands, so we took the ship's launch (the motorized lifeboat on the merchant ship) and did a little exploring at another island. We discovered an abandoned Japanese ammunition dump and camp. The Japanese must have left in a hurry because of the material they left behind—live ammunition and shells. We souvenir hunters tore into these items, took the shells apart, emptied the shell cases of powder, and detonated the primers. It was a wonder we didn't blow ourselves up. I got home with my souvenirs—an ammunition box, helmet, and various shell casings.

After the ship was unloaded we went to the New Caledonia which was another island in the Coral Sea (French). We took on some supplies there and then sailed to Australia.

Christmas 1943 on the high seas in the southern hemisphere! This was my first Christmas away from home as it was for most of us. Armed Forces radio was playing, "I'll be home for Christmas," which didn't help our homesickness any. We did have a Christmas dinner.

On to Australia—Townsville, and Brisbane. We entered the Great Barrier Reef and for the first time sailed with the running lights on and the blackout shutters removed from the portholes. We had been in enemy territory before that and were not allowed lights of any kind—not even illuminated numbers on a watch—for fear of revealing our presence to the enemy.

After unloading supplies at Australia, we returned to the States empty. We encountered some very rough seas and with the ship empty, it was riding high in the water and did some very bad pitching. Our quarters were on the stern and at times, we almost had to tie ourselves in our bunks. The ship would pitch forward and then back, which was up and down about twelve feet. It was quite a sensation!

Back to the States through the Gold Gate to San Francisco, spring 1944. I went home on leave and found my parents doing well. We were not allowed to divulge where we were, what we were doing, or anything which could harm the war effort. All mail was censored, and I was shown one of the letters I had written. It looked like it had been cut up for paper dolls. It was a rough time for those on the home front as well.

I renewed the acquaintance I had made with my wife-to-be and after two shorts weeks, reported back to Treasure Island. Very shortly, another crew was formed and I was assigned to another ship, the SS Jean Lykes, which was a much more advanced ship than the Liberty Ship, the SS Dunham Wright. This ship had the same amount of guns as the previous ship; two 3 in 50s and eight 20mm cannons. I manned the 20mm on both ships.

I knew that we would be welcomed wherever we were going, for the bulk of our cargo was PX beer! There was also whiskey for the Officers' Clubs in the deck lockers, which needless to say, was very heavily padlocked.

Off again for the South Pacific, summer of 1944, when we learned New Guinea was our destination. We crossed the equator again, but this time, I was a Shellback and it was my turn to help with the initiation of the Pollywogs. This time I knew what was going on.

We arrived in New Guinea at the Port of Lae and as I predicted, we were very welcomed. When it came time to unload the whiskey, they had MPs watching MPs in case they decided to take what didn't belong to them!

I knew my brother, Wendell, was in the South Pacific, but had no idea where. The only clue I had was his APO number, the number used for mail. I checked the APO number at Lae and found the number very close to his number. We went from Lae to Langemak Bay and I found that his number was only one number off the APO number there. From Langemak we went up the coast to Finchhaven. When we docked there and were unloading cargo, I found that their APO number was the same as my brother's. I knew Wendell had something to do with the motor pool, so I asked one of the truck drivers of the trucks that was being loaded if he knew anything about Mr. Webster in charge of the motor pool, and he said, "He is my officer! I am going by his tent and I will drop you off there."

He dropped me off and I walked in on him! He didn't have any clue that I was anywhere close to New Guinea! I ate with him, went to a movie, and stayed the night. Wendell told me that several thousand Japanese were isolated in the interior and had not surrendered. They would occasionally catch one sneaking into the chow line or into the movie theater. I didn't see any, but Wendell said they just left them alone. They weren't going anywhere and they weren't hurting anyone. I suppose that eventually they surrendered or starved. The next morning he took me back to the ship and he had a meal with me before I left.

From Finchhaven, we went up the coast to Hollandia which had just been secured. We were just there for a short time and we didn't get off the ship.

We left New Guinea and headed for Australia—Brisbane, Sidney, and Melbourne. I have fond memories of Australia. What time we spent there was very enjoyable and the people were friendly—especially the girls!

Leaving Australia, we found out that we were going to India and on our way, about midway between Australia and India, the news came on the radio that the war with Germany was over, May 1945. What good news!

We proceeded on up to India, to Calcutta, and were there for a few days. This was an eye opener! Most of us had never seen living conditions such as this. As bad as it was during the depression at home, it didn't compare to what we saw in Calcutta. I saw an old man sitting on the street curb where there were open sewers in the gutters. He was brushing his teeth and dipping the toothbrush in the sewer water. We saw a "dead wagon" going around every morning picking up the bodies of those in doorways and on the streets who had died during the night. The bodies were taken to a funeral pyre where they were burned. Young boys, nine or ten years old, were all up and down the street, herding customers into the market and pimping for their sisters who were thirteen or fourteen. Many were users of a substance called betel nut, which when chewed, gave them a high like any other drug. It made their

VISIT YOUR U.S.S. CLUB !

JAIN TEMPLE

AMERICAN MERCHANT SEAMEN'S CLUB
14, Sudder Street, Calcutta

mouths blood red and evidently did something to their teeth. Most of the users had no teeth.

From Calcutta, we went down to Colombo Ceylon (Sri Lanka). After a short stop there, we headed up around the coast to a small Portuguese province called Angoa. Portugal was neutral during the war with Germany, and therefore, had no commerce with any of the warring countries. We were the first American ship to come into Angoa since the start of the war. As we were coming into port, we noticed freighters that were half submerged in the middle of the bay. We found out they were German merchant ships whose sailors had been interned by Portugal (held like prisoners) when the war started. We didn't know why the ships had been sunk.

Years later, as I was watching the History Channel, I happened to catch a documentary of the event which explained what had happened to the German ships. Angoa was just a small pocket in the country of India. It seems that a group of British cricket players in neighboring India got together one night and in the dead of night, sneaked across the bay and sunk these ships. Mystery solved!

In Angoa, December 4, 1945, we took on a load of peanuts (yes, peanuts!) and left for the city of Marseilles in France. In crossing the Indian Ocean, we ran into a bad typhoon. The bow of the ship was under water as much as it was out. We learned later that the three forward holds had leaked water and ruined the peanuts. We learned later, too, that several ships were lost in that storm.

We came up the Red Sea to Port Said, Egypt, which was the gateway to the Suez Canal. While anchored over night, we were surrounded by hucksters selling everything you can imagine. I wound up buying two leather purses. In the morning, we went up through the Suez into the Mediterranean Sea. The Suez is nothing but a huge ditch; no locks as in the Panama. We sailed into Marseilles and there unloaded the peanuts. (I don't know what they did with the spoiled peanuts.)

From Marseilles, we went to Leghorn, (or Livorno) Italy and while there the news of the Japanese surrender was broadcast August 14, 1945.

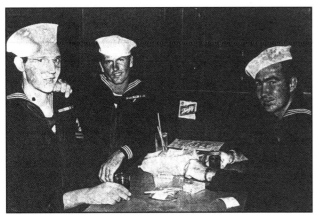

What a celebration! We reached Boston!

My sister-in-law and me driving to California.

After Italy, we sailed across the Atlantic to Boston! No matter where I was all over the world, mail reached me. The only address I ever recorded was Farragut, Idaho, from where I was originally deployed. The Coleman Company newsletters found me no matter where I was. Somehow, the Navy kept track of me.

I had accumulated a lot of things, including leather goods from India and Egypt, perfume and unmentionables in France, three pistols and ammunition, and various other things. I went downtown and bought the largest, cheapest suitcase I could find, loaded all my materials in it, and sealed it with steel bands. I walked off the ship with that suitcase, and no one even checked me!

From Boston in September 1945, I went home on leave and while there I bought a car. My sister-in-law (wife of my brother Wendell whom I visited in New Guinea) and her baby and I drove to California. Wendell didn't see his daughter until she was well over two years. My sister-in-law delighted in calling me Daddy, much to my embarrassment.

I reported in at Treasure Island in California and there was held as a witness in a general court marital trial to be held in New York. I was sent to New York and was a witness. This was an experience, and one I wouldn't want to go through again. It was an embarrassing situation that I had witnessed and therefore had to attend the trial. Fleet Admiral Leahy served as the military judge. He was the first US military officer ever to hold a five-star rank in the US Armed Forces. I had never seen so much gold braid and brass.

From there, I went to St. Louis to Lambert Field where I was discharged, January 18, 1946.

Two of my brothers were discharged about this time also. My oldest brother, Winston, took a look at the weather in Roxbury, which was pretty bad, and decided he didn't care to become a civilian again and work in such conditions, so he re-enlisted and stayed in the Army for thirty years!

My brother Wendell and his wife and baby were visiting our parents and needed to go back to California. I had left my car with my sister-in-law in September 1945, and needed to go back to California to pick it up, so I rode along with them.

Back to being a civilian again. I stayed at home about a month and helped build the American Legion building in Roxbury which was to house the newly formed Legion.

I went back to work at Coleman. I was on the production line that made a civilian version of the GI Pocket Stove. This little gadget was first made for the war, to be used by the military in the field to cook small quantities of food. It was popular, and

Coleman decided to make a version for the general public. The military version was Army olive drab; the civilian, bright shiny chrome.

I left Coleman in the fall to attend Bethany College on the GI bill. My wife-to-be (Margaret) and I were married January 24, 1947, and I graduated from college in 1951.

I have been asked if I ever saw action, and I have to admit that I never fired a shot at the enemy.

The service I was in, the type of ships I was on, were not meant for action. Our job was to deliver the materials to the Armed Forces, not to engage in battles which we were not meant to be in. We were where the action was, were in the danger zones, but our mission was to deliver the goods. In fact, I think the Merchant Marine motto was "We Deliver." The guns on merchant ships were not there to do battles, but were there for defense only.

This is my story; only one from the thousands of young men who have their own stories.

MY AFTER THOUGHTS:

What about the mothers, fathers, and wives of the service men? We don't know what their feelings were or how they coped with the unknown. Their loved ones were somewhere. As a general rule, they did not know where they were or what danger they were in. They hoped and prayed that the envelope being delivered to their door was from their son or husband saying that he was all right, not a Western Union telegram with the words, "I regret to inform you that….." Their thoughts, we could never know, until we had family of our own.

AUTHOR PAGE

Warren was born March 20, 1923 in Roxbury, Kansas. After the war, he came home from Italy in August, 1945 where he had been sent. He attended Bethany College where he earned a teaching certificate in history. While waiting to obtain a teaching job, he began work at the Rodney Flour Mill in McPherson. By the time a teaching job opened, he was making too much money at the mill in a management position to consider changing to teaching.

Warren married Margaret Spongberg January 24, 1947, following his offer to take friends home on leave to McPherson, since he was the only one with a car. On the trip back to Lindsborg, his car had a flat tire. With rubber rationing, he did not have a spare. While the group was deciding what to do, Margaret put out her thumb and hitch hiked a ride for all of them. Warren was impressed.

After sixteen years at the mill, it was closed and moved to Crete, Nebraska. Warren still thought he would get into teaching and attended Emporia State

Warren and his son, Larry.

Warren Webster, now.

University to renew his certificate. Again, he was distracted by a job at Kit Manufacturing in McPherson, a mobile home manufacturer. He spent nineteen years there until he retired. He and Margaret had five children: Sandra, Larry, Denise, Gary, and Jerry. Margaret died February 9, 2010. They had eleven granddaughters, and the twelfth is a step-grandson.

Warren says, "It is ironic and food for thought that we, while coming out the Great Depression, went into the greatest war the world had ever known, and in five years, emerged as the greatest power in the world. I like to honor what I did and what so many did for our country by serving as a member of the honor guard. I attend and present the flag at patriotic events and do honor rites at veterans' funerals. At 18 and 20 years old, I had no idea about the importance of serving or the dangers. Now, I have a different view that comes with the passing of time and the wisdom gained from living for many years."

Throughout the years, Warren has concluded that Uncle Sam doesn't owe him a thing. He truly believes he had a unique experience as a young high school graduate that he never could have had any other way.

ACKNOWLEDGEMENTS

Project Personnel:

Many thanks to the individuals and groups who contributed to these wonderful World War II stories written by Smoky Valley Writers. Without their help and contributions, we would still be trying to get started.

Specific thanks to:

Ann Parr, Lindsborg writer and published author, who initiated the idea of a senior citizen writing project and coordinated efforts throughout.

Marla Elmquist, executive director of U.S.D. 400's new Vision Tek Center, who directed all technological efforts to make the books look good and read well.

Lauri Denk, high school technology teacher at Vision Tek who stepped in at all steps along the way.

Jenica Rose, technology center manager, who kept our schedules and equipment up to date and in place.

Superintendent Glen Suppes who willingly made the center and its equipment available to us day and night throughout the project.

Holly Lofton and **Mary Swenson** who served as support staff to aid in fund raising and public awareness of our project.

Syd Dippel whose eighth graders did a companion project with Bethany Home residents, capturing their stories and sharing their history.

Gretchen Norland and **Jill Huebele** who coached twelve of their sixth graders to partner with senior writers to interview and key their stories into computers.

Dr. Marlysue Holmquist who loaned Bethany College students from her classes to refine the story formats, place pictures, and help with printing the book.

Contributors:

The following individuals and groups believed in us enough to put their money where their heart is. We thank them for making this project possible.

Smoky Valley Community Foundation
Bethany Home
Bob Dole
Farmers' State Bank
National Cooperative Refinery Association
Lindsborg State Bank
Home State Bank
Scott and Susan Auchenbach
Don Ferguson
Don Heline
Anonymous donors